THE
TROUBLE
WITH
BILLIONAIRES

ALSO BY LINDA McQUAIG

Behind Closed Doors: How the Rich Won Control of Canada's Tax System ... And Ended Up Richer

The Quick and the Dead: Brian Mulroney, Big Business and the Seduction of Canada

The Wealthy Banker's Wife: The Assault on Equality in Canada

Shooting the Hippo: Death by Deficit and Other Canadian Myths

The Cult of Impotence: Selling the Myth of Powerlessness in the Global Economy

All You Can Eat: Greed, Lust and the New Capitalism

It's the Crude, Dude: War, Big Oil and the Fight for the Planet

Holding the Bully's Coat: Canada and the U.S. Empire

ALSO BY NEIL BROOKS

The Quest for Tax Reform: The Royal Commission on Taxation Twenty Years Later (*editor*)

A Capital Gains Tax for New Zealand (*with Rick Krever*)

The Canadian Goods and Services Tax: History, Policy and Politics

THE
TROUBLE
WITH
BILLIONAIRES

LINDA McQUAIG
and NEIL BROOKS

VIKING
CANADA

VIKING CANADA

Published by the Penguin Group

Penguin Group (Canada), 90 Eglinton Avenue East, Suite 700, Toronto, Ontario, Canada M4P 2Y3
(a division of Pearson Canada Inc.)

Penguin Group (USA) Inc., 375 Hudson Street, New York, New York 10014, U.S.A.
Penguin Books Ltd, 80 Strand, London WC2R 0RL, England
Penguin Ireland, 25 St Stephen's Green, Dublin 2, Ireland (a division of Penguin Books Ltd)
Penguin Group (Australia), 250 Camberwell Road, Camberwell, Victoria 3124, Australia
(a division of Pearson Australia Group Pty Ltd)
Penguin Books India Pvt Ltd, 11 Community Centre, Panchsheel Park, New Delhi – 110 017, India
Penguin Group (NZ), 67 Apollo Drive, Rosedale, North Shore 0632, New Zealand
(a division of Pearson New Zealand Ltd)
Penguin Books (South Africa) (Pty) Ltd, 24 Sturdee Avenue, Rosebank, Johannesburg 2196, South Africa

Penguin Books Ltd, Registered Offices: 80 Strand, London WC2R 0RL, England

First published 2010

1 2 3 4 5 6 7 8 9 10 (RRD)

Manufactured in the U.S.A.

Library and Archives Canada Cataloguing in Publication data available upon request to the publisher.

ISBN: 978-0-670-06419-9

Visit the Penguin Group (Canada) website at **www.penguin.ca**

Special and corporate bulk purchase rates available; please see **www.penguin.ca/corporatesales**
or call 1-800-810-3104, ext. 2477 or 2474

For my precious Amy: daugher, editor, best friend
—L.M.

To Marlane, with love
—N.B.

CONTENTS

THE
TROUBLE
WITH
BILLIONAIRES

1

RETURN OF THE PLUTOCRATS

Imagine this: you are given one dollar every second.

At that rate, after one minute, you would have sixty dollars. And after twelve days, you would be a millionaire—something beyond most people's wildest dreams.

But how long would it take to become a *billionaire*?

Well, at that rate, it would take almost thirty-two years.

Being a billionaire isn't just beyond most people's wildest dreams, it's likely beyond their comprehension.

Another way to grasp the sheer size of billionaires' fortunes is to imagine how long it would take Bill Gates, generally considered the world's richest man, to count his $53 billion. If he counted it at the same rate—one dollar every second—and he counted non-stop day and night, he'd have it all tallied up in 1,680 years. Or still another way to look at it: if Bill Gates had started counting his fortune at that rate back in AD 330—the year the Roman emperor Constantine had his wife boiled alive and chose Byzantium as the empire's new capital—he'd just be finishing up now.

NO ONE EVER ACCUSED Wall Street bankers of being modest, unassuming, or prone to self-doubt. Still, their decision to collectively pay themselves a record $140 billion in 2009—outstripping even their 2007 record—seemed perverse, given that they'd just brought the world economy to its knees. But then, many in the elite have seemed determined to shake off any responsibility for the 2008 financial meltdown, not just those who directly engineered it, but also those who dismantled the regulatory walls or who simply encouraged the culture of greed that brought it about. By the beginning of 2009, the only thing scarcer than jobs for the masses was *mea culpas* from the elite.

This was evident at the annual elite gathering that January in the Swiss town of Davos, where business leaders, financial innovators, political shakers, and other big thinkers have been coming for years to celebrate the globalized world of liberated financial markets, shrunken government, and reinvigorated capitalism. The benefits this new world offered were evident by looking at the members of this dazzling crowd, whose financial holdings typically matched their bulging intellectual endowments. Naturally, there was some bewilderment in Davos in January 2009, even a few questions about why markets had done such a poor job of policing themselves. A dispatch posted on the website Slate captured the mood: "DAVOS MAN, CONFUSED." Still, as journalist Julian Glover noted in the U.K.'s *Guardian*: "The shock is real, the grief has hardly begun, but no one in Davos seems to think [this] means they should be less important or less rich."

That would have involved a deep change of mindset, which was not what these economic overlords seemed inclined toward. After all, a key concept behind the economic order of the past few decades has been the central importance of individual talent, and the need to nurture it with abundant financial rewards. That way, the brilliant in our midst would be lured into the top jobs running the world. Ensuring the active participation of these giants among us was clearly understood to be worth a lot, and pay scales were adjusted accordingly, going through the roof at the upper end. Just because the global economy was now in a free fall hardly seemed like grounds to go beating up the very people who'd played key roles in designing it.

So, in Manhattan, then Merrill Lynch CEO John Thain apparently saw no irony as he explained why he'd felt it necessary to pay $4 billion in executive bonuses to keep the "best" people on staff—right after those same over-achievers had steered the company to a staggering net loss of $27 billion and in the process helped trigger the global economic meltdown. (One wonders what some less capable types might have done—just carry on regular banking?) And there was particular outrage over a media report in October 2009 that a member of the kitchen staff of bailed-out Wall Street firm AIG had received a $7,700 bonus. (Surely that was less outrageous than the million-dollar bonuses paid to those who'd carried out the firm's financial business. After all, the kitchen helper had presumably produced something that at least could be eaten.)

Away from the rarified air of Davos and Manhattan, the high fliers who had so recently basked in the respect and awe of the less gifted underwent a precipitous drop in regard. Some of those less-gifted types were now clamouring for change, even suggesting that cutting executive pay might induce the hyper-talented to seek more socially useful employment in areas like teaching or health care. But a letter to *The New York Times* clarified the danger of this approach, making a compelling case for maintaining extravagant pay, even huge executive bonuses: "Without them, Wall Streeters will all look for other jobs. Do we really want these greedy, incompetent clowns building our houses, teaching our children or driving our cabs?"

AS A RESULT of the increasing concentration of income and wealth at the top during the last few decades, the United States, Britain, and Canada have become extremely unequal societies.

Before going any further, we should point out that we are not against all inequality. On the contrary, we believe that some reasonable degree of inequality is not only acceptable but even desirable, reflecting different levels of individual effort and contribution. But what exists today in the Anglo-American countries is an excessive level of inequality that has rarely been seen in modern history.

In the past few decades the middle and lower classes have experienced almost no growth in income. Virtually all the income growth has been at the top, particularly at the very top. The top-earning 1 percent of Americans now enjoys a whopping 24 percent of the national income. These high rollers make up an enormously rich and powerful class that can best be described as a plutocracy—not unlike the plutocracy of financial interests that dominated America back in the 1920s, when the opulence of the wealthy and their disproportionate influence over the political process was particularly pronounced.

America's return to plutocracy is all the more striking because, between the extreme inequality of the 1920s and the extreme inequality of today, something very different happened. During the intervening years—particularly the early postwar period, from the end of World War II until 1980—the United States achieved, along with many other industrialized nations (including Canada), a degree of equality and egalitarian distribution of income rarely seen in any period of modern history. Since the 1980s, though, the revival of plutocracy has had sweeping effects, profoundly changing the nature of American society and the lives of Americans (and pulling Canadians in the same direction). Yet, even as this remarkable transformation has taken place, the issue of inequality and its consequences has largely disappeared from public debate, rendering it strangely invisible.

OF THE WORLD'S 1,011 BILLIONAIRES, it seems fitting to begin with John Paulson, who made a fortune betting against the subprime mortgage market.

Mild-mannered, dark-suited, and with a mysterious half smile somewhat reminiscent of the Mona Lisa—one of the few objects on the planet with arguably a higher net worth—Paulson exudes a kind of normalcy. This in itself is odd because, as the forty-fifth richest individual in the world with a fortune of $12 billion, Paulson (no relation to former U.S. Treasury secretary Henry Paulson) is certainly not average in any meaningful sense of the word. Still, there's nothing in the outward appearance of this fifty-four-year-old hedge fund manager that would suggest anything other than a middle-aged man, married with two children, quietly going about his business. Though he moves in elite circles and has all the trappings of wealth, he doesn't keep a chauffeur waiting for him, and is known to travel by cab and even public transit. He doesn't appear to suffer from the syndrome that, as journalist Matt Taibbi notes, causes some Wall Street high rollers to "start seeing Brad Pitt in the mirror." John Paulson probably doesn't much bother looking in the mirror. Why would he, when he could spend that time more profitably pondering which defective subprime mortgages inside a collateral debt obligation would be most likely to yield an unconscionable rate of return?

A dedication to making a serious amount of money has always been a guiding influence for Paulson, who grew up in a middle-class neighbourhood in Queen's, New York, but whose family on both sides has a background in money management. Particularly influential in shaping Paulson's mindset was his maternal grandfather, Arthur Boklan, a successful Wall Street banker who, even during the Depression, managed to house his family in grand style in the elegant apartment building that still stands at 93rd Street and Central Park West.

Paulson always knew he wanted a large fortune, and he systematically went about laying the groundwork for acquiring one, applying himself sufficiently at New York University to graduate first in his finance class and then winning top honours in the Harvard MBA program. From there he soon gravitated, as water down an incline, to the money-making palaces of Wall Street, opening his own hedge fund in 1994 in order to best make use of his unusual talent for spotting the biggest money-making opportunity going. The ultimate one came his way in April 2005, when he developed a hunch that the ultra-hot subprime mortgage market was headed for spectacular collapse. Keeping that particular insight to himself, he turned his research staff loose on the problem and figured out how to make money betting that the millions of people signing up for mortgages they could only dream of actually affording would soon start defaulting. When they did, Paulson was there, watching money flood into his hedge fund with the torrential force of a great deal of water travelling down a very steep incline. In 2007 he personally pocketed $3.7 billion, giving him the record—perhaps of all time—for financially profiting from the misery of others.

But no sooner had Paulson nailed that record than another challenge arose; competition for the title of top-earning hedge fund manager. Hedge funds—pools of capital restricted to wealthy investors—are the ultimate symbol of the new Gilded Age that's emerged in the last few decades. They barely existed before 1980, but have quickly become key vehicles for unregulated financial speculation by the super-rich. By the end of the 1990s, there were 515 of these funds, managing $500 billion; by 2005, there were 2,200 funds, handling almost $1.5 trillion for the world's wealthy elite. Since hedge fund managers take a percentage—generally 2 percent of the value of their accounts and 20 percent of the profits—these individuals have catapulted themselves into a stratosphere of income compensation that is in a league all of its own, vastly higher than even the wildly extravagant CEO pay levels at leading multinational corporations.

And the financial crisis of 2008 turned out to be nothing more than a brief downward blip for the hedge fund industry. As the Wall Street meltdown pushed the world economy into a brutal recession in 2008, hedge fund managers' pay fell by about 50 percent. Even at that dramatically reduced level, the top twenty-five managers still earned *an average* of $464 million each. To put that in perspective (as much as it's possible to put something like that in perspective), let's stack it up against the income of John D. Rockefeller, who in his day and for many decades afterward served as the legendary Richest Man Imaginable. In 1894, at the height of the Gilded Age, Rockefeller had a staggeringly large income of $1.25 million ($30 million in today's dollars)—which was *7,000 times* the average U.S. per capita income at the time. Yet in 2008 the average income of the top twenty-five hedge fund managers (not the top guy, just the average of the top guys) was *12,000 times* that of the average American.

And by 2009, while the world economy remained deeply mired in recession, the hedge fund industry had bounced back fully; the total pay of its top managers exceeded even the record year of 2007, when Paulson alone, in the top slot, had received $3.7 billion. The top spot was now claimed by hedge fund manager David Tepper, who collected $4 billion, basically by betting that the U.S. government would likely come to the rescue of the big banks (Paulson ranked fourth, with a piddling $2.3 billion). Overall, the top twenty-five hedge fund managers made $25.3 billion in 2009—*averaging a little more than $1 billion each*, more than double the $464 million average of the previous year. This meant that the average income of the top twenty-five hedge fund managers in 2009 had risen to the point that it was now more than *24,000 times* that of the average American.

Paulson and Tepper vividly illustrate the sheer scope of today's top incomes, and how far they outstrip that of the very top earners in the past. Indeed, Paulson and Tepper are among an elite group that financial historian Charles Geisst has called "the highest earners of all time." As these numbers reveal, it's not just that the rich are getting richer, but that they're pulling so dramatically ahead of the rest of society. With North American workers experiencing little or no growth in their real wages over the past few decades, middle-class families now typically need two earners to keep up the material standard their parents achieved with one. So if they're holding their ground, they're doing so by working much harder.

The extreme concentration of income at the top is by no means confined to the hedge fund industry. Consider, for instance, how the pay of the average CEO compares to that of the average worker. In the 1970s the gap was about 30 to 1; by 2007, it had risen to 340 to 1. But even this understates the size of the gains made by the very top rung of CEOs. If we look at the average pay of just the 100 highest-paid CEOs and compare it to the pay of the average worker, we find that the gap in the 1970s was about 45 to 1. By 2006 that gap had become *1,723* to 1.

Sometimes referred to as "Winner Take All," this gravitation of pay toward the very top has become the new normal in a wide range of fields. For athletes and entertainers, the pay at the top is now enormous. *Sports Illustrated* compiles an annual list of the incomes of the highest-paid athletes; in 2007, the average for this select group was $25 million. At the pinnacle Tiger Woods, two years before his fall from grace, was making more than $100 million a year. In celebrity rankings by *Forbes* magazine, more than fifty movie stars earned in excess of $20 million in 2007–8, while Steven Spielberg made $130 million, Oprah Winfrey $275 million, J.K. Rowling $300 million.

Then there's *Forbes* annual list of the four hundred wealthiest Americans, ranked by net worth. In 1982, the first year the list was published, it was topped by fourteen billionaires. Twenty-five years later, in 2007, all four hundred individuals on the list were billionaires. Anyone with a net wealth below $1.3 billion didn't even make the cut. And again, as in the case of the hedge fund managers, we can see that the 2008 financial crisis created little more than a temporary drop in the wealth of billionaires, with a quick recovery the following year. Gates's fortune—the world's largest for most of the past fifteen years— dropped in value from $58 billion to $40 billion on the *Forbes* 2009 list. But by 2010, it had bounced back to $53 billion (just slightly behind the world's new richest man, Mexican Carlos Slim Helú, with $53.5 billion).

In Canada, where the pattern is similar although less extreme than in the United States, there's also been a stunning surge of income and wealth at the top. Over the past dozen years, while incomes of ordinary Canadians have stagnated, compensation for the fifty highest-paid CEOs has risen by 444 percent. In 1995 the ten top-earning CEOs took home $60 million, a total that had more than quintupled to $330 million by 2007. The top-paid CEO in 1995 was Gerald Pencer of Cott Corporation, with an income of $13 million. But by 2007 twenty-five Canadian CEOs were making at least $13 million, and the pay of the top earner (newcomer Mike Lazaridis, co-founder of Research in Motion) had almost quadrupled, to $51.5 million.

The ranks of Canada's billionaires also continued to swell, rising from twenty-five in 1999 to fifty-five in 2009. Far out in front of the Canadian money pack was the Thomson family (they rank number ten on the *Forbes* worldwide list, with a net wealth of $21.99 billion), followed by the Irvings ($7.28 billion), Galen Weston ($6.47 billion), Jimmy Pattison ($5.07 billion), and the Rogers family ($4.7 billion), just to name the top five.

One can perhaps grasp the sheer size of billionaires' wealth by imagining how lavishly they are able to spend, just by living off the *interest* from their fortunes. If they were to indulge in the wildest orgies of consumption, diligently sustained over long periods of time, it would be a struggle for them to make even a small dent in their capital. Take Larry Ellison, CEO of business software giant Oracle, with a net worth of $27 billion. Assuming a 10 percent rate of return, Ellison could spend $51 million a week—or $303,000 *an hour*, every hour of the day, seven days a week—and still not dig into his principal at all. Moreover, at that same 10 percent return, the taxes on Ellison's sprawling twenty-three-acre California estate could be entirely paid from his interest payments in just six hours, during one night's sleep. Nevertheless, in 2008, Ellison contested the tax bill for the estate and won a $3 million refund, which had to be repaid by local school boards and municipalities. The Portola Valley School District in northern California was ordered to repay the billionaire some

$250,000, roughly the cost of hiring several new teachers. For Ellison, the tax refund was yet more pocket money—enough, for instance, to increase that week's *hourly* spending from $303,000 to $321,000. [1]

THESE DOLLAR AMOUNTS become numbing after a while. To get a clearer sense of how very rich the top income earners have become—and how dramatically they've pulled ahead of the population at large—it's helpful to create a visual image. To do so, we've borrowed a concept created by Dutch statistician Jan Pen. Pen's idea was to present the distribution of income as a national parade in which everyone in the country marches. The height of the marchers is determined by their incomes. The entire parade takes one hour, during which time the entire nation marches by very quickly, in order of height, starting with the shortest marchers (the lowest income earners) at the front and ending with the tallest ones (the highest income earners) at the rear.

What's striking about the parade, as Pen noted when he first applied it to British incomes in the early 1970s, is how short just about everyone is—that is, how much the national income is concentrated in the hands of a few incredibly tall marchers who appear at the very end. Indeed, Pen dubbed it "a parade of dwarves (and a few giants)." And of course that was more than thirty years ago, before the post-1980 revolution that dramatically increased inequality in the United States, Britain, and Canada. If we really want to appreciate the huge jump in top incomes that has occurred here in recent decades, it's best to compare the Canadian income parade of the late 1970s to what such a parade would look like today.

In the 1978 version, nothing but very tiny people—less than a foot tall—were visible for the first six minutes. This low-income crowd, all earning less than $7,000, included welfare recipients, part-time workers, and old-age pensioners. The height of the marchers rose ever so gradually. By about fifteen minutes there were fast-food workers, retail clerks, and parking lot attendants, all less than three feet tall.

Eventually, slightly taller receptionists, factory workers, and truck drivers appeared. But they were still awfully short, not measuring more than four feet. Their ranks seemed never-ending.

The parade had been going on for almost forty minutes before we started to see people of normal height—reflecting average income levels.[2] It was only in the last ten minutes that really tall people started to appear. These were typically high-income professionals—doctors, lawyers, accountants, engineers—and they stood well above the crowd, seven or even eight feet in height. In the last six minutes, the marchers became taller still—more than fourteen feet tall.

But it's what happened in the last minute that was truly eye-catching. With only twenty-five seconds remaining, the marchers had reached heights of thirty feet. Then, in the last few seconds, some real giants walked by. Among these, standing 167 feet tall, was Ian David Sinclair, CEO of Canadian Pacific, with an income of $334,725. Then came Edgar Bronfman, chairman of Seagram's, with take-home pay of $397,582, standing 199 feet tall. But towering even above him was the final marcher in the parade: John Armstrong, CEO of Imperial Oil, with an income of $453,820, and reaching a commanding height of 224 feet.

Now let's re-run the parade, using today's income earners.[3]

Actually, for the first fifty minutes, this parade is strikingly similar to the 1978 one. But with just ten minutes to go, it starts to look very different, with the people noticeably taller.

As in the 1978 parade, the real giants appear only at the very end, particularly in the last few seconds. But in today's parade, they aren't just very tall, they're truly gigantic. We can recognize some prominent CEOs in the crowd—except that the faces are so high up that it's hard to see them. Way up there, for instance, is Siegfried Wolf, CEO of Magna International, with an income of $13 million, standing 2,054 feet tall—more than nine times as tall as John Armstrong, the tallest person in the 1978 parade. Indeed, Wolf is so immense, he is actually taller than the CN Tower. Then there's Paul Desmarais Jr., CEO of Power Corporation, with a $29 million income, standing more than twice as high at 4,582 feet, and Jim Balsillie, CEO of Research in Motion, at $32 million and 4,980 feet tall. Robert Milton, the former CEO of Air Canada, who took home pay of $42 million even as the company suffered terrible losses and thousands of Air Canada workers lost their jobs, is there too, standing 6,636 feet tall, well over a mile high. Then finally, at the very end of the parade, is the tallest man in Canada, Michael Lazaridis, another CEO of Research in Motion, with a take-home pay of $51 million, standing 8,058 feet tall—more than a mile and a half high. From the viewing deck at the top of the CN Tower, we don't even come up to his knees.

Most Canadians probably regard extreme inequality as a thing of the past. But while kings and nobles of pre-industrial times enjoyed a standard of living that was wildly lavish and grand compared to the poor in their day, that gap was not as extreme as the one that separates Canadian billionaires from the homeless living in Toronto, Calgary, and Vancouver today. The lives of the destitute may not have changed that much over the past few hundred years, with today's homeless often living on streets or in makeshift shelters in ravines. But the rich have become vastly richer than their pre-industrial counterparts. Here, for instance, is what an income parade would have looked like in the year 1688 in England.[4] While it's definitely a parade of dwarves (and a few giants), the level of inequality back then was considerably less extreme than it is today.

At the outset of the 1688 parade, we see some very tiny characters— vagrants, gypsies, rogues, vagabonds—who manage to collect about two pounds a year, begging or performing magic tricks for village gatherings. These extremely little people are followed by a large number of paupers and cottagers, who are still very low to the ground. Following close behind, about fifteen minutes into the parade, are household servants and common labourers, with incomes of about fifteen pounds a year, measuring about two feet tall.[5] Eventually we start to see the middle class—blacksmiths, silversmiths, masons, tinkers, tailors, weavers, cobblers, cordwainers (leather workers)—all earning about thirty-eight to forty pounds a year and standing about normal height. Just slightly taller are prosperous shopkeepers, ale-sellers, and innkeepers. Then come the naval officers, about ten feet tall. Only in the last few minutes do we see some giants—successful merchants and sea traders, measuring above fifty feet. Then in the last seconds, heavily armoured knights appear, standing 108 feet tall. Behind them, in heavy church garb, are pious-looking archbishops and bishops, earning 1,300 pounds a year and soaring up to 175 feet, even as they proclaim that the poor will inherit the earth. Finally, a couple of dozen magnificently attired dukes and earls, with incomes above six thousand pounds, stretch a lordly 815 feet into the air—a fraction of the height of today's mile-high giants.

As stupendous as the growth in top Canadian incomes has been in the last few decades, we still have not reached the extreme level of inequality that exists today in the United States. The rise in incomes at the very top in the U.S. has been simply colossal. It's possible to really zoom in on this phenomenon by looking at U.S. government data on the top four hundred incomes in the United States each year. The growth of these very top incomes over time is startling—especially compared to the paltry growth in the incomes of the bottom 90 percent. In 1961, for instance, the average income of these very top earners was $13.7 million (in 2006 inflation-adjusted dollars). By 2006, the average income of this top-earning crowd had risen spectacularly to $263 million—more than nineteen times bigger. Yet over that same time period, the average income of the bottom 90 percent grew (in inflation-adjusted dollars) from $22,000 to $31,000—only 1.4 times bigger.[6]

But once again, we can capture the feel of this runaway inequality much better if we assemble Americans into a parade.

As we watch Americans march past us, we see that, like our own parade the U.S. version consists of many dwarves and a few giants. And, like our parade, it's the end that is a sight to behold. Recall that Mike Lazaridis, the final giant at the end of the Canadian parade, stood a mile and a half high. But he's tiny compared to some of these American giants. In the last fraction of a second of the parade, we need a set of binoculars to see the faces now appearing: Tiger Woods, with an income of $100 million, measuring 2.9 miles high; Jerry Bruckheimer, creator of the hit TV series *Without a Trace* and *CSI: Crime Scene Investigation*, $145 million, 4.3 miles high. As the very end approaches we get a glimpse of the hedge fund crowd—or at least of their feet. Their knees are utterly beyond view, even with high-powered binoculars. Then, finally, we're directly facing the soles of the shoes of the tallest man in the parade: John Paulson. With a 2007 income of $3.7 billion, Paulson stands 110 miles high. A high-flying airplane is about at his chest level. His head juts well into outer space.[7]

2

WHY PORNOGRAPHY IS THE ONLY TRUE FREE MARKET

For the most part, Western governments did little to clip the wings of bankers, who continued to reward themselves exorbitantly even after they'd devastated the global economy in 2008. The one exception was Britain. After bailing out its banks for more than $1.6 trillion, Britain's Labour government slapped a 50 percent tax on bank bonuses in the fall of 2009. The move prompted howls of protests from the banking elite, including foreign banks operating in Britain.

As the furor grew, Goldman Sachs, the legendary Wall Street firm, quietly informed a key British media outlet that it was considering relocating its massive London operation to Geneva, signalling that its top officials had no intention of submitting to higher taxes. Goldman CEO Lloyd Blankfein, who received $73 million in compensation in 2007 and had amassed some $500 million in Goldman stock, revealed how little the crash of 2008 had affected bankers' perception of themselves and their role in society. In an interview with *The Sunday Times* of London, Blankfein steadfastly defended his company and himself, explaining that he was just a banker "doing God's work."[1]

Britain's tax on bank bonuses was actually its second move to raise taxes on the rich in the wake of the 2008 crash. In the spring of 2009, the government had raised the marginal tax rate[2] on high-income earners from 40 to 50 percent, prompting similar howls of protest and threats from the rich that they would abandon Britain. Theatre impresario Andrew Lloyd Webber appealed to the public to reject what he characterized as a tax increase on those who create wealth: "The last thing we need is a Somali pirate-style raid on the few wealth creators who still dare to navigate Britain's gale-force waters." Film star Sir Michael Caine, seventy-six, echoed the outrage, threatening to leave Britain if taxes at the upper end went even one percentage point higher. (The star of *Jaws: The Revenge* and *The Swarm* also threatened to retire if he wasn't given better film roles.) In a sympathetic article about Caine's tax complaints, journalist Iain Martin noted that Caine, the son of a charlady and a porter in London's fish market, personified the rags-to-riches success the government should be trying to encourage. What we need is not higher taxes, Martin asserted, but to clear "the rubble of the interfering state out of the way."[3]

In fact, Martin—and just about every other critic of high taxes on the rich—conveniently overlooks one key fact: without "the rubble of the interfering state," the rich would have nothing.

It's a simple and unassailable point, but it's almost always ignored: it is only possible for anyone to own anything—money, land, jewellery, yachts, and so on—if there is a state to create laws and enforce those laws.

This is the logical starting point for any serious discussion about income and wealth and who is entitled to what.

Without government, there would be chaos and anarchy, or what seventeenth-century English philosopher Thomas Hobbes called "a war of all against all." Not only would life under such circumstances be rough and disorderly—or, in Hobbes's words, "nasty, brutish and short"—but there would be no reliable way to enforce ownership. As another English philosopher, Jeremy Bentham, succinctly put it: "Take away the laws, all property ceases." Under such conditions, everyone's welfare would be fairly minimal—and roughly equal. Accordingly, philosophers Liam Murphy and Thomas Nagel argue that it is wrong to "pretend that the differences in ability, personality, and inherited wealth that lead to great inequalities of welfare in an orderly market economy would have the same effect if there were no government to create and protect legal property rights."[4]

By imagining the complete removal of government, we can quickly dispose of the notion that the "interfering state" has been hard on the rich. On the contrary, that interfering state has been their best friend. Without it, they'd be scrounging around in the bush with the rest of us, worried about when the next marauding gang was going to pounce on the buffalo they had just speared in an attempt to feed their children. Only with the complex set of laws governing property, inheritance, contracts, banking, stock exchanges, and other commercial relations—not to mention criminal prosecution of those trying to seize their buffalo—can the rich be secure in holding their possessions and enjoy the comfortable lives that come with those possessions.

Indeed, a government-enforced system of property rights, while theoretically benefiting all, provides far greater benefits to the rich than to the rest of us. As American legal scholar Robert Hale put it: "One owner, as the result of the entire network of restrictions inherent in property rights, gets the benefit of finding that liberty to use a particular ragged suit of clothes will not be interfered with by the acts of non-owners. Another owner gets the liberty of wandering over a large estate and using a large number of automobiles without interference from others.... The benefits conferred by these rights are not equal in any important sense."[5] It could be added that the police would likely respond somewhat differently to a call from the homeless man saying that someone was making off with his ragged suit than they would to a call from the estate owner reporting that his mansion was being robbed. While the state theoretically serves us all, it serves some more readily and fully than others.

In fact, those who lack resources will quickly find the state and all its resources lined up against them. Hale notes that while there is no law which forbids a man to eat food, "there is a law which forbids him to eat any of the food which actually exists in the community—and that is the law of property." Unless the individual has the money to buy the food available, he will have to go without. Similarly, he can't take possession of the delightful swing set in someone's yard and then tell the police that he was simply exercising his right to acquire private property. Private property is a special privilege, backed up by state power, conferred exclusively on those who have control over sufficient resources.

Of course, the rich have no quarrel with government interference when it comes to enforcing property rights. They are only irked when the government interferes by imposing taxes on their incomes, particularly when those taxes are progressive, that is, impose a higher rate on higher levels of income. But in protesting this taxation as unjust—in suggesting that it amounts to a "Somali pirate-style raid"— the rich are implying that the income they received *before tax* was somehow just. There they were, minding their own business, receiving their just compensation due to their talent and effort, and then along came the tax system and disturbed this otherwise intrinsically fair distribution. The assumption is that the way the "market" distributes income is fair.

This assumption is based on the notion that the market operates according to basic, natural principles—supply and demand—that are not subject to the sort of human whims that shape the tax system. In other words, the market is what would just happen if the interfering hand of government were removed, if things were simply allowed to happen, free of human interference. Hence the term *laissez-faire* ("let act" or "leave alone"). In fact, this is a bit of fiction. The "market" is a creation of the state, every bit as much as the tax system is. Both are based on an elaborate series of laws devised by humans and enforced by governments.

The profit level of a company, for instance, is determined by a whole range of laws: environmental laws that determine how much it may pollute or what fines it will face if it exceeds those levels, labour laws that determine whether its employees are allowed to form a union and whether they are permitted to withdraw their services, contract laws that determine what it can collect from a client who fails to live up to the terms of an agreement or what it must pay a landlord if it wants to break the lease held on its factory. After these (and many other) laws determine the company's profit level, there are a whole different set of laws governing how owners of the company will transfer those profits to themselves—what rights shareholders have in determining how the profits will be divided, who will get paid and who won't in the case of the corporation's bankruptcy, and so on. (The very existence of the company, for that matter, is made possible by laws that allow for incorporation, thereby limiting the personal financial vulnerability of the company's officers and owners in the event of a lawsuit.)

Once a shareholder is allotted his share of the company's profits, he may perhaps invest some of this money in bonds. Once again, the hand of government will be involved in determining how much he will profit from his investment, since the return he receives on his bonds will be determined by interest rates, which are determined by the actions of government-appointed central bankers. Their decisions affecting interest rates will hinge on whether they (and ultimately the government that appointed them) give priority to controlling inflation (as wealth-holders tend to want) or to encouraging employment (as those without wealth tend to want).

Similarly, lawyers, doctors, accountants, engineers, architects, and other professionals enjoy elevated incomes because of laws that give these groups monopoly power over their occupations. By giving them the legal power to license those practising in their fields, governments enable these professionals to restrict the number of participants, thereby ensuring high demand and high prices for their services. While such laws may be necessary to protect the public from quacks and charlatans, they also clearly bolster the incomes of a small group of professionals. Certainly, these professionals are operating in tightly controlled situations governed by a set of laws—far from what is conjured up by the expression "free market."

The point is that there's no simple, natural thing called "the market." The market is the result of the complex set of laws that regulate commerce and financial exchange in a particular jurisdiction. It can take any number of forms, depending on decisions made by government officials and parliamentarians who design, approve, and implement those laws. If the government tilts toward the interests of business owners, it may ensure strong property rights by, for instance, enacting laws that make it very difficult for workers to unionize or that make work stoppages or strikes illegal. In doing so, the government is not simply letting nature takes it course, as implied by the phrase *laissez-faire*; rather, it is actively intervening in a way that restricts the rights of workers, preventing them from combining with other workers or from withdrawing their labour in order to maximize their bargaining power.

If a new government takes over and tilts more toward workers' interests, it might revise those laws to ensure the right to unionize, thereby strengthening the bargaining power of labour in its struggle with business owners. There is a wide range of legal possibilities just on issues dealing with unionization—and unionization represents just one area of the vast array of laws that determine how any particular "market" will operate. All these variations represent different ways that the goalposts can be moved around within any particular "market." Each movement will generate a somewhat different result. So, for instance, we can see that different versions of the law affecting unionization will result in significantly different incomes for workers and for business owners. The different incomes that result from various possible versions of the law could all be said to be determined by the "market." But which market?

In other words, the market doesn't just fall from the sky. It is created. And the details of the laws that create it play a significant role in determining the income of the many different individuals in a society. Ultimately, the size of one's income is not just determined by abstract notions like supply and demand, but by the details of the particular laws that govern all economic exchanges and transactions in a particular jurisdiction. Change those laws—even just a little bit— and you can end up with significantly different incomes.

How much less, for instance, would Goldman CEO Lloyd Blankfein have earned in 2007 had there been a different set of laws governing financial markets?

To answer this question, it's useful to briefly review some recent history. Only a few decades earlier, financial markets had been much more carefully regulated. Financial houses were subjected to stricter capital requirements, greatly limiting the amount they could leverage in financial deals and therefore limiting their potential rewards.

For that matter, it was because of changes in the rules governing the financial marketplace that the big Wall Street firms grew to become such colossal—and wildly profitable—giants in the last decade. In the early postwar period, the major Wall Street firms were considerably smaller, because they were restricted to operating as private partnerships. This meant that a firm was owned by its senior partners, who shared all the profits, but who also were jointly responsible for all the firm's debts and liabilities. As a result, the partners were careful in their investing practices, knowing that they would personally be on the hook in the event of big losses. They also held each other in check, since the reckless behaviour of one individual could lead to losses that affected all the partners in the firm.

But things began to change after 1970—because the rules governing the marketplace changed. Up until 1970, the New York Stock Exchange had prohibited investment banks from becoming public corporations listed on the stock exchange, effectively limiting them to the partnership model. When this ban was repealed, the major investment banks began to switch over to the public model.

Merrill Lynch went public in 1971, followed by Bear Stearns in 1985, Morgan Stanley in 1986, Lehman Brothers in 1994, and Goldman Sachs in 1999.

As public corporations, investment banks were now able to raise money from investors through the stock exchange. This gave them access to far more cash and enabled them to grow into much bigger operations. By the time Lehman Brothers went bankrupt in September 2008, it had amassed $600 billion in debt—an amount far greater than anything it could have accumulated as a partnership. The change also meant that the senior executives of the investment banks were no longer personally liable for their firms' debts. When individuals within a firm—or whole trading divisions—indulged in rogue behaviour in pursuit of ever-bigger profits, there was none of the vigilance that existed in the days when the fate of all the firm's partners was on the line. Now bankers could use other people's money to award themselves massive pay packages even as they gambled recklessly, without facing any personal risk.

There were other advantages to the investment banks' new status as public corporations. Their bigger size and the fact they were dealing with the public's money meant that government now deemed them "too big to fail." If their irresponsible behaviour risked undermining the stability of the entire financial system, government would have to step in and bail them out. For the bankers, it was a dream world: they could take enormous risks, knowing that whatever gains they made would be theirs alone, while any losses they suffered would be assumed by the taxpayers.

All this suggests that the more stringent laws that governed financial markets in the early postwar period had been eminently sensible, and their removal greatly contributed to the 2008 financial crash—a subject we'll return to in the next chapter. But for now, the point we want to emphasize is that today's elite earns much of its income in ways that would simply not have been possible under the particular set of market rules that existed only a few decades ago. Without a whole new set of man-made laws governing the financial marketplace, Lloyd Blankfein would undoubtedly have earned considerably less than $73 million in 2007, and his Goldman Sachs stock would be worth a lot less than $500 million today—probably hundreds of millions less.

Under a different set of market rules, doing "God's work" would have been a lot less profitable.

WE MAY NEVER KNOW how well Sir Michael Caine would have fared had he become a porn star, but his income would have certainly been smaller.

This is relevant because it helps unpack the mythology that allows Caine, Andrew Lloyd Webber, and other big earners in the entertainment world to believe that their large incomes are simply the result of the exercise of their talents in the free market. Make no mistake about it: their good fortune has come about because of government intervention in the marketplace. And no, we are not talking about government subsidies for the arts, but rather something much more basic and enriching—the elaborate set of copyright laws that allow artists and performers to receive royalties for their creative efforts. Without these laws, the movies Michael Caine appears in could be copied and sold to people all over the world, without Caine receiving a penny. Under such a wide-open system, no movie production company would be willing to pay Michael Caine a huge fee for his performance, or much of a fee at all.

This indeed is the fate of porn stars. No matter how great their talent, porn stars earn far less than stars in the regular movie business. That's because the porn business, which by its very nature operates outside legal boundaries restricting sexually explicit material, isn't able to take advantage of the huge protection the state offers movie-makers and other creative artists in the form of copyright laws. If a porn producer contacted police to report that his videos were being reproduced without permission, the police might chuckle before arresting him for violating laws against displays of nudity and sexually explicit behaviour. As a result, porn producers don't bother reporting cases of copyright infringement, and porn videos are freely ripped off by others. The internet abounds in freely available pornography. This wide-open system is closer to what an actual "free market" in movies would be like.[6]

But it's not a market that allows performers to get rich, as American economist Dean Baker has noted. The huge incomes enjoyed by stars like Michael Caine and Andrew Lloyd Webber would be impossible without an elaborate set of government laws that provide them with property rights over their own artistic works—rights that are enforced by police and the courts. Baker notes that copyrights and patents are really government-granted monopolies, and that they have their origins in the feudal system of guilds.

It's straying a bit from our point, but it's worth briefly noting that it would be possible to do without copyright and patent laws, which form a large part of our legal system. The justification for these laws is that, without them, there would be little investment of time and money in creating new works of music, film, or writing—or, for that matter, developing new pharmaceutical drugs. But as Baker argues, there are other forms of government intervention that could ensure adequate investment in these areas, while creating fewer negative consequences due to the monopoly power of copyrights and patents. For instance, Canadian laws permitting generic equivalents of brand-name drugs to be produced under licence have helped restrain brand-name manufacturers from using their monopoly power to earn astronomical profits on drugs badly needed by the public. The consequences of monopoly power are less serious in the field of the creative arts, but Baker argues that the monopolies created by copyright laws are enormously costly to enforce, and becoming more so as the technology for video and music reproduction becomes ever easier. He proposes instead a system of individual vouchers, under which each taxpayer would be given a fixed sum that he or she would pass on to individual artists each year through the tax system. That may sound like it would involve a great deal of government intervention, but then so does the system of copyright and patent laws.

The point here is that government intervention in the form of copyright laws benefits stars like Michael Caine and Andrew Lloyd Webber. They have gotten rich not by exercising their talents in some mythical "free market" but by exercising those talents within a tightly regulated, government-enforced monopoly, heavily enforced at great cost by police and the courts. Without the interfering rubble of this aspect of the modern state, Caine and Webber would be no richer or more famous than the giants of the porn world, no matter how much natural talent they were endowed with.

So it is bizarre to isolate the possible tax increases faced by Lloyd Blankfein, Michael Caine, or Andrew Lloyd Webber and condemn them as the actions of an interfering government. The market is nothing but a complex web of government interventions. The income tax hike stands out in these people's minds only because it's an intervention that goes against their interests, whereas so many of the other laws and government policies favour them. As Murphy and Nagel wryly put it, "people care more about what unjustly harms them than about what unjustly benefits them." The favourable interventions tend to become invisible to their beneficiaries, as if they were just part of the natural order of things.

THE NOTION that it should be possible to become a billionaire is rooted in the idea that there are some uniquely talented people whose contribution is so great that they deserve to be hugely, fabulously rewarded. Some spectacularly wealthy individuals, such as American businessman Leo J. Hindery Jr., have articulated this point themselves. Hindery, whose contribution was to found a cable television sports network (a clear example of a government-granted monopoly, by the way), put it this way: "I think there are people, including myself at certain times in my career, who because of their uniqueness warrant whatever the market will bear." Similarly, Lew Frankfort, chairman and chief executive of the high-end handbag company Coach, argues that today's extraordinary pay packages can be justified because of the extraordinary skills required by the individuals running corporations in the "technological age." As he told *The New York Times* in 2007, "To be successful, you now needed vision, lateral thinking, courage, and an ability to see things, not the way they were but how they might be." Sanford I. Weill, long a towering figure on Wall Street, is also impressed with the contributions of billionaires like himself: "People can look at the last twenty-five years and say that this is an incredibly unique period of time. We didn't rely on somebody else to build what we built."[7]

What is so striking about such statements, beside the absence of modesty, is the lack of acknowledgment of the role society plays in the accumulation of any great fortune. These men apparently fail to see society's role in constructing a market that favours their interests. More broadly, they seem unaware of the pervasive role played by society in general (as well as by specific other people) in every aspect of their lives—in nurturing them, shaping them, teaching them what they know, performing innumerable functions that contribute to the operation of their businesses and every other aspect of the market and indeed every part of life around them. Weill's statement that "We didn't rely on somebody else to build what we built" can be quickly tested. Would Weill, having built everything from scratch, be able to reproduce his fortune if stranded on a desert island?

If so, it strikes us that he should be able to keep every bit of it for himself, having been solely responsible for its creation. If not, then it is reasonable to ask what portion of it was created by Weill, and what by others?

The Desert Island Test is a useful one to keep in mind, since those justifying large fortunes tend to see the individual in splendid isolation, achieving great feats on her own. In fact, no such reality exists. Humans are, above all, social beings who make their way in the world with the assistance and involvement of countless others who play roles of varying importance. This point is so obvious that it seems ridiculous, even trite to mention it. Yet it is typically left out of the formulations of those invoking the inherent right of individuals to accumulate large fortunes.

Philosophers have conjured up the notion of the individual, alone in a state of nature, choosing to enter into a contract with society. But this is clearly a metaphor with no basis in reality. No individual ever existed first in a state of nature and then decided to join society. Her involvement with society came first and, except in the most unusual circumstances, continued throughout her life. The primacy and ubiquity of society—so casually erased by billionaires and others justifying their fortunes—must be restored if we are to have any meaningful discussion of income and wealth, and where an individual's claim ends and society's begins. The restoration of society into the equation allows us to meaningfully explore the question of the proper relationship between the individual and the community— and who owes what to whom.

One of the crucial ways that society assists individuals in their ability to generate wealth lies in the inheritance from previous generations. In other words, in addition to all the benefits individuals derive from the society that has nurtured them and continues to sustain them today, there is the inheritance of all previous human societies, stretching all the way back to the beginning of human history. This inheritance from the past is so vast it is almost beyond calculation. It encompasses every aspect of what we know as a civilization and every bit of scientific and technological knowledge we make use of today, going all the way back to the beginning of human language and the invention of the wheel. Measured against this vast human cultural and technological inheritance, any additional marginal advance in today's world—even the creation of a cable television sports network—inevitably pales in significance.

The question then becomes: who is the proper beneficiary of the wealth generated by innovations based on the massive inheritance from the past—the individual innovator who adapts some tiny aspect of this past inheritance to create a slightly new product, or society as a whole (that is, all of us)?

Under our current system, the innovator captures an enormously large share of the benefits. Clearly, the innovator should be compensated for his contribution. But should he also be compensated for the contributions made by all the other innovators who, over the centuries, have built up a body of knowledge that made his marginal advance possible today? How do society and its contribution fit in? What share of the newly generated wealth correctly belongs to the society that has not only nurtured him but also provided him with this rich past inheritance, without which he would not have been able to create anything?

It is our position that society—and, by extension, all of us—should be entitled to a much larger share of the benefits. This could be accomplished through a decision to raise taxes at the upper end, thereby adjusting the economic goalposts—a decision no more arbitrary than the decisions made to determine the current location of the goalposts.

Some will protest that raising taxes on the rich isn't worth the effort, since the extra revenues collected would, in the grand scheme of things, be trivial. In fact, this isn't true. The sums involved are potentially immense. Virtually all the economic gains of the past few decades have gone to the top; that's where the money is. But even so, the goal is not just to find a new revenue source. The goal here is more basic: to determine a morally valid basis for the distribution of income, rather than accepting on faith the moral validity of the way income is distributed by the set of man-made laws that make up the current version of the "market."

We will return to this important subject later in the book. But for now, we want to emphasize that the need for a goalpost adjustment is particularly compelling today, when huge amounts of the wealth currently being generated stem from the enormous technological gains of the past. Technological breakthroughs related to the development of the computer in the past half-century have made possible the whole new range of information-age products that flood consumer markets today, generating much of the new wealth.

For example, a large number of today's successful entrepreneurs became fabulously wealthy building businesses based on the internet. None of these businesses would even exist—let alone have made people spectacularly wealthy—if the internet hadn't been developed. Yet the entrepreneurs reaping these enormous benefits played no role whatsoever in developing the internet. That technology was simply a gift from the past, the product of the work of thousands of other people who came before them.

An equally impressive set of technological breakthroughs related to the development of the internal combustion engine occurred early in the 1900s, paving the way for a similarly lucrative payoff with the rise of a consumer market for cars and airplane travel following World War II. The difference was that, back in that early postwar era, the enormous economic gains that resulted were more widely shared, due to the more egalitarian ethos and a more equitable tax system. Today, the stupendous gains made possible by the technological advances of the information age have been almost entirely captured by a tiny elite.

So we take issue with Lew Frankfort, the CEO of Coach, who argued that today's billionaires deserve their fortunes because they figured how to manage in the "technological age." We think he's got things fundamentally backward. The enormous pay at the top hasn't come about because those in today's elite have come up with innovative new ways to adapt to the technological age. Rather, it reflects the fact that they have succeeded in capturing for themselves virtually all the immense gains made possible by the technological age—a vast inheritance that could and should be more widely shared with the rest of society.

Today's gigantic fortunes seem to be less a reflection of the innovative genius of current billionaires and more a reflection of how uniquely adept they've been at elbowing their way to the front of the trough.

EVEN WHEN BILLIONAIRES aren't being actively lauded (by themselves and others) for their contribution to society, there's a tendency to regard the rise of a fabulously wealthy elite as healthy, or at least benign. At worst, billionaires are regarded as harmless fodder for the celebrity gossip tabloids and glossy magazines. This is highly misleading.

There is a growing body of evidence showing that extreme inequality imposes a number of very negative consequences on society. It increases the incidence of a wide range of health and social problems—including crime, stress, mental illness, heart disease, diabetes, stroke, infant mortality, and reduced longevity. It's no accident that the United States claims the most billionaires but also suffers from among the highest rates of infant mortality and crime, the shortest life expectancy, and the lowest rates of social mobility and electoral political participation in the developed world. There is also extensive evidence that the emergence of an extremely wealthy elite seriously impairs the functioning of democracy. Simon Johnson, a business professor at MIT and former head of research at the International Monetary Fund (IMF), argues that the financial elite has managed to effectively take control of the U.S. government, just as surely as oligarchies take control of governments in countries we typically dismiss as "banana republics." We'll explore these important findings about the adverse effects of extreme inequality later. Here we'd just like to highlight one dramatic and probably unexpected consequence of extreme inequality—reduced social mobility.

The notion that it is possible for anyone to get ahead, to do better than one's parents, to some day live in comfort and ease, lies at the very heart of the American Dream (shared by Canadians as well). The up-from-nothing dream lives in us all, energizing our society with a vitality and dynamism and sense of possibilities. In the most extreme version of this dream, one can rise from poverty to become a billionaire. Such a journey (although obviously rare) is theoretically possible in our society today in a way that it wasn't really possible, for instance, in the rigid, class-based European societies of earlier centuries. So that part is good. But it turns out that the country that fostered that dream has become a society in which even minimal upward mobility is effectively blocked for the vast majority of citizens. The reality is that there is more *actual* upward mobility for more individuals in societies with more equal income distributions—such as America in the early postwar years or Scandinavia today.[8]

The significance of this should not be underestimated. Every situation in which an individual is unable to realize an ambition—of going to university, of pursuing a career, of earning enough to support a family, of developing his or her talents to their fullest—is a dream denied, just as surely as the billionaire's fortune is a dream realized.

A society top-heavy with billionaires may seem like a paradise of upward mobility, but it's actually closer to being a boneyard of broken dreams for all but a lucky few. Those wanting to give their children a real chance to live the American Dream would be well advised to move to Sweden.

AS NOTED, the level of inequality in America today is extreme by historical standards. In 2008, the top-earning 1 percent of Americans collected a whopping 24 percent of the national income. The last time income was distributed that unequally in America was 1929.

It's interesting to note that the two moments of greatest income concentration in America over the last century coincide with the two infamous Wall Street crashes. Indeed, even the extent of the income concentration in the years 1929 and 2008 is virtually the same. In both years, the top-earning 1 percent of Americans enjoyed 24 percent of the national income. (By comparison the top-earning 1 percent enjoyed only about 9 to 10 percent of the national income during the early postwar years.)

Yet oddly, there's been little speculation about the role extreme income inequality may have played in the recent crash. Of course, there's been plenty of discussion of the role of individual rich people—certainly, the villains in this tale are all very rich. And there's been ample talk about the problem of "greed." But there's been little consideration, at least in the mainstream media, of whether the crash was related to the structural reality of the rich having an unusually large share of the national income.

This lack of focus on extreme income inequality is evident in an analysis done by the Congressional Research Service (CRS) in a 2009 report to Congress.[9] In this broad overview of the media and academic literature on the causes of the crash, the CRS singled out twenty-six different causes that had been identified, and also provided commentary and additional reading references for each one. All the familiar culprits are here, including the housing bubble, financial innovation, deregulatory legislation, excessive leverage, even "human frailty." But nowhere in this supposedly exhaustive review is there any mention of income inequality, or the unusually large share of income going to the rich. We're not suggesting that the CRS is suppressing anything. Rather, it simply reported to Congress the factors that are widely considered to be the main causes of the crash. In the popular debate, extreme income inequality just doesn't figure.

But then, extreme inequality passes largely without comment in the mainstream media. While poverty is treated as a problem, inequality in itself is rarely considered an issue, or even a subject for public debate. Its negative consequences go mostly unnoticed, or at least unmentioned.

Could it be that the rise of a new class of billionaire was the real cause of the Wall Street crash—with its devastating and lingering economic impacts for just about everyone in the world? In our attempt to probe the trouble with billionaires, this seems like a good place to begin.

3
MILLIONAIRES AND THE CRASH OF 1929

There was more than the usual secrecy as Frank Vanderlip and Henry P. Davison arrived at the White House on a cool evening in the fall of 1911. The men were two of Wall Street's most senior figures, and their meeting with President William Howard Taft was to be strictly confidential. A conservative Republican, Taft was known to have close ties to members of America's economic elite. But his advisors were constantly urging him to be careful not to appear too accommodating to the wealthy. So it was considered best that the public know nothing about this meeting. After all, Vanderlip and Davison were top officials in the nation's leading banks, and they were there representing two even more wealthy and powerful men, John D. Rockefeller and J.P. Morgan, who not only ran the banks but, between them, exercised control over just about every corner of the American economy.

On the agenda at that White House meeting was a matter of considerable concern to the banking interests of Rockefeller and Morgan: the Taft administration was on the verge of shutting down "bank securities affiliates." These were companies set up by banks to get around restrictions that barred banks from becoming involved in the risky business of trading in stocks and bonds. Taft's solicitor general, Frederick J. Lehmann, after a review by his department, had concluded that these affiliates violated the nation's banking laws. Spotting the potential for them to become vehicles for dangerous speculative ventures, Lehmann had notified the banks that he was planning to shut them down.[1]

Lehmann's decision had come as a surprise to Rockefeller and Morgan, who were used to getting their way in political matters. When Taft had taken office in 1909, a top Morgan official had wired Morgan, then vacationing with a massive entourage in Egypt, to confirm that the new Taft cabinet was in line with the recommendations made by the Morgan empire: "Franklin MacVeagh Chicago has been selected for Secretary of the Treasury. Wickersham will be Attorney General and other places are filled to our entire satisfaction."[2]

But now it seemed that one of those cabinet members, Frederick Lehmann, had proved too zealous in pursuing his duties. The only remedy at this point was to appeal to the president himself. Taft was someone they presumed they could prevail upon—even though they were aware that he was sensitive about appearing too close to the powerful—something even his wife advised him against. While Taft golfed with the influential industrialist Henry Clay Frick, he drew the line at playing a round with the even more powerful oil magnate John D. Rockefeller. Similar discretion was required in his dealing with banking colossus J. Pierpont Morgan, who quietly visited Taft's summer home, Beverly, on a number of occasions without the visits becoming public. Taft's prudence in these matters was understandable. The public was agitated about the extraordinary clout wielded by these titans, and the president felt it necessary to at least appear intent on breaking up their giant monopolies or "trusts"—just as his popular predecessor, Theodore Roosevelt, had been. As with Roosevelt, there was a lot of antitrust talk and some antitrust action during the Taft administration, but also a lot of accommodating the business tycoons.

Certainly Taft had a freer hand to accommodate members of the elite when the issues were less in the public eye, as in the case of this "bank securities affiliates" matter. While the issue of trusts was highly controversial, much talked about in Congress and the press, bank affiliates were really on nobody's mind, except the bankers.' So when Taft met at the White House with Vanderlip, president of the Rockefeller-controlled National City Bank, and Davison, a high-ranking partner in J.P. Morgan & Company, the president knew he had some leeway. If he were to acquiesce to their demands, the public wouldn't have to know. He didn't need to fear that loudmouths like Congressman Charles A. Lindbergh (father of the famed future aviator) would have another opportunity to denounce the "Money Trust" as the most sinister power of all, or that muckraking journalist Lincoln Steffens would spot another chance to decry Pierpont Morgan as "the boss of the United States." No, what happened at this meeting—even the fact that it ever took place—would never have to become an issue.

And so it was that the stout, moustached Taft, all three hundred pounds of him, settled comfortably into a large sturdy chair. In the cozy secrecy of the White House, he assured Vanderlip and Davison that he would overrule his own solicitor general, thereby handing his guests—and beyond them, the potentates for whom this bone was really intended—the power to wreak havoc in the financial markets for almost two decades.

IN MANY WAYS, the seeds of the 1929 Wall Street crash were sown in that quiet White House meeting. What the president agreed to—in overruling his prescient solicitor general—amounted to a significant deregulation of the financial markets. The restrictions that kept banks out of trading in stocks and bonds had been a crucial pillar of the post–Civil War banking system. Given their important role in handling the public's savings, banks had been considered too central to the economy to be allowed to play in the notoriously fast and loose trading world, which more closely resembled the world of gambling. Taft's decision to allow banks into this lucrative area essentially eliminated a deliberate safeguard that had been built into the 1864 U.S. National Bank Act, which had been modelled on British banking practices.

Not only did Taft's decision free up banks to use their vast deposits in risky ways, but it also allowed the banks to raise even more money from members of the public by selling them stocks and bonds. Ordinary citizens were much more likely to trust a securities firm connected to a well-established bank than a lesser-known player in the securities field—a field that was known to be full of shady characters. This greater public confidence in the banks (which turned out to be undeserved) helped draw many unsophisticated investors into the financial marketplace, fuelling what became a gigantic speculative bubble in the late 1920s.

But it's important to note that this key act—Taft's willingness to allow banks to venture into stock trading—came about because of the immense political power of a few extremely rich financiers. That Rockefeller and Morgan were able to get the president to agree not to enforce the nation's banking laws was a reflection of the extent to which control over the nation's wealth had become highly concentrated in a very small number of hands.

Certainly, the country of small yeoman farmers that had existed in colonial times and that the founding fathers had envisioned as a permanent feature of American democracy had largely disappeared by the early decades of the 1900s. Instead, the United States had become a highly stratified, top-heavy society dominated by a few dozen incredibly wealthy "robber barons." Ferdinand Lundberg captured the extent of the economic concentration that prevailed in the early years of the twentieth century in the title of his book on the phenomenon: *America's 60 Families.* It was an age of stunning, conspicuous inequality, with grand, ornate mansions rising along Fifth Avenue and the ultra-wealthy occupying a world of their own, whiling away their time in luxuriant splendour on sprawling country estates, waited on by legions of servants, or congregating for glittering costume balls at the glamorous Waldorf-Astoria Hotel.

Part and parcel of this concentration of wealth was the emergence of a dominant banking elite, personified by the rise of John Pierpont Morgan. The son of a banker who had made a fortune raising British capital for American industrial expansion, Morgan ended up becoming America's richest and most powerful banker. An intense and domineering man who barked orders at underlings and vacationed with members of the British royal family, he became a symbol of the growing concentration of money and power in banking.

Morgan's reach extended far beyond what he actually owned. Through dominant positions on boards and executive committees, he and his close associates eventually controlled some thirty-five banks and insurance companies and sixty non-financial institutions, including such diverse corporate giants as the United States Steel Corporation, American Telephone and Telegraph, the Chesapeake and Ohio Railroad, the General Electric Company, International Harvester Company, Consolidated Edison Company, the Niagara Hudson Power Corporation, Standard Brands Incorporated, and the United Gas Improvement Company. In all, Morgan effectively controlled companies worth a total of $17 billion—equivalent to about $370 billion today. And there were dozens more financial and non-financial entities in which Morgan was a dominant influence, even without holding direct control. Writer Anna Rochester compared his sprawling empire to a medieval fortress whose "inner stronghold is surrounded by open stretches on which maneuvers can take place only with the knowledge and goodwill of the ruling lord."[3]

Indeed, Morgan had all the imperiousness of a medieval lord. In open defiance of the nation's antitrust laws, he and Rockefeller had brazenly created a giant holding company that knit together all their interests, raising fears that the entire American economy could end up under the control of one corporation. When Theodore Roosevelt's administration initiated an antitrust action against the holding company in 1902, Morgan was highly annoyed, telling guests at a dinner party he had been assured that the new president, for all his trust-busting talk, would do the "gentlemanly thing." Morgan appears to have regarded the antitrust action almost as a matter to be sorted out privately by two equally powerful potentates; meeting with Roosevelt at the White House, he reportedly told the president: "If we have done anything wrong, send your man to my man and they can fix it up." Although the antitrust case did proceed (and eventually resulted in the dissolution of the holding company), the president assured Morgan at the White House meeting that Morgan's many other monopoly interests were safe from government intervention.[4]

Along with Morgan, two other banking interests had come to dominate Wall Street early in the twentieth century—National City Bank, controlled by Rockefeller (with J.P. Morgan being the second-largest stockholder), and First National Bank of New York, controlled by financier George F. Baker, the eleventh richest man in the country. Concern over the influence of these three enormously potent banking interests prompted a 1912 congressional investigation. Led by Congressman Arsène Pujo of Louisiana, the lengthy probe documented the extraordinary financial reach of this banking triumvirate: together, their principals held 341 directorships in 112 corporations, with aggregate resources or capitalization of $22 billion ($482 billion in today's dollars). This gave this inner circle of Wall Street interests a degree of control over the economy that was shocking even to an American public that had become used to the power wielded by the big industrial monopolies of the time—the oil trust, the railroad trust, the steel trust, the copper trust, the sugar trust, and so on. The Pujo committee charged that, of all the trusts, this one—the "money trust"—was the most threatening to the public welfare: "Far more dangerous than all that has happened to us in the past in the way of elimination of competition in industry is the control of credit through the domination of these groups over our banks and industries."

The clout of the House of Morgan was most nakedly displayed in the infamous "Bankers' Panic" of 1907. After a series of moves that suggest Morgan may have deliberately created a panic in the markets, President Theodore Roosevelt put $25 million in treasury funds under the control of J.P. Morgan & Company, hoping that the banker would use it to calm the markets down. When the market tumult continued, Roosevelt realized Morgan wanted more from the White House—specifically, approval for U.S. Steel to absorb Tennessee Coal and Iron, a takeover that would amount to a serious violation of the Sherman Antitrust Act. As the Wall Street panic grew, the president met with high-level Morgan emissaries at the White House and assured them his administration would take no action in the event of a Tennessee Coal takeover. Calm was very quickly restored to the markets, for which Morgan was widely credited. Roosevelt delivered on his end of the implicit deal as well; U.S. Steel was permitted to take over Tennessee Coal while frustrated government antitrust lawyers were obliged to look the other way.[5]

In the wake of the Bankers' Panic, the power of the moneyed interests had become so flagrant that there were widespread calls for something to be done. Congress set up a commission to consider banking reforms—only to have Morgan interests quickly capture control of it. Indeed, from the outset, the commission was effectively under the thumb of the House of Morgan. It was chaired by Republican senator Nelson Aldrich, a wealthy Rhode Island financier who moved in elite business and social circles and whose daughter Abby married John D. Rockefeller Jr. As a senator, Aldrich was known for vigorously championing the causes of the wealthy, and he immediately appointed Henry P. Davison, a trusted Morgan associate, as his advisor on the banking commission. (Davison was the banker who would later represent Morgan in the 1911 meeting with Taft at the White House.) This meant that Davison would have ample opportunity to influence the Aldrich commission in the direction favoured by Morgan and the Wall Street clique—a clique that Aldrich was already closely allied to. As a cable sent to Morgan from one of his officials noted: "It is understood that Davison is to represent our views and will be particularly close to Senator Aldrich."[6]

The key reform to be considered by the Aldrich commission was the creation of a central bank. The House of Morgan had effectively been operating as one, but it was now widely appreciated that this gave Morgan far too much clout over the American economy. The important question for the commission was what form such a bank would take. Should it be under the control of private interests, similar to the Bank of England, or under government control? Some reformers, notably the farmer-dominated Populist movement, weren't keen on a central bank at all, fearing it would end up dominated by Wall Street, no matter who technically ran it.

But among the small group of insiders with input into the Aldrich commission, the matter was never in doubt. In 1910, Senator Aldrich, along with his close advisor Henry Davison and a small cabal of Wall Street bankers, departed for a secret retreat at the Jekyll Island Club, a favourite Morgan hideaway off the cost of Georgia. There, in secluded splendour, ostensibly on a duck-hunting vacation, they devised a plan for a fully private central bank, involving a system of private regional reserve banks to be governed by a board of private bankers.

When Aldrich presented his plan, it was widely denounced as a Wall Street scheme and blocked by Democrats in Congress. Several years later, the Democrats brought forward legislation for the Federal Reserve System, a central banking system modelled along the lines of the Jekyll Island plan but with the modification that the private regional banks be placed under the authority of a government-appointed board based in Washington. Although the creation of the Federal Reserve System in 1913 was aimed at limiting Wall Street's power, in reality, things turned out much as the Populists had feared. Despite the government board at the top, the New York Reserve Bank dominated the system, largely setting the nation's monetary policy to suit Wall Street interests. Benjamin Strong, who served for many years as governor of the New York Reserve Bank, was a Wall Street banker who had been part of the Jekyll Island cabal. Author Ron Chernow argues that, far from seeing its power diminished, the House of Morgan was able to "skillfully harness the Fed and use it to amplify its powers."[7]

By the 1920s, the power of the financial elite had become even more entrenched than it had been in the preceding decades. The labour and agrarian protest movements that had sprung up in the late nineteenth and early twentieth century had largely petered out as a significant force in American politics. Their leader, William Jennings Bryan, had proved unable to win the White House, despite three attempts as the Democratic presidential candidate. By 1924, the badly divided Democrats abandoned any pretense of being a reform-oriented party and, on the one-hundred-and-third ballot at their convention, selected as their leader John W. Davis—a senior attorney for J.P. Morgan.[8] Meanwhile, wealthy interests unabashedly dominated the Republican Party. As Lundberg wryly noted, the contest between Herbert Hoover and Andrew Mellon for the 1928 Republican presidential nomination "was strictly one between Morgan finance capital and Mellon finance capital."[9] Indeed, with no pressure from the left, the Republicans happily drifted even farther to the right. After two decades of feeling the need to at least appear concerned about the problems posed by the giant monopolies, the three Republican presidents who held office in the 1920s—Warren Harding, Calvin Coolidge, and Herbert Hoover—settled into the comfortable niche of simply accommodating the interests of the wealthy.

Nowhere was this more evident than in the area of tax policy. Arguably more important than the rather lacklustre Republican presidents themselves was Andrew Mellon, a wealthy Pittsburgh banker who served as treasury secretary in all three Republican administrations of the 1920s, and whose extensive financial and business holdings made him the fifth richest man in the nation. Mellon used his position and personal influence to work tirelessly to reduce taxes on the well-to-do. Although opposition from progressives in Congress thwarted some of his early attempts, Mellon succeeded in pushing through a 1926 revenue bill that dramatically cut taxes on the rich. Under the bill, someone earning $1 million a year saw his tax bill plummet from $600,000 to $200,000.[10] Mellon also brought down taxes on estates to a maximum of 20 percent, a rate that kicked in only on estates worth more than $10 million (equivalent to $121 million today).[11]

Not content to massively reduce their taxes in the present and the future, Mellon reached back into the past as well, quietly signalling to wealthy taxpayers (particularly Republican friends) that the Treasury Department would happily review any requests they might have for reductions in their taxes going back to 1917. (It was Mellon's view that the rich had paid too much tax on the enormous wartime profits they'd made during World War I.) Not surprisingly, wealthy people and corporations responded keenly to the offer, and before long some 27,000 lawyers and accountants were presenting tax rebate cases to the Treasury.[12]

Under Mellon's guiding hand, the Treasury proved very accommodating to the desires of the rich to get back whatever financial contribution they had made to the war effort. The list of tax refunds eventually totalled $1.27 billion and filled some twenty thousand pages. Incredibly, $7 million went to Mellon himself, and $14 million to his corporate interests.[13] Altogether, between the reduced tax rates and the refunds, Mellon's Treasury Department handed over an astonishing $6 billion to the wealthiest Americans—equivalent to $72 billion today—a massive windfall that was to act like gasoline in fuelling the stock market bubble of the late 1920s.

AS THE NATION'S ELITE devoured an ever-larger share of the national income, far below them, the majority of Americans lived extremely modest, austere lives with little political power. Unionization efforts had been fiercely opposed by the great industrial titans of the late nineteenth and early twentieth centuries, with strikes ruthlessly suppressed, sometimes with state support. Workers returning from the battlefields of World War I came home to high unemployment and stagnant or falling wages. With union power on the decline, dissenters within union ranks turned to radicalism and even anarchism, making it easier for authorities to vilify and clamp down on labour.

So, although the 1920s proved to be a decade of significant techno-logical advances, workers were in such a weak bargaining position that they were unable to demand a meaningful share of the gains. From 1919 to 1929, worker output in manufacturing rose by 43 percent, but wages by only by 8 percent. With the costs of production falling and workers getting only a small share of the benefits, most of the gains of this improved productivity flowed into corporate coffers. As John Kenneth Galbraith noted, "The rich were getting richer faster than the poor were getting less poor."[14]

This left vast segments of the working population unable to afford the amazing new consumer goods that the technological advances were making possible—notably cars, refrigerators, radios, and vacuum cleaners. The more prosperous workers could only afford these luxuries by buying them on credit through popular new installment plans. With consumer demand constrained by the limited buying power of the masses, there was little incentive for corporations to invest their huge profits in expanding their factories. Those factories were already highly productive, efficiently producing as much as could be sold to a population whose appetite for the new consumer items wasn't matched by its ability to pay for them.

This left corporations looking for other places to invest their surplus funds. Like wealthy individuals, whose pockets were also bulging after

Mellon's generous 1926 tax cut, corporations increasingly directed their funds toward Wall Street. There was certainly money to be made there. Corporate stocks, reflecting the substantial productivity gains, were rising impressively. For instance, shares in Radio Corporation of America (RCA) shot up from $85 to $420 in the course of 1928, feeding the notion that Wall Street was a place where money quickly multiplied. As more and more money flowed in, stock prices rose ever higher with seemingly unstoppable momentum.

The glittering lives of the very rich and the upward surge of the stock market set the tone for the era, creating the impression that getting rich quick was just another exciting feature of the Roaring Twenties. Middle-class Americans who had been weaned on ideologies of hard work, honest effort, and doing without were suddenly mesmerized by the thought that, by investing just a little bit, they too could get wildly rich. Speculation pushed up Florida land prices to feverish heights in the mid-1920s, with investors snapping up unseen swamp properties far from any beach—only to have the market come crashing down, in part because of a brutal 1926 hurricane. Undeterred by the sobering losses, the focus of the speculative fever simply moved elsewhere. Wall Street bankers fanned the flames and the press, much of it owned by the wealthy Hearst and Pulitzer families, helped out with their own keen promotion of the wealth-making possibilities on Wall Street. Even the Democratic Party, having abandoned any pretense of being a promoter of progressive causes, pushed Wall Street schemes as the solution to the nation's problems. Writing in *Ladies' Home Journal* in 1929, Democratic national chairman and prominent financier John J. Raskob expressed the new zeitgeist of the party in an article full of investment tips, under the title "Everybody Ought to be Rich."

It was an almost irresistible notion, made tantalizingly possible by Wall Street's offer of allowing investors to buy largely on credit. This was a variation of the installment plans being peddled to middle-class consumers to help them afford cars and appliances. Just as they could put down a little money toward buying a car, Wall Street was inviting them to put down a little money toward getting very rich, offering to sell them stocks "on margin" for a fraction of the price. With just $10, it was possible to buy an $85 share in RCA at the beginning of 1928, with the remaining $75 provided by the Wall Street broker in the form of a loan. By the end of the year, the share was worth $420. So, after repaying the broker's loan with interest, the purchaser was left with a whopping profit of about $330—all from a mere $10 down.

Wall Street was keenly peddling endless variations of this sort of scheme. But while there were real opportunities to make a lot of money quickly, the risks were also tremendous. One obvious risk was that the stock price would fall, leaving the investor in considerable trouble. If he'd put up $10 to buy the $85 RCA stock, and the stock fell to $60 by the end of the year (instead of rising to $420), he would lose his initial $10 and would also owe another $15 (plus interest) to the broker for his loan.

But this less attractive scenario was far from the minds of those playing in the giant gambling parlours of Wall Street. As the market kept rising and more and more money flowed in, there was an eagerness to believe that this cornucopia was real and had only to be seized. And so caution was largely thrown to the wind. The miracle profits that were possible by buying on margin were only the beginning. These profits could be infinitely multiplied by adding layer upon layer of investments—all bought on margin. This was accomplished through "investment trusts"—paper companies that did nothing but hold stock in other companies. A purchaser could buy a share in an investment trust, which would then, on margin, buy stock in another invest-ment trust, which would then, on margin, buy stock in yet another investment trust, and so on. A giant pyramid could be constructed without investors ever actually putting down much real money. As long as the stock prices kept rising, the profits simply multiplied. On the other hand, if prices were to collapse, the whole edifice would come tumbling down, and the investors would owe a great deal of money to those providing the loans.

The nation's leading banks, liberated by President Taft from their legal responsibility to stay out of this world of gambling, had jumped in fully. Their presence only helped drive the frenzy. After all, the major Wall Street banks seemed to know what they were doing. So, for instance, the public was inclined to trust the National City Company, a securities affiliate of the powerful National City Bank, which was controlled by Rockefeller with a major share held by J.P. Morgan. At the height of the boom, National City Company had some 1,900 salesmen out aggressively selling its financial products, including some highly risky Latin American loans that were offered to the public as largely risk-free bonds. Whereas potential investors would have likely been skeptical of bonds offered by unknown dealers from Brazil, Chile, or Peru, they put aside such fears and eagerly bought up the near-worthless bonds when they were offered by an affiliate of the prestigious National City Bank, with its top-drawer Wall Street pedigree.

The banks were only too pleased to take advantage of such trusting naïveté, selling shares in investment trusts to the investing public at greatly inflated prices. In 1927, the public bought more than $400 million worth of stock in investment trusts; in 1929, that number rose to $3 billion. The ultimate scam, launched in the final gasp of market frenzy leading up to the crash, involved a Morgan-sponsored investment trust known as Alleghany Corporation selling shares in a holding company that went on a massive binge of railroad and real-estate takeovers.[15] The company created a giant pyramid scheme in which each new purchase was used as collateral for the next. The scam was made all the more curious by the fact that the holding company was managed by two Cleveland real-estate brokers, Otis and Mantis Van Sweringen—strange, inseparable brothers who lived in a sprawling empty mansion, where they slept in the same bedroom. The brothers ended up as figureheads of a giant railway conglomerate worth $3 billion. In fact, the real owner was J.P. Morgan & Co., which, it was later revealed, had cheated public investors out of $16 million. Meanwhile, a select group of Morgan associates and friends had been allowed to buy shares at a heavily discounted advance price, providing these insiders with instant profits when the shares were offered to the public. Among those who cashed in on such windfalls as part of the Morgan "preferred list" were a host of political figures from both parties, including just-retired president Calvin Coolidge.

As the stock market rose to dizzying heights, funds flowed in from around the United States and even around the world. All this had a choking effect on the "real" economy, as money was sucked from corporate coffers and the bank accounts of the wealthy into the speculative bubble. Much of the money loaned to investors for essentially gambling purposes actually came from the treasuries of major corporations. By late 1928, as the Fed pushed up interest rates in a belated attempt to cool the dangerously overheated market, the going rate for these loans to the "call market" shot up to 12 percent—a rate of return that was almost impossible to achieve by investing in the actual production of goods but that speculators, anticipating mammoth returns, were willing to pay. By 1929, many of the leading corporations—including Standard Oil, Bethlehem Steel, United Gas Improvement Company, General Foods, General Motors, and the Chrysler Corporation—had made multimillion-dollar loans in the "call market," seeing that as the most profitable place to put their money. The involvement of such major companies in the Wall Street markets was unprecedented.[16]

The relationship between the financial world and the broader economy had been turned upside down. No longer was there any notion that the financial community was performing the useful function of acting as the brains of the economy, directing capital to where it could be most productively employed and helping to spread risk in the process. Instead, the financial markets were sucking money directly out of productive places and feeding it into a giant speculative bubble—a bubble that would eventually burst, with devastating repercussions for the whole economy.

WHEN A SWEET-LOOKING thirty-two-year-old female midget crawled into the lap of banking magnate Jack Morgan, the 1933 Senate hearings into the banking disasters of the previous decade did, almost literally, turn into a circus. Jack Morgan wasn't quite the legendary character his father had been but, as head of the sprawling financial empire built by his father, he had emerged as a famous and feared Wall Street titan in his own right. He was even called J.P. Morgan, just as his father had been, providing a continuity that helped perpetuate the dominance of the Morgan dynasty. So the stunt, dreamt up by newsmen covering the hearings to provide them with a dramatic photo, caught the reserved, late-middle-aged banker completely off guard and somewhat flustered. As the professional circus midget planted herself firmly on his knee, photographers got their dream photo, and the broader public saw for the first time a scene in which the usually imposing and haughty head of the House of Morgan was no longer calling the shots.

In many ways, the moment dramatically captured a power shift that was underway in America. For the first time, the head of the most powerful set of money interests was being forced to submit to something almost completely unfamiliar to him: public authority. The 1929 Wall Street crash and the painful downturn that followed had fundamentally altered the political landscape. By 1933, there were thirteen million unemployed (about 25 percent of the labour force), with thousands of homeless men riding the rails searching for work. The enraged American public was not only hungry for food, but also hungry for answers about what had gone so terribly wrong.

The bank hearings, held right after Franklin D. Roosevelt took office, served up the villains angry citizens were looking for. Conducted by a tough, uncompromising former New York assistant attorney general called Ferdinand Pecora, they pried open the scheming world of Wall Street. Even the grand, graciously chandeliered House of Morgan at Wall and Broad streets was obliged to open its doors to Pecora's inquisitive agents, giving the public its first real look inside the highly secretive world. With the public intently following the hearings, which were covered in salacious detail by the scandal-mongering press, Pecora unveiled just how elitist these aristocratic banks truly were. They didn't handle just anybody's money, but rather regarded a Morgan account as a privilege they only bestowed upon those inside their social circle. Duncan Fletcher, the powerful chairman of the Senate Banking and Currency Committee under whose auspices the hearings were being held, prodded Morgan with questions about his bank's aloofness. Morgan simply confirmed that, no, the bank would not accept deposits from strangers. Frustrated, Fletcher pressed on: "I suppose if I went there, even though I had never [seen] any member of the firm, and had $100,000 I wanted to leave with the bank, you would take it, wouldn't you?"

"No, we should not do it," Morgan calmly replied. "Not unless you came in with some introduction, Senator."[17]

Public rage grew as the hearings wore on. The unrelenting, cigar-smoking Pecora unearthed the fact that President Taft had met secretly with the Rockefeller and Morgan representatives in 1911 and promised them he wouldn't enforce the ban on bank securities affiliates. There were revelations that the banks, through these securities affiliates, had been involved in more than four hundred stock pools—syndicates that actively manipulated stock prices, often with the help of publicity agents or even financial reporters taking bribes. Perhaps the most egregious fact unveiled by the relentless Pecora hearings was that Jack Morgan—who in the midst of the Depression still took home a princely salary of $5 million a year, lived on a lush, 250-acre island estate and sailed on the world's most elaborate yacht—had paid absolutely no federal income tax in 1930, 1931, or 1932. (For that matter, none of the twenty wealthy Morgan partners had seen the need to pay any income taxes in 1931 or 1932.) With so many Americans destitute, this was the final straw. When headlines about "tax evasion" blared across the country the next day, the stage was set for a historic move aimed at bringing Wall Street to heel.

Barely a month later, in June 1933, President Roosevelt signed a bill that had been working its way through Congress. Known as the Glass–Steagall Act, after sponsors Senator Carter Glass and Representative Henry Steagall, the legislation restored the safeguard that President Taft had so cavalierly tossed aside in 1911. Banks were once again to be kept out of the volatile, speculative arena of stock trading. A strict wall of separation was erected to separate investment houses from commercial banks, which handled the savings of the public. Wall Street fiercely protested the move. But this time, with an irate public watching closely, the bankers weren't able to prevail. Despite his wealthy pedigree (and past employment at a Wall Street firm), Roosevelt did not capitulate.

Indeed, the following year, Roosevelt angered Wall Street further by appointing maverick Utah banker Mariner Eccles to be chairman of the Federal Reserve. Eccles believed in Keynesian-style economic stimulus as a cure to the Depression—an approach that was anathema to conservative Wall Street bankers. Worse still from Wall Street's point of view, Eccles encouraged an overhaul of the Federal Reserve Act that transferred power from the New York Fed to the Federal Reserve Board in Washington, stripping Wall Street of its effective control over the nation's central bank. The best-laid plans of the Jekyll Island banking clique lay in ruins. Wall Street had been reduced to a faint shadow of its former self.

4

BILLIONAIRES AND
THE CRASH OF 2008

The humbling of Wall Street in the 1930s was a key part of the sweeping changes that significantly reduced the power and wealth of the very rich in the decades that followed. As a result, the United States became a considerably more egalitarian society dominated by a large and thriving middle class.

Of course, many racial, ethnic, and gender prejudices remained, blocking a number of groups—notably blacks and women—from sharing fully in the move toward economic equality. Still, overall, the change from the pre-1929 Age of Riches was striking, remaking America in ways that would have been barely imaginable a few decades earlier. And, as Nobel Prize–winning economist Paul Krugman has noted, the rise of a significant middle class in these postwar decades wasn't a gradual process that evolved due to market forces, but rather a sudden development that had more to do with the changing balance of power.[1] Widespread anger at Wall Street for bringing on the Depression had brought an end to public resignation about the privileges of the rich. There was now a determination that wealth and power should be more broadly shared with the rest of society.

The once-cozy relationship between Wall Street and the White House had been severely strained, as the Roosevelt administration now promised a "New Deal" that would include ordinary Americans. At a speech at Madison Square Garden in 1936, President Roosevelt unabashedly expressed antagonism toward the wealthy interests that had brought chaos to Wall Street: "Never before in our history have these forces been so united against one candidate as they stand today. They are unanimous in their hate for me—and I welcome their hatred." His secretary of the interior, Harold Ickes, described America as locked in a struggle between the power of money and the power of the democratic instinct: "This irreconcilable conflict, long growing in our history, has come into the open as never before, has taken on a form and an intensity which makes it clear that it must be fought through to a finish—until plutocracy or democracy—until America's sixty families or America's 120 million people win."[2]

With strong public backing, the Roosevelt administration took steps that greatly strengthened the hand of organized labour, bringing an end to the days when government automatically sided with the corporate elite. FDR signalled the beginning of a new labour-friendly era in 1935 by signing the Fair Labour Relations Act, a far-reaching bill aimed at ensuring workers the right to organize and bargain collectively, and giving government a role in enforcing those rights. During World War II, he used the sweeping powers of the National War Labor Board to raise wages, particularly for the lowest-paid workers, in a range of industries. With government actively backing unions and pushing up pay, unionization increased dramatically, almost tripling from 12 percent of the workforce in 1935 to 35 percent a decade later.

In the new climate, unions flourished, winning deals at the bargaining table from employers who now saw co-operation with their workforces as the sensible approach. In a precedent-setting 1949 deal dubbed the Treaty of Detroit, the United Auto Workers (UAW) and General Motors agreed to labour peace in exchange for workers receiving wage hikes and benefits in line with productivity gains. The deal set the tone for labour relations in the postwar years, allowing the gains of the UAW to push up wages across the economy. Among other things, this meant that workers came to form a vast consumer block with considerable buying power. As a result, corporations had plenty of incentive to invest in making products to sell to these eager consumers, rather than directing their capital into the speculative dens of Wall Street.

As the middle class became more prosperous, there was a relative decline in the fortunes of the rich. Indeed, as mentioned, the share of national income going to the top 1 percent fell from 24 percent to about 10 percent. To some extent, the rich had lost ground as a result of the financial cataclysm of 1929 and the severe downturn that followed. However, even when the rest of the economy bounced back robustly after 1945, they didn't recover their former predominance. As economists Thomas Piketty and Emmanuel Saez have shown, the declining fortunes of the wealthy were due in part to government action.[3] Among other things, Washington dramatically increased taxes on the rich.

In the 1920s' heyday of pro-rich tax policies under Andrew Mellon, the top marginal tax rate had been a mere 24 percent. But Roosevelt pushed that top rate up to 63 percent, and then to 79 percent. As this more egalitarian ideal became the established norm in the postwar years, successive governments—even Republican ones—followed suit. Under the Eisenhower administration, the top marginal rate rose to a striking 91 percent. (Some commentators try to dismiss the significance of these high rates, suggesting that loopholes allowed the wealthy to avoid paying them. While the rich certainly did take advantage of loopholes, the simple truth is that, in the early postwar era, they paid a significantly larger share of their incomes in tax than they did in earlier times, or than they do today.) Estate taxes followed a similar pattern, with the top rate rising from 20 percent in the 1920s to 77 percent in the 1950s, making it more difficult for the ultra-wealthy to perpetuate family dynasties. There were still rich people who lived very comfortable lives, but the super-rich—the ones living fairy-tale lives on sumptuous estates groomed by armies of servants—were increasingly relics of bygone days.

The overall result was a more egalitarian society, as the wage increases of working people and heavier taxation of the rich led to greater equality in income distribution. The egalitarian reality also contributed to a new ethos of equality, fairness, and public empowerment. This was reflected in support for government, which was called upon to defend and promote the public interest. No longer regarded as simply an instrument for protecting the interests of a small wealthy class with which it had been so closely allied, government was now seen as an institution with a duty to represent the interests of the population at large. Having proved itself capable and effective in defending the population in fighting the war and pulling the country out of the Depression, government came to enjoy respect as a central and beneficial force in society.

The very notion that there was such a thing as a public interest, and that government had an obligation to serve it, was part of a profound change in attitudes. Among other things, the new mood removed the well-to-do from their protected bubble at the top of society and brought them more into the mainstream. No longer giants who strode unchallenged across the economic skyscape, the wealthy were pushed closer to the ground. They were now subject to economic as well as social constraints, facing greater regulation in their business affairs, heavier taxation of their incomes, and public disdain for any behaviour that seemed excessively self-interested or greedy. Under the new social contract, everyone was expected to contribute to the community. J.P. Morgan had once famously said, "I owe the public nothing."[4] In the egalitarian heyday of the early postwar years, the self-centred banker would have been regarded as the crassest of boors.

THE NEW ERA cast a pall over Wall Street. In line with the Glass–Steagall Act, commercial banks were now required to divest themselves of their lucrative investment divisions, which were sold as separate investment banks. The idea was that commercial banks, which received deposits from the public, were to be subject to a tight new set of regulations. In exchange, they were to be protected from bank failure by government, which would provide insurance covering deposits, so that members of the public wouldn't rush to pull their money out in the case of a financial panic. There was thus a trade-off for the commercial banks: although they were now subjected to strict regulation, they got the full protection of government, ensuring they wouldn't fail. Commercial banks were also prevented from holding significant equity stakes in companies. Along with these new restrictions, higher estate taxes clipped the wings of the banking elite's favoured clientele. As Ron Chernow notes, "the glue that compressed companies, banks, and rich families into a coherent financial class was coming unstuck."[5]

For those who had enjoyed great clout, the restrictions no doubt felt like a blow. But for all the bemoaning and the vilification of FDR as an enemy of his class, the big Wall Street banks and investment houses continued to function and even thrive. What had changed was that they were now performing the function that they were supposed to perform: raising and allocating capital so that the economy could operate efficiently. In Chernow's words, investment banks in the postwar era "functioned according to a textbook model in which capital was tapped for investment, not financial manipulation."

The result was an era of remarkable financial stability, with the lowest level of bank failure in American history.[6] In the ten years of the 1970s, only seventy-nine banks failed—compared to two thousand during the seven-year period between 1985 and 1992.[7] Indeed, banking was transformed into a fairly dull, predictable enterprise. "Postwar commercial banking became similar to a regulated utility, enjoying moderate profits with little risk and low competition," note economist Simon Johnson and analyst James Kwak.[8] The lack of excitement in the banking world was captured in what became known in banking circles as the "3-6-3 rule": pay depositors 3 percent, make loans at 6 percent, and hit the golf course by 3 pm. (Recently, there's been a new appreciation in some circles for this postwar dullness. Following the wildly volatile events of September 2008, Mervyn King, governor of the Bank of England, urged a group of British bankers "to join me in promoting the idea that a little more boredom would be no bad thing. The long march back to boredom and stability starts tonight."[9])

No longer the hotbed of action it had been in the 1920s, banking now had trouble luring talent from other fields. Doug Peters, who went on to become chief economist and senior vice-president of the Toronto Dominion Bank in the 1990s, recalls the sleepy nature of the banking world in the 1950s and '60s. Peters got his start in banking almost by accident, because as a young man he'd been kicked out of university with a 40 percent average and was told by the government employment office in Winnipeg that "the only place for someone with no education and no skills is a bank." Peters got another shot at redeeming himself academically a couple of years later when he was accepted at Queen's—and then soon thrown out for failing two courses. Once again, banking seemed the only option; this time he ended up as a loans officer at the Bank of Montreal.[10]

But while the financial world may have lacked glamour and drama in the early postwar years, bankers were performing their proper role as intermediaries, connecting capital to the real economy. As a result, American industrial interests in automobiles, steel, aluminum, and oil took centre stage, providing the basis for a period of strong, sustained economic growth—and one in which labour was allowed to share.

This early postwar era—an era of restrained banking, reduced incomes for the rich, and a rising middle class—was also a time of extraordinary economic growth and prosperity. It should be acknowledged that the rapid growth of those decades proceeded with little attention to the severe environmental consequences that were unfolding. By stressing the prosperity of the period, we don't mean to minimize the seriousness of this environmental degradation, but simply to note that it is a separate issue. Certainly there is no evidence to suggest that the rich would have done more to protect the environment if they had remained dominant in the early postwar years. (On the contrary; since the environment became an issue in the 1970s, environmentalists have received far more support from labour than from business for their campaign to reduce pollution and adopt green solutions.)

But our focus here is on inequality, and our point is that the measures that reduced inequality in the early postwar period did not in any way hamper economic prosperity. This is worth highlighting, because in recent years conservatives have made the case that measures to reduce inequality lead to a decline in prosperity. But the evidence quite simply suggests otherwise, as we'll see in more detail later. For now, we just want to emphasize that the early postwar era, with its strong regulations and income redistribution measures, was a period in which the United States and Canada witnessed extraordinarily high levels of economic growth as well as great financial stability.

HOWEVER, there were always those who wanted to unravel the postwar deal. On Wall Street, the yearning for the old days remained alive. And with the rise of less-regulated financial markets in Europe (Euromarkets) in the early 1960s, there was increasing resentment in New York toward the restrictions imposed by the Glass–Steagall Act. By investing in these overseas markets, banks got a taste of being able to operate freely again, tossing aside bothersome New Deal rules requiring them to hold mandatory reserves and pay deposit insurance premiums.

The appetite for such freedom only grew as time went on, particularly with the innovation of leveraged buyouts (LBOs) in the 1980s. A throwback to the pyramid-style holding companies championed by J.P. Morgan & Company in the 1920s, LBOs made Wall Street bankers key players in corporate takeovers. Typically, bankers would provide funding to a company's management team and a group of outside investors who were trying to take control of the firm, using the company's own assets as collateral for the loans. The deals were incredibly dangerous to the health of the targeted company, which would be left holding high levels of debt after the takeover, but not very risky for the bankers and its takeover partners, who put up only a small part of the money. As merger mania spread through the corporate community, bankers were transported back to the heady world of the 1920s—playing lucrative self-enriching games with other people's assets and shifting the risk onto others.

Meanwhile, the emergence of the new discipline of academic finance seemed to provide an intellectual basis for a return to a more freewheeling era. Economists and finance professors at the leading universities started developing arcane new financial innovations— using high-yield debt, securitization, arbitrage trading, and derivatives—based on highly complex mathematical models that gave a scientific veneer to the old game of gambling. Out of this new discipline came the Efficient Market Hypothesis, which seemed to prove that markets are always right, and that there is therefore little need for regulation. Those who mistrusted the new theories and products were dismissed as Luddites unable or unwilling to seize the exciting new wealth-making opportunities.

This blind faith in the market was highly reminiscent of the irrational Wall Street confidence of the late 1920s. But whether or not the dangers had been properly appreciated in the 1920s, they should have been clearly evident by the 1980s. A number of meticulous investigations—most notably those headed by Pujo and Pecora— had left little doubt what the banking world would do if given the freedom to indulge in risky, unregulated behaviour. The need to hold the line would seem obvious, but the forces pushing to knock down the walls that penned in Wall Street had gained strength. Indeed, the re-emergence of an aggressive Wall Street was part of a broader resurgence of wealthy interests, made possible by the 1980 election of Ronald Reagan.

Although packaged to the public as a folksy straight-talker, Reagan had elevated himself from B-movie-star status mostly on the basis of his Hollywood union-busting. His rise had been championed by business and conservative forces anxious to roll back the restraints and egalitarian policies of the postwar era. These wealthy interests had never given up resisting the New Deal. After failing dismally in their bid to put conservative extremist Barry Goldwater in office in 1964, they became more focused and better organized, bankrolling an array of Washington think-tanks that aggressively attacked liberalism and promoted ideologies favouring less regulation of business. They finally scored with Reagan, whose down-to-earth manner connected with voters. And Reagan delivered for them. From his early move to crush the air traffic controllers' strike to his massive tax cuts for the rich—reducing the top rate from 50 to 28 percent—Reagan's message of "morning again in America" was a sweet one for the country's financial and corporate elite.

The Reagan era brought significant change to America—notably a dramatic rise in inequality and an ethos that supported this increased inequality. Indeed, it's hard to identify which came first—the inequality or the ethos that made it palatable to the public. They clearly worked in tandem, reinforcing each other like a vicious circle. The more tax rates were cut and the rich became richer, the more money flooded into think-tanks promoting the new conservative ideas, and the more the corporate-owned media felt comfortable promoting these ideas to the public. As the new conservatism took hold, creating a culture of rewarding "success," there was increased momentum for changes favouring corporate America and for still deeper tax cuts for the rich, leaving labour and ordinary working people ever more marginalized.

The result was a significant decline in the clout and income of workers. The captains of the corporate world, empowered in the new environment, adopted a more adversarial approach toward organized labour, and successfully pressured government to let labour protections lapse and the minimum wage languish. As a result, unions were no longer able to ensure their members a share of productivity gains, and the positive ripple effects once felt by the broad middle class came to an end. This in turn meant declining support for unions, which were no longer seen as key vehicles for advancing the interests of middle-class workers.

As a result, there was virtually no growth in the real wages of American workers—even as incomes at the top soared. The middle class managed to retain some of its buying power after 1980, largely thanks to the Federal Reserve's looser monetary policy, which kept real interest rates low and made borrowing more affordable. But easier credit simply encouraged the middle class to fall deeper and deeper into debt, with many living on their credit cards or borrowing against the equity in their homes. All this made ordinary Americans particularly vulnerable to a serious downturn. It also meant that there was less incentive for corporations to invest in products to sell to middle-class consumers, whose incomes were mostly stagnating.

The bleak prospects for the middle class were spelled out in a newsletter that Citibank sent out to its well-heeled clients in 2005. The newsletter noted that the United States, Britain, and Canada had become "plutonomies"—economies where financial growth is largely restricted to the rich. The Citibank analysts who wrote the newsletter actually expressed surprise at their findings. They said that they'd been shocked to discover the level of income concentration at the upper end—a level that they noted was matched by only a few other epochs in history (one of them being the Roaring Twenties in America). But their point wasn't to criticize or provoke controversy; certainly not to suggest the need for any income redistribution. On the contrary, it was simply to advise their wealthy clients to focus their investment strategies on products catering to the rich—the only place the analysts foresaw substantial growth. (One of the analysts, Ajay Kapur, later left Citibank to start his own hedge fund.[11])

But of course the rich, even though they take consumption very seriously, can only consume so much. Even if every wealthy family buys ten or twenty cars—plus similar numbers of high-end barbecues, walk-in refrigerators, or massive flat-screen TVs to grace their multiple homes—there simply aren't enough wealthy families to keep up consumer demand. And with limited prospects for consumer spending among the masses, American business responded by ceasing to invest in its own expansion. James Livingston, a historian at Rutgers University, notes that through the years of George W. Bush's administration, business invested less than its retained earnings for a period of six years—the longest stretch since World War II.[12] Instead, as in the 1920s, the action drifted to Wall Street. Whereas the financial sector accounted for just 2 percent of the economy in the early postwar years, by 2006 it had grown to 8 percent. Similarly, while the financial sector attracted only 5 percent of Harvard undergraduates in the 1960s, it was enticing more than 20 percent of them by the mid-2000s.[13]

Wall Street was both the beneficiary of the new conservatism and an active promoter of its agenda. With the wind at its back, it pushed more aggressively to dismantle the regulatory controls of the New Deal. Up until the Reagan years, banks had tried to undermine regulations by essentially ignoring them, carrying on forbidden banking activities in the hope that regulators and Congress would turn a blind eye. But now the bankers felt emboldened to try to actually get the controls removed. Not surprisingly, the House of Morgan was in the forefront of the attack, laying out its case in 1984 in a pointed document called *Rethinking Glass–Steagall*.[14] A key player in the campaign was Alan Greenspan, then a Morgan director as well as the former chairman of President Gerald Ford's Council of Economic Advisors (and later, of course, chairman of the Federal Reserve).

This was just the opening salvo of a massive and abundantly funded campaign for financial deregulation that was to become part of the vicious circle favouring the wealthy. As the rich became richer, they became bolder and more confident in their demands, and put more and more money into achieving them. And as they won more tax reductions for themselves, they had yet more money to sink into lobbying and campaigning. Between 1998 and 2008, financial companies donated $1.7 billion to federal political campaigns and spent another $3.4 billion on lobbyists. That's more than $5 billion in a war chest dedicated to dismantling decades-old regulations aimed at protecting the public from manipulation and speculation by the financial industry.[15]

Emboldened by the new political environment, Wall Street became more flagrant in its violations of Glass–Steagall. In 1998, financial services giant Travelers Group bought out Citibank, creating a sprawling conglomerate combining banking and insurance and openly defying Glass–Steagall. The following year, Congress passed legislation, championed by then Texas senator Phil Gramm, to repeal key sections of Glass–Steagall, making the Citibank merger retroactively legal. Gramm followed up soon after with the Commodity Futures Modernization Act, which made it impossible to regulate the exploding and highly speculative market for the new craze—credit default swaps (CDS)—which now, thanks to the repeal of Glass–Steagall, were being eagerly bought up by regular banks. The floodgates were open. Things had come full circle back to 1911, when Morgan and Rockefeller interests had managed, in one secret meeting with the president, to overturn longstanding rules barring banks from participating in high-risk trading.

Deregulation mania raged for the next decade, liberating every corner of the American financial industry from what were patently sensible regulations aimed at protecting the public from reckless bankers, speculators, hucksters, and just the blind stupid greed of the herd on a rampage. Deregulation can't simply be chalked up to the alleged imperatives of globalization or the existence of freer financial markets offshore. There were international efforts to rein in the financial anarchy, but instead of joining them—even taking a leadership role—the U.S. government actively resisted attempts to bring order and caution to the markets. When the European Union tried to bring the foreign operations of America's five big investment banks under stricter European regulations in 2004, the Bush administration helped ward off such interference, siding with the banks' request to be left alone to decide how best to regulate their own risky behaviour.

Indeed, with billions of dollars of deals being made daily on Wall Street, regulation largely disappeared. And so it was that AIG, a global insurance colossus holding insurance policies for millions of people and businesses, ended up being regulated by the modestly equipped Office of Thrift Supervision (OTS). (In a fit of deregulation mania, Congress had passed legislation that enabled certain kinds of companies to choose the patently inadequate OTS as their regulator.) It's a bit understated to note that the OTS was understaffed; its one insurance specialist, C.K. Lee, later acknowledged he had been wrong in assuming that AIG's $500 billion worth of credit default swaps, backed up by nothing of real value, were "fairly benign products."[16] Surveying the damage in March 2009, U.S. Treasury Secretary Tim Geithner observed that there had been a serious lack of "adult supervision."

WHAT GEITHNER DID NOT POINT TO—but that strikes us as key—was the role played by extreme inequality.

As in the 1920s, the enormous concentration of income and wealth after 1980 placed a stunning degree of power in the hands of a small crowd of financiers, and they used this power to, among other things, shape the financial landscape to suit their interests. Indeed, as the rich have become richer in the past three decades, they have attained a virtual stranglehold over the domain most important to them: the financial sector. As MIT business professor Simon Johnson has noted, the rising wealth of the rich in America in the past twenty-five years has enabled them to consolidate political power, giving the United States not just the most advanced economy, military, and technology in the world, but also "its most advanced oligarchy"—similar, it could be added, to the extremely powerful financial elite of the early part of the last century.

This extraordinary political clout has enabled the wealthy few to effectively disable government when it comes to regulating financial markets. So when Brooksley Born, head of the U.S. Commodity Futures Trading Commission, tried in the late 1990s to bring greater oversight to the wildly gyrating derivatives market, she was stopped in her tracks. It was almost a foregone conclusion that her efforts would be defeated, since she was opposed by the three most powerful government officials in the financial domain: Treasury Secretary Robert E. Rubin, Securities and Exchange Commission Chairman Arthur Levitt Jr., and Federal Reserve Chairman Alan Greenspan. Significantly, these men had all earned their wealth via Wall Street and all were dedicated to the Wall Street creed of deregulation. Indeed, as noted, Greenspan, in his days as a J.P. Morgan director, had played a pivotal early role in the campaign for the repeal of Glass–Steagall.

In fact, by the early 1990s, prodigies of Wall Street had effectively taken over government by being appointed to its top economic management positions. A virtual revolving door now connects the power corridors of Wall Street and Washington, with Goldman Sachs practically serving as a training school for those running the U.S. Treasury. Robert Rubin spent twenty-six years at Goldman Sachs, rising to co-chairman of the firm before becoming Treasury secretary under Bill Clinton; Henry Paulson, a one-time Goldman CEO, became George W. Bush's Treasury secretary. Then there's Lawrence Summers, Barack Obama's top economic advisor, who earned $5.2 million in 2008 from hedge fund D.E. Shaw. And Greenspan left the Federal Reserve to become a financial consultant to Pimco, a key player in international bond markets. Given these interconnections—which are multiplied at lower levels as Wall Street titans bring their associates and bright underlings with them to fill positions throughout the Washington bureaucracy—it's not surprising the two worlds now share a mindset and a worldview, built around freeing up the market and loosening controls on financial capital. And it's not hard to imagine how this nexus of power between Wall Street and Washington filtered down to encourage a "belief system," as Simon Johnson puts it, that gave Wall Street's power and influence a legitimacy throughout the broader culture.

IT'S BEEN SAID that much of the foolishness and excess on Wall Street in 2008 happened out of ignorance, that few players even understood the nature of the bets they were taking and the extent of the gambles they were making with other people's money. But that could never be said of Angelo Mozilo, the garrulous and cocky former CEO of Countrywide Financial Corporation—a company close to the centre of the financial crisis. Countrywide was one of the leading peddlers of subprime mortgages, offering the treacherous loans to thousands of Americans who, by any reasonable measure, couldn't possibly make the payments they were signing up for. If Mozilo didn't know the details of every case, he certainly knew the broad arc of the problem he was instrumental in creating. He knew that some of Countrywide's mortgages were, as he described them in internal emails, "poison," "toxic," or, not to put too fine a point on it, "the most dangerous product in existence."[17]

What makes the Mozilo story particularly interesting is not just his role so close to the epicentre of the meltdown, but his apparent reluctance to be there. In the early 1990s, Mozilo, perhaps heeding the wise counsel of his long-time business partner, David Loeb, and perhaps his own inclinations, resisted the temptation to take Countrywide into the lucrative subprime market, steering sensibly clear of a product that was a danger to his company as well as to homeowners who would soon be defaulting on their payments. But his resistance only lasted so long.

As the market heated up in the late 1990s, and his partner retired in 2000, Mozilo saw his chance to finally make it into the top banking circles he'd always felt excluded from. Wall Street was hungry for the risky subprime mortgages, with their obscenely high interest rates that only clicked in after months of rock-bottom "teaser" rates and that were only spelled out in very fine print. Mozilo moved aggressively into the subprime market, setting up a subsidiary specializing in them with thirty offices across the country and even cloaking the company's blatant opportunism in the mantle of social activism. "Homeownership is not a privilege but a right," he declared in a speech in Park City, Utah, as he peddled "the most dangerous product in existence" to tens of thousands of unsuspecting, low-income folks. So, while Countrywide had insisted on 20 percent down on mortgages a few years earlier, it was now offering them for zero down—and to people who had no proof of having any sort of income. The full tragedy of the situation—beyond the fact that people who could barely afford a trip to the laundromat were being lulled into believing that they too could own a home of their own—was the fact that some borrowers with good credit ratings were redirected into the subprime market, where they ended up losing homes they could have afforded. This was done because it offered more profit for the likes of Mozilo and the Wall Street clan.

Countrywide became a stunning success story. By 2003, Mozilo had a personal compensation package of $33 million. He had more than realized his dreams of acceptance and achievement, being welcomed into the ranks of the big bankers. In 2005, Countrywide made it onto *Fortune*'s list of "Most Admired Companies." Mozilo—whose Italian immigrant father had hoped his son would someday take over his butcher shop—was now being identified by *Barron's* as one of the thirty best CEOs in the world.

It's easy (and appropriate) to condemn Mozilo for his seemingly bottomless greed. But it might be more useful to try to understand him as a cultural phenomenon—a product of a culture (or even a cult) of greed in which, over the past few decades, the desire for material accumulation has been applauded, fanned, and stimulated to an extraordinary extent. Wall Street has been the engine room of the cult, a kind of hothouse of avarice, an experimental lab in which the normal restraining impulses—caution, prudence, common sense, not to mention common decency—were sliced and diced along with the toxic assets being peddled, and everyone was urged to join in a wild, rapturous romp aimed at snagging an ever-bigger pot of gold.

The ability to set cultural norms and attitudes is part of the power wielded by the dominant forces of society. In times of great wealth concentration, the financial elite not only captures political control of the mechanisms of government, but also more broadly establishes the tone and defines the mores of the era. In both the pre-1929 period and in recent decades, a culture celebrating greed and wealth accumulation dominated, with notions of social responsibility and public spiritedness shunted to the sidelines, even sneered at as a kind of political correctness. Wall Street traders routinely boasted about "ripping the face off" clients, an expression that meant making profits by selling derivative deals so complicated the buyers couldn't possibly understand them.[18] Such indifference to clients, let alone other members of the public, promoted an ethos in which greed and an obsessive focus on self-interest were considered normal and acceptable, even laudable and beneficial. It was this deadly combination—a political agenda controlled by the rich, reinforced by a culture celebrating greed and saluting billionaires—that encouraged thousands of apparently normal people to take part in the subprime mortgage scam, either as participants preying on the vulnerable or as political authorities failing to stop the brazenly predatory behaviour.

It could be argued that, in a more egalitarian era, a different group—perhaps the middle class or, more specifically, organized labour—captures control of the political agenda and sets the tone of the times. There's some truth to this, although conservative commentators generally exaggerate the amount of power ever wielded by labour. The notion of labour as a powerful "special interest" has been used to justify anti-union attacks in recent decades. In reality, workers are always at a disadvantage to corporate interests, which, by definition, have power over their employment. Even in the heyday of labour power in the early postwar decades, corporations remained enormously potent and there was considerable inequality. Back then, CEOs weren't earning the massive incomes they are today, but they were still bringing in about thirty times more than the average worker, allowing them to enjoy substantially more comfortable lives. So to the extent that labour wielded some power in the 1940s and '50s, this provided nothing more than a bit of healthy rebalancing, tipping the scales less overwhelmingly in favour of corporate interests, who had called all the shots before 1929.

In any event, the point at issue here is the role extreme inequality played in the stock market crashes of 1929 and 2008.

As noted, income inequality hasn't generally been considered a factor in the 2008 crash. Nor has it attracted much attention as a factor leading to the 1929 crash and the Great Depression. Indeed, income inequality doesn't figure at all in the explanation of the Great Depression that has been most widely accepted in mainstream circles in recent years. The dominant thesis is the one put forward by Milton Friedman and Anna Jacobson Schwartz, who blame the Depression on inappropriate actions by the Federal Reserve, particularly the contraction of credit between 1930 and 1932, which they believe turned what would have been just another downturn in the business cycle into a full-fledged depression. This theory, embraced by current Federal Reserve chairman Ben Bernanke, considers management of the money supply the key to managing the economy and has led to the notion that the Fed can ward off depressions through sensible policies. As Bernanke, then a member of the Fed board, told the crowd at a ninetieth birthday party for Friedman in 2002: "I would like to say to Milton and Anna, regarding the Great Depression: You're right. We did it. We're very sorry. But thanks to you, we won't do it again."

But the notion that things would have worked out fine back in the 1930s if only the Fed had properly managed the money supply seems less convincing in the wake of the 2008 Wall Street collapse, which happened despite the apparently greater sophistication of those running the Fed today, who had the benefit of hindsight. Rather, the striking similarity in the inequality levels in both 1929 and 2008— and the lack of financial crises in the more egalitarian intervening decades—suggest a causal relationship between inequality and financial crashes. For that matter, while the Friedman–Schwartz thesis has become the dominant view in recent years, there have always been analysts who pointed to inequality as the key factor in the 1929 crash. In his book *The Great Crash 1929*, economist John Kenneth Galbraith identified five factors he considered had a particular bearing on the 1929 disaster, the first one being "The bad distribution of income." Historian Robert S. McElvaine agrees. "The causes of the Great Depression were many…. In the end, though, the greatest weight must be assigned to the effects of an income distribution that was bad and getting worse," McElvaine wrote in *The Great Depression*. "Maldistribution was only one among many roots of the Great Depression, *but it was the taproot* [italics added]."[19]

Recently, a number of analysts have also pointed to the significance of inequality as a factor in the 2008 crisis. "The real cause of the crisis," wrote World Bank economist Branko Milanovic in the spring of 2009, "is not to be found in hedge funds and bankers who simply behaved with the greed to which they are accustomed (and for which economists used to praise them). The real cause of the crisis lies in huge inequalities in income distribution which generated much larger investable funds than could be profitably employed."[20] Historian James Livingston has also pointed to the similar patterns of extreme income concentration in the late 1920s and the run-up to the 2008 collapse. Livingston, rejecting the Friedman–Schwartz thesis, argues that the "underlying cause" of the Great Depression "was not a short-term credit contraction engineered by central bankers …[but] a fundamental shift in income shares away from wages/consumption to corporate profits that produced a tidal wave of surplus capital that could not be profitably invested in goods production." He notes that in the past twenty-five years there has been a similar shift away from wages and consumption and toward corporate profits. For a while, government transfer payments offset wage stagnation, but this only delayed the gathering storm, according to Livingston, who teaches at Rutgers University. "The moment of truth reached in 1929 was accordingly postponed. But then George Bush's tax cuts produced a new tidal wave of surplus capital, with no place to go except real estate."[21]

The evidence suggests that a high level of inequality sets up a dynamic that contributes to financial instability. Lack of buying power on the part of the mass of citizens leads to a lack of good investment opportunities in the real economy, driving capital toward the financial sector and concentrating wealth and power in the hands of financiers. This elite uses its clout to both create a social ethos that condones greed and to directly shape the political agenda to facilitate the amassing of great fortunes. A crucial element in this political agenda is the freeing up of financial markets for lucrative speculative activities. While these speculative activities are clearly orchestrated by the financial elite, segments of the broader public are drawn in, and bear most of the risks and the ultimate costs of a financial collapse.

By contrast, when income is more widely dispersed, as in the early postwar era, there is strong consumer demand for goods and services, attracting capital into the real economy. Political power is also more widely held. Middle-class citizens and organized labour aren't inclined to use their political clout to press for freer financial markets, but rather to protect and enhance their own incomes and buying power. This creates a political agenda and a social ethos that has a restraining effect on financial markets. As we've seen, Wall Street investment banking continued to function in the more egalitarian postwar era, but it did so, as Chernow noted, "according to a textbook model, in which capital was tapped for investment, not financial manipulation." In other words, Wall Street functioned as it should—as a vehicle for raising and allocating capital for the broader economy—not as a vehicle for highly destabilizing financial speculation.

It could perhaps be added that eras of extreme inequality have a certain zesty drama about them that may seem lacking in more egalitarian times, with their textbook virtue, restraint, and rule of law. "Money has lost its mystique and banking, therefore, has lost a bit of its magic," wrote Chernow almost wistfully at the end of his massive 1990 history of the J.P. Morgan empire, apparently saddened by the idea that "there will never be another barony like the House of Morgan." True, a larger-than-life financial titan running roughshod over the economy, vacationing with royalty, and whipping presidents into line does provide a lot of colour—as do today's rogue billionaires accumulating the riches of kings even as they fleece society's most vulnerable citizens. On the other hand, a little less drama in the lives of bankers might be a reasonable trade-off for a lot less devastation in the lives of millions of others.

5

WHY BILL GATES DOESN'T DESERVE HIS FORTUNE

At latest count, Bill Gates's fortune was worth some $53 billion.

One of the key arguments of this book is that Gates, like other billionaires, only "deserves" a fraction of his fortune. Of course, even if his fortune was much smaller—say, just a couple of billion—Gates would still be a fabulously wealthy man, and his other billions could be spent in ways that would dramatically improve the lives of millions of others.

Let's start by noting that there's a difference between the concept of what one *deserves* and the concept of what one is *legally entitled* to. Presumably, Bill Gates has good tax lawyers, so he probably hasn't broken any tax laws. And if he were to run afoul of any tax or other laws affecting property, the matter would be sorted out through proper legal channels. Therefore we can assume that his $53 billion is legitimately his, under the law. So he is *entitled* to it. But the question remains: does he *deserve* $53 billion? The question is essentially a moral one, a question about what society considers fair. Does Gates— or any other immensely wealthy individual—really deserve to be so much richer than everyone else?

There's a further question that will come into play: is it necessary for society to allow huge discrepancies in income and wealth in order to provide incentives to motivate people to work hard, so that the economy will grow and everyone will benefit? This is a crucial question, but it's an economic one, and we'll get to it in the next chapter. First, let's consider the more basic question of whether Bill Gates's massive fortune passes the basic test of fairness.

Gates is, in many ways, a good test case for the question of whether billionaires deserve their fortunes because he sets the bar high. As billionaires go, he seems like a rather deserving one. He didn't just inherit a fortune; he went out and made one on his own in the marketplace. He not only has great natural talents but, by all accounts, he worked extremely hard to get where he is, making full use of his abilities and every opportunity he encountered. Furthermore, his accomplishment is nothing less than coming up with the operating system for the personal computer—the most widely used innovation of the past century and one that few of us would want to do without. So Gates has made a substantial contribution to society. And, to top it off, he's become a significant philanthropist, donating huge sums of money not just to concert halls where rich people gather but to causes that help truly needy people, like AIDS victims in Africa. It wasn't surprising then that *Time* magazine elevated him to one of the 100 most influential people of the twentieth century, and in 2005 chose him (along with wife, Melinda, and rock star Bono) as Persons of the Year. If there's anyone who seems to deserve his fortune, it's Bill Gates.

Indeed, at first glance, he's just about a perfect role model—lots of talent and effort, a major social contribution, and a generosity toward the needy. Not surprisingly, Gates has become an almost mythical character, one who makes wealth accumulation look justified. He's a kind of poster boy for billionaires.

Like most legends, of course, there's more to the story. Certainly the point has been made, including by Malcolm Gladwell in his bestselling book *Outliers*, that Gates's success was dependent on luck, which immediately makes him seem less heroic. Indeed, Gates had the great luck of being born into a well-to-do family, opening up possibilities that would almost certainly not have been available to a child of low-income parents. His father was a successful Seattle lawyer, and his maternal grandfather a rich banker. As a result, he was sent to a private school, Lakeside, which happened to have a computer club—something unusual in the late 1960s. A fundraising drive by the savvy mothers of Lakeside students didn't just raise chump change for hockey sweaters or school outings. Rather, drawing on the school's wealthy clientele, they raised enough money—and were sufficiently forward-looking—to buy a three-thousand-dollar computer terminal for the school in 1968. This made Lakeside one of the few high schools in the country, and probably the world, with a computer terminal in the 1960s. And it was a particularly good one. Bill Gates, who hadn't been very interested in schoolwork, took readily and enthusiastically to the technology and was soon spending all his time in the school basement playing with the exciting new machine.

As it turned out, his timing was perfect. Society was on the cusp of a revolution that would shortly bring computers into the lives of millions of people. Decades of technological advances had led to the development of giant IBM mainframe computers, which had spectacular powers but were enormously costly and big enough to fill a room. By the late 1960s, the technology was evolving rapidly. In particular, a project done for the U.S. Air Force in the early 1960s, called "Augmenting Human Intelligence," made possible the development of miniature computers that could be programmed to process data in response to commands. This created the possibility that, in addition to giant machines used by government and the military, computers could be personal devices used by individuals in their own lives. The prospects were breathtaking. Bill Gates, just thirteen years of age and in grade eight, was getting ample access to rare and expensive computer time, enabling him to experiment for hours on end with a technology that was about to change the world.

Over the next few years, Gates got a number of important lucky breaks that greatly helped him get a grounding in the emerging technology. A mother of one of the Lakeside boys happened to be involved in computer programming at the University of Washington. She and some colleagues had set up a small business developing software to sell to companies wanting to lease time on the university computer. They decided to let the students in the Lakeside computer club come down to their office and test out the company's software programs after school and on weekends.

That meant more access to free computer time, and Gates and the others grabbed the opportunity. Soon they had an even better deal with another Seattle company, Information Services Incorporated (ISI), which had its own mainframe and was willing to give them free time in exchange for testing out software it was developing for processing company payrolls. In addition, the Lakeside gang discovered that they could get free time on the computer at the University of Washington in the middle of the night. Again, they jumped at the chance, becoming regular nocturnal visitors.

The ISI connection proved crucial. When Gates was in his final year of high school, a company looking for programmers to help it develop a computer system for a state power station approached ISI. The assignment required experience with a particular type of software—software now very familiar to Gates after hours of work on the ISI computer. He managed to convince the teachers at Lakeside to let him move to the southern part of the state to work on the power project as an independent study program. The following year, Gates went off to Harvard, where computers remained his obsessive focus. After a couple of years there, he dropped out and in 1975 set up Microsoft with former Lakeside computer pal Paul Allen.

For the first few years, Microsoft was a relatively small, aggressive technology company with several dozen employees—one of a number of such companies working in the emerging field of small, desktop computers. At this point, desktop computers were fairly primitive and hard to operate, and the market for them, while growing, was still limited. Gates was successful in the field, but not a leading figure. He was certainly far behind Gary Kildall, a brilliant computer innovator thirteen years his senior who had already developed an operating system, known as Control Program for Microcomputers or CP/M, which had become the most widely used operating system for desktops at the time. Kildall's company, Digital Research, had sold hundreds of thousands of copies of CP/M and was pulling in revenue of more than $100,000 a month. Microsoft's main business was selling computer programming language that ran on Kildall's CP/M.

But Microsoft caught a huge break in 1980 that was to launch it into the stratosphere of corporate success as the dominant force in the computer industry. That year, IBM had set up a secret internal task force, code-named Project Chess, to consider developing a desktop computer for the mass market. Crucially, the company would need an operating system for its new minicomputer. By any logic, the task force should have turned to Kildall, who was the acknowledged leader in the field. As writer Harold Evans puts it: "Everybody in the computer field knew that Kildall had created CP/M—everybody, it seems, except the biggest beast in the mainframe jungle, in which personal computers had hitherto been invisible." Instead, oddly, the IBM task force headed to Seattle to see a secondary player, Bill Gates.[1]

Gates received members of the IBM team enthusiastically, but when they tried to buy the licence for CP/M from him, he was obliged to tell them that it wasn't actually his. Gates referred them to Kildall, whom he knew personally; he'd been to dinner with Kildall and his wife at their home in Monterey, California. The IBM project team flew down to see Kildall and tried to negotiate a licensing deal with him. Kildall wouldn't immediately accept their terms, which weren't particularly favourable, but he shook hands with them before heading off on holiday with his family, assuming he had an agreement in principle for a deal. Instead, the IBM team headed back to Seattle, where Gates now assured them that Microsoft would be able to come up with an operating system to meet their requirements. He then quickly bought the rights to another operating system—an adaptation of Kildall's CP/M developed by Tim Paterson and produced by a Seattle company. When Kildall got back from holiday a week later and was told by one of his colleagues that Gates was negotiating with IBM, he replied, "Bill's a friend of mine. He wouldn't cut my throat."

Friend or not, Gates was certainly willing to cut a deal. He flew down to IBM's southern headquarters in Boca Raton, Florida, to meet with the IBM project team for lunch. The meeting went well. Project leader Don Estridge told Gates that the new IBM chief executive, John Opel, was delighted to hear that the company might be doing a deal with Gates, whose mother he knew personally. (Opel sat on the board of the United Way with Mary Gates.) Certainly Bill and his mother fit much more comfortably into the upscale corporate culture of IBM than did the hippie-like and free-spirited Gary Kildall.

In the end, IBM did a deal with Gates—even though Kildall's system was far superior. Indeed, Kildall, who was years ahead of everyone else in the field, had already developed the capacity for multi-tasking—a function that it would take another decade for IBM and Microsoft to come out with. According to Evans, Kildall was "the true founder of the personal computer revolution and the father of PC software." But of course it was Gates who was to get the credit, and in the process become one of the world's most famous and celebrated men—and the richest person on the planet.

BUT DOES HE deserve that fortune?

Although Gates was a go-getter who maximized every opportunity that came his way—to the point of pushing aside a friend who apparently should have gotten the big deal—he wasn't the inventor of the operating system of the personal computer, as he's often celebrated for being. If anyone deserves that title, it's Gary Kildall. And this is by no means the first time an actual inventor has been pushed aside by a more opportunistic, less ethical rival who's simply more adept at manoeuvring himself to the front of the line. The history of inventions is full of such stories. But the point isn't that Gary Kildall should have ended up with the $53 billion (in fact, Kildall, although not in the same league as Gates, did do well financially). Rather, the point is to question whether *anyone* should end up with such a vast fortune as a reward for inventing a system that was in fact developed through the collective contributions of many, many people.

Our culture inculcates us with the notion that important advances are the product of individual genius. We tend to see the development of human civilization over the centuries as the history of spectacular achievements by individual Great Men (and the occasional Great Woman), virtually eliminating the role that society plays. This notion gives credibility and legitimacy to the accumulation of vast fortunes. If Bill Gates—or, for that matter, Gary Kildall—was responsible all by himself for an invention that changed the world, then our winner-take-all system of rewards might make sense.

But in fact Gates and Kildall are only two of the legions of people who in some way contributed. The personal computer didn't just spring whole from either of their brains. On the contrary, it was the product of a long series of technological developments going back decades (or even centuries), each one making possible the advance of science to the point that the next breakthrough became possible, indeed almost inevitable. Let's just take a minute to think of some of the more significant contributors.

In many ways, the story of the personal computer begins in France in the early 1800s with the invention of a superior loom for weaving silk. The intricate brocaded fabrics that were fashionable at the time could be produced by an instrument known as a drawloom, but only with extremely difficult and complex hand weaving. Joseph Marie Jacquard, the fifth of nine children of a master weaver from Lyons, devised a loom that allowed the weaving function to be done without manual effort. The key to his invention was a series of punched cards. These were inserted into the loom, where metal rods attached to individual threads would hit against them. If a rod encountered a hole in a card, it would activate a thread; if it encountered solid card, it would do nothing. So the actions of the loom were determined by the placement of a series of holes in the punched cards. With the insertion of the cards, the loom could effectively be *programmed* to carry out the complex weaving tasks on its own. The Jacquard loom, notes technology historian James Essinger, "was a machine of a caliber and sophistication that had never been seen before. In fact, when it was patented in 1804, it was unquestionably the most complex mechanism in the world."[2] Its punched-card technology was the germ of the idea for the computer. (Indeed, the first computers Bill Gates worked on as a student still used punched cards.)

Jacquard's loom not only transformed silk weaving—allowing the daily output of a weaver to increase dramatically, from one inch of intricately woven fabric to two feet—it was the inspiration for an ambitious calculating machine that is now considered to be a Victorian-age "computer." Developed by British scientist and mathematician Charles Babbage, the machine was an attempt to adapt the punched-card technology of Jacquard's loom for the task of mathematical calculation. Babbage, who was well known in London's literary and scientific circles in the 1840s, openly acknowledged that his idea was derived from Jacquard, and indeed displayed a magnificent portrait of the French weaver in his home, made of silk using the Jacquard loom.

One of the enormously frustrating problems for mathematicians and scientists in the early nineteenth century was the great difficulty and tedium in calculating accurate mathematical tables. At the time, for instance, tables used to calculate the movement of stars and planets were prepared slowly and painstakingly by clerks who were known, interestingly enough, as "computers." Babbage wanted to create a machine that would avoid this time-consuming manual process and also produce more reliable results. In the same way that Jacquard had used punched cards to control the metal rods on his loom, Babbage's machine used punched cards to control metal rods that in turn activated cogwheels carrying out calculating functions. His "Analytical Engine" even had a *memory* that he called "the store" and a *processor* that he called "the mill." Babbage developed highly sophisticated portions of his machine as well as detailed plans and drawings for its completion, but he failed to actually make it operational. More than a century and a half later, in 2004, scientists built a full model of his extraordinary apparatus—with eight thousand parts and weighing five tons—based faithfully on his drawings. Babbage is now considered the father of the modern computer.

The next key step was taken by Herman Hollerith, an American engineer who used the punched-card technology of Jacquard's loom to create a machine that was actually able to process information. Hollerith originally developed his machine, known as the "tabulator," to simplify the massive task of processing data gathered by the U.S. census. When it was applied to the 1890 census, allowing the entire counting process to be automated, it quickly carried out tasks that had previously taken hundreds of clerks two years to complete. The tabulator was also able to easily produce complicated tables identifying relationships between different variables. Hollerith had some success adapting his machine for commercial purposes, and his company later merged with three others and surfaced under a new name in 1911: International Business Machines, or IBM.

It was under IBM, and specifically its high-powered, sales-oriented president Thomas John Watson, that Hollerith's punched-card tabulating machine became a widely used business tool. By the 1930s, IBM had developed an advanced automatic tabulation machine and was manufacturing some fifteen hundred of them a year. The Depression hurt sales, but the introduction of the Social Security Act in 1935 as part of the New Deal created a bonanza for IBM. Suddenly, the U.S. government needed to automate the employment records of the entire nation, and it soon ordered five hundred machines from IBM.

IBM got even more help from the government during World War II, when the U.S. Army funded it to carry out special projects. In January 1943, IBM produced its first real computer—the first automatic digital calculating device—for use by the U.S. Navy. The device consisted of a massive steel frame fifty-one feet long and eight feet high containing five hundred miles of wire and three million wire connections, but it was still based on the central punched-card technology.

Meanwhile, two engineers from the University of Pennsylvania, J. Presper Eckert and John Mauchly, with funding from the U.S. government, succeeded by the late 1940s in developing an all-electronic computer. It could carry out five thousand operations per second—compared to just three for IBM's wartime computer. The development of transistors in the late 1940s allowed computers to get more powerful still, and they could soon perform up to one hundred thousand tasks per second. At the same time, the devices were getting smaller.

By 1955—the year Bill Gates was born—the computer revolution was well underway, drawing the intense interest of some fifteen thousand enthusiasts intent on devising ways to develop and widen the use of these powerful machines. It was this loose group of computer professionals and hobbyists that Gates would join in the early 1970s. But before he was finished kindergarten, there was a whole host of advances that set the stage for his upcoming role in the rise of personal computers. Almost all these advances were the result of work funded by the U.S. government and military, and most were the result of teamwork, with individual contributions often hard to identify. Notes Essinger: "Ever since the late 1950s, this has tended to be the pattern for breakthroughs in computing: they have been the result of collaborative and joint effort by large teams composed of often anonymous people rather than by individual pioneers."[3]

Some individual pioneers do stand out, most notably Douglas Engelbart, a visionary engineer driven by a desire to develop computers to help solve the urgent problems facing humanity, rather than just as commercial tools enabling people to work faster. With funding from the U.S. Air Force in the early 1960s, Engelbart, along with engineer Bill English, invented some of the key features that we associate with personal computers today, such as the mouse.[4] Up until this point computers, though immensely powerful, were essentially inaccessible to humans, except a few initiates possessing sophisticated programming skills. Engelbart and others got around this problem by devising ways for people to interact with these potent machines—through the keyboard, the screen, the mouse, the menu, and other items of what's known as the graphical user interface (GUI)—so that individual users could easily instruct computers to carry out specific tasks.

These devices—absolutely essential in transforming the computer into the ubiquitous machine that is central to the lives of hundreds of millions of people today—were developed by Engelbart and dozens of others, long before Apple Computers (and later still, Microsoft) simply repackaged them for the mass market. (Before Microsoft developed Windows, it used MS-DOS—short for Microsoft Operating System—a much less user-friendly system in which users typed command words on the keyboard.) In a 1994 interview with *Playboy* magazine, Bill Gates acknowledged that one of the keys to Microsoft's incredible success was "committing to the graphics interface"—an array of tools developed not by him but by many others, who remain largely obscure and considerably less rich. Engelbart, who has been sadly disappointed by the commercial direction of the computer revolution, held the patent for the mouse, although he never actually received any royalties for it because he allowed it to expire in 1987, on the cusp of the desktop revolution.

So if we were to present the story of the development of the personal computer as a stage play, it would be a rich and complex drama with a long list of characters. From early scenes featuring Joseph Marie Jacquard and his punched-card technology that transformed silk-weaving in post-revolutionary France, the play would go on to include starring roles for Charles Babbage, Herman Hollerith, Thomas John Watson, J. Presper Eckert, John W. Mauchly, Douglas Engelbart, and Bill English, with a host of other largely unidentified characters playing crucial supporting roles onstage and off. Toward the end of this rather long drama, there'd be an intriguing subplot about how Gary Kildall went on holiday in 1980 thinking he had a deal with IBM only to come back and discover the company was negotiating with Bill Gates to use an adaptation of Kildall's own operating system for the first mass-market personal computer. Indeed, it would only be at this point late in the final act that we'd get our first sight of Gates. And he'd come across as a rather unsympathetic character, pushing aside a far more talented computer innovator (and friend) in a bid to convince IBM to use his (or rather, another company's) inferior operating system. At the end of the production, it's hard to imagine Bill Gates getting a curtain call or stealing the lion's share of the applause, let alone walking away with the entire box office.

AMONG OTHER THINGS, the story of the personal computer suggests that inventions and innovations are the result of an evolutionary process involving many players, rather than being the product of one brilliant individual. As Isaac Newton famously remarked in a letter to scientific rival Robert Hooke: "What Descartes did was a good step. You have added much several ways.... If I have seen a little further it is by standing on the shoulders of Giants."

Indeed, an invention typically occurs when the scientific body of evidence has accumulated to the point that the breakthrough is almost apparent—at least to the scientists closely engaged in the field.

As political economists Gar Alperovitz and Lew Daly put it: "What commonly happens is that a field of research reaches a certain point in time when 'the next step' is obvious to insiders—and because it is obvious, it is also inevitable that somebody, or more likely many somebodies, will take the step. Someone will connect the dots (but only, it is important to note, when the requisite dots have developed to the point where they can be connected.)"[5]

This truth is illustrated by the fact that a number of major inventions appear to have been "invented" by different individuals at virtually the same moment. One striking case is that of Alexander Graham Bell, forever credited with inventing the telephone. Bell did file a patent on February 14, 1876, but that same day, an American electrical engineer named Elisha Gray filed a caveat—a statement of intent to patent—for a similar apparatus. In the log book at the patent office, Bell was no. 5, while Gray was no. 39, which would seem to suggest Bell won the race to develop a telephone, if only by a hair. But two things throw that claim into question. Many of the patents were received by mail, and it's not clear from the patent office logs at what point in the day on February 14, 1876, the submissions by Bell and Gray were received. More importantly, it turned out that the mechanism outlined by Bell in his original patent wouldn't have actually worked—he had to file another patent soon afterward, correcting some of his design problems—while Gray's original submission *would* have worked! After years of unsuccessful litigation by Gray, Bell's claim now stands unchallenged in popular history.[6]

Clearly, Alexander Graham Bell was not indispensable to the invention of the telephone. In fact, he may not deserve any credit at all. There's evidence that half a decade before 1876, when Bell and Gray were virtually tied in the race to "invent" the telephone, Antonio Meucci, an Italian stage technician, had already quietly crossed the finish line. Meucci had already essentially developed a telephone, which he called the "teletrofono." It appears that he had been able to establish voice transmission between his Staten Island workshop and his nearby home as early as the 1850s. By 1871, Meucci had filed a caveat for his apparatus, but in 1874, unable to afford the $10 renewal fee, he allowed it to lapse. Had he not, Bell would have raced his application to the patent office only to discover that the telephone had already been invented years earlier.[7]

It's also clear that the personal computer would have been developed with or without Bill Gates. Indeed, as we've seen, Gates didn't really invent anything; rather he landed the big deal with IBM by elbowing aside Kildall, who had actually developed the key ingredient: an effective operating system. Gates later adapted other brilliant innovations (like the graphical user interface) that had also been developed by others. Not only would the personal computer revolution have gone ahead without Gates, it would likely have gone ahead sooner and better without him. For instance, innovations like multi-tasking, which were part of Kildall's more advanced operating system, would have become widely used much earlier if Gates hadn't been in the picture. As Harold Evans notes, "Multi-tasking was thus delayed in America for more than a decade by the IBM–Microsoft hegemony."

Furthermore, it's possible that, without Gates, the revolution in personal computers would have evolved along less commercial lines. A number of the early pioneers were committed to developing personal computer software for the public realm, free from corporate domination. Engelbart, for instance, was deeply motivated by the idea of using the computer primarily as a tool to advance human capacities to cope with the enormous problems facing the world. But despite his brilliant innovations, Engelbart was never able to realize his vision. Nor were dozens of other talented pioneers with aspirations of collectively building computer operating systems freely accessible to all. Their dreams were blocked in part because of the supremacy of Bill Gates. As Gates achieved greater and greater market dominance, he was able to use his power to relentlessly squeeze out others, prompting years of government antitrust actions that ultimately failed against Microsoft's deep pockets. In the process, Gates took control of the computer revolution, which could have been a vehicle for human empowerment or betterment, and turned it instead into a commercial Shangri-La, where virtually every computer user in the world is obliged to contribute to the enlargement of his ever-growing personal jackpot.

So, once again, does Bill Gates deserve his massive fortune?

The key point in this discussion of Gates and the rise of the personal computer has been to emphasize how relatively minor his contribution was in the grand scheme of things, compared to the collective contribution of so many others. And this is true not just of the personal computer but of just about all advances. Patent law expert Alfred Kahn argues that no invention is the work of one individual but is rather "the aggregate of an almost infinite number of individual units of invention, each of them the contribution of a single person. It is little short of absurdity to call any one of the interrelated units the invention, and its 'creator' the inventor."[8]

Indeed, any comprehensive assessment of our technological inheritance would include more than a simple list of the many breakthroughs that led to any individual invention, but rather the whole history of the development of technology. For that matter, it should include the entire record of the development of human thinking or even human civilization. Whatever Bill Gates's contribution to the development of the personal computer, it was only possible because of innumerable developments starting well before Jacquard's invention of punched-card technology, including a vast range of scientific and mathematical developments that preceded them for centuries: the invention of everything from geometry and algebra to the printing press, and even the development of human writing, beginning in ancient Mesopotamia.

It is this enormous knowledge and technological inheritance—which has grown at a particularly breathtaking rate in the last hundred years—that accounts for so much of the wealth we enjoy today. The Nobel Prize–winning economist Robert Solow clarified this in a groundbreaking study in 1957 when he identified that the key element in the phenomenal productivity growth between 1909 and 1949 was not the contribution of either capital or labour, as was commonly believed. Instead, Solow attributed the lion's share of the growth—about 88 percent—to "technical change in the broadest sense."[9] Herbert A. Simon, another Nobel Prize–winning economist, referred to the huge store of knowledge from the past as "social capital," and argued that access to it was our main source of wealth, responsible for about 90 percent of national income.[10] Still another Nobel laureate, George Akerlof, points to the economic significance of this technological inheritance in noting that "our marginal products are not ours alone…[but] are due almost entirely to the cumulative process of learning that has taken us from stone age poverty to twenty-first century affluence."[11]

Indeed, it's hard to figure out the rationale for the huge discrepancies in today's incomes when so much of what any of us are able to accomplish is due to all the learning and knowledge accumulated in the centuries preceding us. As Alperovitz and Daly put it, "Before anyone is a 'talented' entrepreneur or a 'menial' labourer, or anything in between, most of the economic gains that get distributed to individuals in a given year or period are derived from what is inherited from the past, not created by them in the present."

All this inevitably raises the question of who should benefit from the wealth made possible by this huge technological inheritance. As Alperovitz and Daly note, "All of this knowledge—the overwhelming source of all modern wealth—comes to us today through no effort of our own. It is the generous and unearned gift of the past."[12]

As things currently stand, the overwhelming beneficiary is whoever (like Bill Gates) manages to adapt some aspect of our technological inheritance into a marginally new product that gains market dominance—often through a combination of luck, opportunism, and ruthlessness. But why should Bill Gates or any other individual take such an extraordinarily large share of the jackpot? Does the technological inheritance that made his marginally new product possible really belong so exclusively to him? If it belongs more properly to all of us, and if this inheritance is the overwhelming source of all wealth today, shouldn't society as a whole enjoy a larger share of the bounty?

This group inheritance is implicitly acknowledged in the tax system, which collects a share of each person's income and deposits it in the national treasury for the general use of society. The question is: does the tax system collect a sufficiently large share of a person's income to compensate for the enormity of the technological inheritance? In the case of low- and middle-income earners, the answer is probably yes. After all, their incomes are not so large, and they need to be left with sufficient funds to support themselves and their families. But what about the very rich? Given the relatively small contribution any one individual is able to make, by what logic do we allow one individual to make off with such a gigantic portion of the spoils?

A number of important social theorists have argued for greater acknowledgment of the role of society in generating incomes— and greater payback through the tax system. John Stuart Mill, the nineteenth-century British political philosopher best known for his writings in defence of individual liberty, also argued, particularly in his later years, for a recognition of the important role society plays in individual earnings. Mill noted that it was society, not just individual effort or labour, that determined what a person was able to do or create, and that society was morally entitled to receive due compensation for its contribution.

In 1870, for instance, Mill was involved in the founding of the Land Tenure Reform Association, considered an important step in the evolution of modern social welfare philosophy. While arguing that private ownership of land might be desirable to achieve optimal production, Mill, in his draft of the association's program, insisted that increases in land values due to the general growth and development of society properly belonged to the community at large.[13] Mill extended this approach to increases in values of all sorts of property that are caused by factors having nothing to do with the contributions of the individual property holder. In a well-known passage from his *Principles of Political Economy*, he explained: "Suppose there is a kind of income which constantly tends to increase, without any exertion or sacrifice on the part of the owners … it would be no violation of the principles on which private property is grounded, if the state should appropriate this increase of wealth, or part of it, as it arises."[14] Mill went on to make the case that the failure of society to appropriate its due would result in property holders receiving undue benefit— thereby bestowing on them an "unearned appendage" to their existing wealth.

Many others have developed arguments along this line. The renowned American revolutionary writer Thomas Paine noted that, if an individual is separated from society, even given a whole continent to possess, "he cannot acquire personal property. He cannot be rich." Thus, continued Paine, "all accumulation … of personal property, beyond what a man's own hands produce, is derived to him by living in society; and he owes on every principle of justice, of gratitude, and of civilization, a part of that accumulation back again to society from whence the whole came." British philosopher and reformer Leonard T. Hobhouse, writing in the early 1900s, developed a similar argument. As great fortunes were being amassed through the industrial revolution, Hobhouse reminded the prosperous business owner to consider "what single step he could have taken" if it hadn't been for the "sum of intelligence which civilization has placed at his disposal" and the "inventions which he uses as a matter of course and which have been built up by the collective effort of generations."[15]

Mill, Paine, Hobhouse, and others were clearly developing a case for the moral legitimacy of taxation as reimbursement for society's contribution. Indeed, as Hobhouse argued, taxation should not be seen as "redistribution" but rather as "just compensation"—the restoration of the unearned, excess wealth to its proper place in the common treasury. "The true function of taxation is to secure to society the element in wealth that is of social origin, or, more broadly, all that does not owe its origin to the efforts of living individuals." Hobhouse went on to suggest that setting taxes on large incomes too low deprives society of its just share of the rewards, and even amounts to a kind of distorted welfare system in which wealthy individuals unfairly receive the fruits of society's industry.

Certainly, if most of what we are able to create is inherited from the past, it seems reasonable that a significant part of any resulting windfall—which happens to come the way of an individual who is often simply lucky—should go back to society. Jacques Turgot, an eighteenth-century French economist, referred to the technological and cultural heritage of the past as a "common treasury."[16] This apt phrase suggests not only that this heritage is something we receive collectively, but also that it is a treasure, a store of riches that should provide benefits for all.

The case for returning a substantial share of large incomes and fortunes to the common purse is based not only on the contribution of the inheritance of the past, but also on the ongoing contribution made by the public treasury. In many cases, inventions are the direct result of substantial government funding of research. So, for instance, in addition to the technological bequest Bill Gates received from Jacquard et al., there was the fact that Gates learned computer programming largely through access to the mainframe computer at the government-funded University of Washington. For that matter, virtually all the early research leading to the development of the personal computer was paid for from the public purse—from Engelbart's Augmenting

Human Intellect project, funded by the U.S. Air Force, to a whole range of path-breaking government-sponsored computing projects in the 1940s and '50s, including those at Harvard, MIT, University of Illinois, the Rand Corporation, the Los Alamos Laboratories, the Stanford Research Institute, and the Office of Naval Research.[17]

More broadly, of course, massive government funding of public education makes possible the advanced society we live in, in which people are literate enough to be able to use a computer. And without government funding of police and fire departments as well as roads and the whole urban infrastructure, our sophisticated economy in which citizens can afford to buy personal computers would not exist. Indeed, as we saw in Chapter 2, government creates the market itself— through laws, regulations, and institutions that govern banking, commerce and international trade, in addition to establishing and enforcing property rights.

Without all this, no one individual could ever make much of a difference—no matter how brilliant, dedicated, motivated, or hard-working she might be. In the overall picture, one person's contribution would still inevitably be infinitesimally small. If this seems to underestimate the importance of individual greatness, consider some of the most outstanding minds in history and try to imagine how far they would have gotten without the benefit of society and all the knowledge accumulated before them. Alperovitz and Daly put it well: "If [Isaac] Newton, in his lifetime, had to learn everything humanity had learned from the time of the caveman to the late seventeenth century—if he had no knowledge inheritance whatsoever to work with—he could not have contributed much more than an insightful caveman could in his lifetime."[18]

And Bill Gates, stranded naked on a desert island, would have his work cut out just figuring how to keep himself warm.

6

WHY OTHER BILLIONAIRES ARE EVEN LESS DESERVING

It was late in 2006 when an aging, little-known economic consultant named Gary Shilling arrived at a tony office in New York's Upper East Side for a meeting with hedge fund manager John Paulson and his team of high-powered analysts. Shilling, who operated out of more modest quarters in suburban New Jersey, may have seemed a little out of place with Paulson and this younger crowd of urbane money traders, but Paulson had sought him out after reading a newsletter Shilling produced. Paulson had been impressed by Shilling's analysis of the nation's economic prospects—and how sharply out of sync it was with the rosy picture painted by others. Just about every other economist and market watcher was adamant that, even after five years of record-breaking growth, housing prices would continue to surge upward. But Shilling wasn't convinced. As he told his intrigued audience at Paulson & Co., housing prices were about to come crashing down. And that, he said, would trigger a sharp increase in mortgage foreclosures. The scene would not be pretty.

In fact, Paulson and his minions had been watching the housing market intently for the past two years, tracking the explosive growth of risky debt that was obscured by the stunning rise in house prices. He had a gut instinct that Shilling, well into his seventies, was on to something, and it didn't take long for the hedge fund manager to figure out where it could lead.

"Boy, if you're right, the financial system will fall apart," said Paulson.[1]

Shilling confirmed that he fully expected that to happen.

As the pieces began to fit into place in his mind, Paulson concluded that the global economy was closer to the precipice than anyone seemed to realize.

At last, the moment he had long waited for seemed to have arrived.

LIKE A FEW OTHER savvy Wall Street players, Paulson had been looking for an opportunity to bet that the housing bubble would burst. There was enough information around about the shoddy nature of many of the subprime mortgage deals—with clients who had little in the way of assets, income, or employment—that a number of close observers realized a lot of "homeowners" would soon be in dire straits, unable to meet their monthly payments. In the betting parlours of Wall Street, this represented a chance to make some serious money.

The best vehicle for betting against the housing market, as Paulson and a few other Wall Streeters had figured out, was to take out "insurance" on packages of mortgages that had been bundled together and sold as a stock. This was an odd concept that twisted the conventional notion of insurance. Typically, for instance, a car owner takes out insurance on his car, paying a small monthly premium to protect himself against the potentially heavy financial loss he would suffer if his car were to be in an accident. In this case, the asset was not a car but a stock. Still, that made sense, since a stock could decline in value, so an investor holding the stock might want to protect himself from the possibility of such a decline. What was unusual here was that the Wall Street types were taking out insurance on something they had no personal stake in, on something that involved other people's assets. It was like buying insurance on a car owned by a stranger, in the hopes of collecting money if the stranger's car crashed. This "insurance"—known as a credit default swap (CDS)—was simply a bet. The fate of thousands of mortgage holders and their dreams of homeownership had become an opportunity for Wall Street hotshots to roll the dice, in the hopes of winning a jackpot.

In some ways, this form of gambling wasn't very risky, because the most the bettor could lose would be the cost of his premiums. (For $1 million a year in CDS premiums, it was possible to insure some $100 million worth of these mortgage stocks.)[2] The problem was that it was impossible to know exactly when the housing market would collapse and cause the mortgage stocks to tumble in value. In the meantime, the cost of paying the premiums would add up. A few bettors had already been badly burned, spending too much on premiums and eventually pulling out of the game, frustrated and bitter that the housing market hadn't yet imploded. Paulson too had been betting on a housing collapse, but he'd assembled a big enough war chest from his wealthy hedge fund clients to keep playing, despite the continued buoyancy of the housing market. After the meeting with Shilling, he was convinced that now was the time to go really big.

One frustration for Paulson was that there just weren't enough of these stocks, known as collateral debt obligations (CDO), to bet against. So he decided to become proactive. He approached a number of investment banks with the request that they create more CDOs to sell to clients, so that he could then take out insurance betting these would fail. The arrangement Paulson had in mind was rife with potential conflicts of interest. He clearly wanted to help pick the mortgages that would make up the new CDOs. And he would obviously favour particularly risky subprime mortgages, thereby increasing the likelihood that the CDOs would become worthless and he would be able to collect on the "insurance" he had taken out.

Bear Stearns, the giant investment bank where Paulson had once served as managing director, said no to his scheme. But Goldman Sachs agreed to the arrangement, providing Paulson with his dream opportunity: a chance to bet on toxic CDOs worth about $5 billion.

And all went according to plan. The housing bubble burst soon afterward, causing untold misery among homeowners and rendering the $5 billion in CDOs worthless—and allowing Paulson to collect $1 billion in "insurance." In fact, that was only a fraction of the money Paulson earned by betting on the collapse of the housing market in 2007. When the winnings from all his bets were counted, he emerged with $3.7 billion, making him the tallest man in that year's income parade.

ALL THIS TURNED PAULSON into a mini-hero on Wall Street. The financial press celebrated him for his cunning moves in scoring the biggest one-year jackpot ever. *The Wall Street Journal* reporter Gregory Zuckerman recounted in stirring detail every step that led to Paulson's winning gamble in a book whose title gives away the author's enthusiasm: *The Greatest Trade Ever.* In the book, Paulson comes across as a sympathetic character, an "underdog" who overcame obstacles and "triumphed over the hubris" of Wall Street. "Paulson was no singles hitter, afraid of risk," Zuckerman writes breathlessly. "Anticipating a housing collapse—and all that it meant—was Paulson's chance to hit the ball out of the park and win the acclaim he deserved."

The acclaim he deserved? The fact that Paulson's hit also helped trigger the collapse of global financial markets, leaving tens of millions suffering around the world, apparently doesn't prevent a financial journalist from concluding that fame and fortune are Paulson's just rewards.

But would that assessment be widely shared outside the financial community? Certainly, the activities of Paulson, and others like him on Wall Street, could in no way be construed as socially beneficial. Their actions do nothing to improve the efficient allocation of capital—the function that financial markets are supposed to perform. Instead, they amount to little more than gambling, which has no social utility. Martin Wolf, a columnist for the *Financial Times* (U.K.), noted that

Paulson's moves served "absolutely no useful purpose."[3] By buying insurance on CDO investments in which he had no ownership stake, Paulson wasn't protecting himself from losses, but rather was placing a bet that the CDO investments would fail—like buying insurance on someone else's car, hoping it would crash. But it was worse than that. Paulson managed to get Goldman Sachs to create faulty CDOs so that he would have excellent odds in betting against them. Paulson was effectively arranging to have a manufacturer build a car with a faulty brake pedal, and then, when the brakes inevitably failed and the car crashed, collecting on the insurance he'd taken out.[4]

In April 2010, the U.S. Securities and Exchange Commission (SEC) charged Goldman Sachs with fraud for selling CDOs without telling buyers that they'd been designed with the help of Paulson, who was betting they would fail. However, no charges were laid against Paulson, since he hadn't been involved in misrepresenting the CDOs to buyers. Still, even if Paulson escapes charges, he was clearly instrumental in getting Goldman to create the toxic and destructive CDOs that lie at the heart of the SEC's fraud case.

Some observers have joked that Wall Street should be regulated, not by the SEC, but by the Nevada Gaming Commission. In that spirit, business professor Simon Johnson says that it appears as if Paulson and Goldman Sachs were running a "crooked roulette table"—something that gets one banned for life from Las Vegas. Johnson argues that, whether or not Paulson is charged, he should be banned for life from securities markets.[5]

Certainly, the Paulson–Goldman scheme set off a series of events with extremely negative repercussions. Investors purchasing the toxic CDOs lost billions of dollars, unaware that they were buying faulty merchandise. Furthermore, the scheme exacerbated the impact of the housing collapse and the near-bankruptcy of insurance giant AIG, which had sold some $64 billion of CDS "insurance" on CDOs related to subprime mortgages. AIG was unable to pay out the money it owed to those, like Paulson, who had bought insurance on now-worthless mortgage-related CDOs. (Goldman too had bought such insurance from AIG, which put the firm in the position of both creating the highly risky CDOs and taking out insurance betting they would fail.) But it gets worse. Insisting that AIG's bankruptcy would devastate credit markets, the U.S. government stepped in to prop up the giant insurance conglomerate. In a deal overseen by then Treasury Secretary Henry Paulson,[6] Washington bailed out AIG with $170 billion. Out of that huge pool of taxpayer money, AIG paid Goldman $14 billion to make good on the insurance Goldman had bought on its CDOs.[7] Similarly, it paid Paulson $1 billion.

This means that a billion dollars of taxpayer money went to ensure that Paulson was able to collect his gambling jackpot. By the logic of the marketplace, Paulson should have been left with nothing when the massive bets he'd made, based on faulty products, helped bankrupt the gambling parlour; instead, in the protected comfort of Wall Street's sheltered casino, he walked away with vast amounts of taxpayer dollars bulging from his pockets.

So Paulson not only helped spark the financial collapse—with its ruinous repercussions for millions around the world—but he made off with $1 billion of the public's money for his role in what appears to be a crooked gambling scheme.

While some in the financial world may celebrate him as a home-run hitter, another view was captured in a handwritten sign held by protestors marching on Wall Street: "Jump, you fuckers!"

SO DOES JOHN PAULSON deserve his fortune?

If Bill Gates is a poster boy for billionaires, Paulson might be considered the opposite: someone who accumulated great wealth in a way that actually harms society. While Gates could be credited with contributing to the development of the personal computer—no matter how small his actual contribution was in the grand scheme of things—Paulson helped trigger a financial meltdown and a worldwide recession. If the case for Gates deserving his fortune seems tenuous, how much less compelling still is the case for Paulson?

For that matter, Paulson is hardly the only billionaire whose overall contribution to society might seem to veer into negative territory. There's also Joseph Cassano, former head of the Financial Products Division at AIG. Cassano was instrumental in peddling some $500 billion worth of CDSs, including the $64 billion connected to subprime mortgages, leading to the collapse and bailout of AIG. Then there's Angelo Mozilo, former CEO of Countrywide Financial, who made a fortune directly peddling subprime mortgages to unsophisticated would-be homeowners. There's also Sanford I. Weill, former head of Citigroup, whose extensive lobbying efforts helped kill the Glass–Steagall Act, thereby undermining regulatory supervision of financial markets and allowing Wall Street to turn itself into a giant casino. Indeed, much of Wall Street would fit one way or another into this non-poster-boy category. (And we haven't even mentioned the likes of out-and-out billionaire crooks such as Bernie Madoff, who, in crossing the line into obvious criminality, have lost any claims to deserving their fortunes.)

Of course, if contribution to society were the criterion for determining an individual's compensation, the income parade would look very different. By most people's standards, the giants reaching up into the clouds would be people like nurses, doctors, teachers, and social workers, while the bankers and hedge fund managers would find themselves among the dwarves. (In reality, however, the pay of the top twenty-five hedge fund managers in 2009 was the same as that of 658,000 schoolteachers.[8]) While few would argue that our system of rewarding people accurately reflects their social contribution by any reasonable measure, our society does implicitly subscribe to the view that there is some connection between social contribution and compensation. According to neo-classical economic theory, which has dominated Western thinking for the past century, a person's compensation is a reflection of his marginal product—that is, his additional contribution to total economic output. So, to make a contribution to society, one doesn't have to be doing social work or directly helping others. By adding to society's economic output, the individual is deemed to have increased the well-being of the community. Under this theory, those who contribute most to economic output receive the largest rewards.

In reality, however, it is hard to make the case that those with the biggest incomes (John Paulson, for instance) have made the biggest contribution to economic output, let alone to any broader goals in society. Supporters of neo-classical theory get around this problem by arguing that a person's contribution to society is simply a reflection of what others are willing to pay him for his services. This has a nice simplicity about it; rather than society making judgments about the value of an individual's input, it is left to the market to determine value. But a problem quickly becomes obvious: under this formulation, a person's social contribution is determined by how valued her services are by those who have money and are therefore able to pay for her services. Is this really a meaningful measure of a person's social contribution? Is a tax lawyer who exploits every ambiguity in the law to benefit his wealthy clients really worth ten to twenty times more than a community clinic lawyer who figures out legal ways to prevent poor families from being evicted from their homes? Is a dentist who performs cosmetic work really worth many times more than a dentist who, responding to pressing community needs, devotes her practice to performing basic dentistry on children? Are politicians who go on to lucrative careers after serving the interests of the rich and powerful really more socially valuable than those who have minimal career prospects after political careers championing the rights of the poor and challenging the status quo? It's hard to see much of a moral principle in a system that rewards people on the basis of how much they're willing or able to pander to the rich.

The flaws in neo-classical economic theory are more evident now than ever, given today's frenzy of pay at the top. Joseph Stiglitz, the Nobel Prize–winning economist, points to the discrepancy between the huge pay of the Wall Street crowd and that of the late agronomist Norman Borlaug, who saved millions of lives by developing methods for improving agricultural productivity: "If neo-classical theory were correct, Borlaug would have been among the wealthiest men in the world, while our bankers would have been lining up at soup kitchens." Stiglitz notes that there appears to be no justification for today's top earners receiving so much more than those who performed similar functions in the recent past. He doubts that the difference is due to any superior skills or talents on the part of the current managerial class. "Does anyone really believe that America's bank officers suddenly became so much more productive, relative to everyone else in society, that they deserve the huge compensation increases they have received in recent years?"[9]

CLEARLY, if we just consider social contribution, it is hard to make the case that John Paulson deserves his fortune. But there's a secondary argument used to justify large wealth accumulations, often made by the rich themselves. It goes like this: I deserve my money because *I earned it.* According to this line of argument, as long as John Paulson made his money without breaking any laws—and he has perhaps just gotten in under the wire on this one—the money is deservedly his.

The notion that a person has "earned" his income is based then merely on staying within the laws. But this seems like a rather flimsy basis for a moral claim to a vast fortune. As we saw in Chapter 2, an individual's income is to a large extent simply a product of the particular set of laws that happen to be in place at that time and in that jurisdiction. So, for instance, if financial markets had been more tightly regulated—as they clearly should have been—Paulson wouldn't have made nearly as much money as he did in 2007. He made his money in CDOs and CDSs, which are part of the largely unregulated derivatives market. As noted earlier, there were serious attempts to regulate this market in the 1990s, particularly by Brooksley Born, then head of the Commodity Futures Trading Commission, the agency responsible for derivatives. While Born's commission regulated certain derivatives traded on exchanges, it had virtually no control over the kinds of custom-made derivatives that Paulson, Goldman Sachs, and AIG were concocting. Born felt there was a need to regulate these as well, but her efforts in this direction were strongly resisted, not just by Wall Street but by high-ranking government officials with close ties to Wall Street, including Federal Reserve Chairman Alan Greenspan. With such powerful forces lined up against regulation, Congress even took the unusual step of actually passing a law that prohibited Born's commission from regulating custom-made derivatives. Had Congress been less beholden to Wall Street (which donates heavily to congressional campaigns) and permitted Born's commission to regulate this highly volatile field of financial speculation, things would have likely turned out very differently, and John Paulson would have probably remained a rather minor figure in the hedge fund business. He was able to collect $3.7 billion in 2007 only because powerful players were able to block badly needed laws regulating the derivatives market. This reality seems to undermine the strength of any moral claim that he "earned" the money.

Similarly, Bill Gates's ability to "earn" his fortune was partly determined by the weak set of laws protecting copyrights in the newly emerging field of computer innovations in the 1980s. Had today's more rigorous legal standards been in force back then, Gary Kildall—the real inventor of the operating system of the personal computer—would have had strong grounds to sue Gates for copyright infringement, according to writer Harold Evans.[10] If Kildall had prevailed in such a lawsuit, Gates would almost certainly not be sitting on a fortune of $53 billion today. Rather, he might be making a comfortable—but unspectacular—living as a software entrepreneur, along with thousands of other individuals with similarly impressive computer skills.

So the notion that a billionaire deserves his fortune because he "earned" it rests on a rather weak moral foundation. The laws that made his fortune possible are the product of the biases and whims of judges who shape the common law, and of legislators who often succumb to pressure and financial rewards from wealthy interest groups. Indeed, as we see in the Paulson case, the laws that enabled him to get hugely rich were simply the product of the enormous political leverage exercised by powerful players on Wall Street.

It strikes us then that the two arguments used to justify a large fortune—that the wealth-holder made an important contribution to society, or simply that he legitimately "earned" it—are both seriously flawed. Of course, these flaws would apply to arguments justifying pay packages at all income levels, not just those of the very rich. Does an advertising consultant, for instance, make a more useful social contribution or "earn" his income more legitimately than a kindergarten teacher? These sorts of questions can and should be raised at all income levels. But the ramifications of undeserved income are potentially so much bigger and more negative to the public interest when the result is enormous concentrations of wealth at the top.

Perhaps the more basic moral question is: *can extreme inequality be justified?* The richest 9.5 million people—0.14 percent of the world's population—control about one-quarter of its assets.[11] What is the moral basis for allowing such a vast amount of the planet's bounty to be held in so few hands? By what right does such a small group of individuals manage to horde such a large share of the earth's resources?

In much earlier times, these sorts of questions didn't really emerge because people's circumstances in life were considered beyond human control. Medieval nobles enjoyed coddled lives while peasants struggled to survive, but there was little concern about justifying such discrepancies. A person's station in life—and the bounty (or lack of bounty) that went with it—were thought to be determined by birth, as part of God's plan. It was therefore everyone's duty, according to medieval thought, to simply submit to God's will and accept one's fate.

All that changed, however, with the transition to the Enlightenment and the modern era. Things that had simply been accepted in earlier times now had to be justified. Inequality was one of those things that seemed to cry out for justification. Why did some people have so much more than others? How could so much deprivation at the lower end be tolerated when there was so much abundance at the top? Was that morally acceptable? Since the gap between the pleasurable lives of the rich and the wretched lives of the poor could no longer just be attributed to a plan ordained by the Almighty, rational justification was now required. Enter John Locke, justifier extraordinaire.

Writing in the 1680s, the renowned English philosopher set out arguments that were to become the basis of the modern world's acceptance of inequality. It's worth reviewing them here, partly to highlight some contradictions in them, and also to show how Locke's position has been misrepresented in an attempt to expand and strengthen the case for inequality.

Locke argued that, while land and resources were originally given by God to "mankind in common," the result of this joint bequest isn't that property is held by all, but rather that it is held by none. However, Locke insists that this can be changed. If an individual applies his own labour to the property, he adds something of value to it, and in so doing develops a legitimate claim to its exclusive ownership: "It hath by this labour something annexed to it that excludes the common right."

There is something intuitively appealing about Locke's reasoning, which perhaps explains why it has resonated so deeply in Western minds for more than three centuries. He is arguing that human labour, or more broadly human effort, is what justifies property ownership. This seems fair and even empowering, since humans have control over their own labour. If they are willing to put forth effort, and exert themselves with the sweat of their brows, they can obtain property. What could be fairer? What a wonderful leap forward from the medieval world, where peasants were stuck in their lowly, impoverished station, on God's orders, no matter how hard they were willing to toil!

But Locke had left out society. In focusing exclusively on the rights of the individual, he brushed aside the rights of everyone else. After suggesting that land and resources were given to "mankind in common," he simply discards the collective nature of the bequest. To observers today, this may seem reasonable, since we're so used to ignoring the broader rights of society in favour of individual rights. But in the seventeenth century, such an approach involved a deliberate omission, an intentional denial of the rights of the many. Traditionally, peasants had enjoyed "common rights" to the land, where they were legally permitted to graze their cattle and forage for wood, peat, berries, and the leftover produce of the harvest. Locke was suggesting wiping out these historic "common rights" and allowing individuals to claim exclusive rights. Political theorist C.B. Macpherson pointed out that in an earlier period there had been two kinds of property rights: the right to exclude others and the right not to be excluded by others. This second one—the right not to be excluded—established a right of access to property. But under the system proposed by Locke—which became the norm in the market economy—only the first right survived. As Macpherson put it: "The very idea of property was narrowed to cover only the right to exclude others."[12]

This was a huge change that swept away the rights of countless people—people who were poor and powerless and "of no importance to anyone but themselves," as historian E.P. Thompson memorably put it. Peasants responded with spontaneous protests and attempts in the dark of night to sabotage the planting of hedges and building of fences aimed at keeping them off the newly privatized land—protests that continued in various forms over several centuries. But since peasants don't get to record history or shape the public debate, their rights were simply eliminated, and have been largely forgotten in the mists of time. Still, the consequence of the removal of these rights is worth pausing over briefly. Political theorist Anatole Anton argues that the "right of exclusion" that Locke championed is a right that "defies moral justification"—or at the very least requires some serious explaining, which Locke never really provides. "Taking something from a group and giving it to a single person ... cries out to the democratic sensibility for reasons," writes Anton. "Private property, from a democratic point of view, amounts to the surrender of democratic control of social resources to private individuals. Surrender might be the right thing to do, but surely some good reasons ought to be given for so doing."[13]

Locke's justification is based on the transformative power of individual labour that, as noted, has some considerable intuitive appeal. But then Locke goes on to develop the argument in a way that seems to weaken his case considerably: "Thus, the grass my horse has bit, the turfs my servant has cut and the ore I have dug in any place where I have a right to them in common with others, become my property." Well, surely, it's one thing for Locke's prototypical man to make a claim to the ore that he has dug with his own labour but quite another to claim ownership of the product of his *servant's* labour. Wouldn't that logically belong to the servant? For that matter, how did the servant end up a servant? And how did the horse come to be in this guy's possession, to be part of his property? If we're supposedly starting from basic principles, examining the legitimacy of the case for private property, how does Locke's prototypical man already happen to own a horse and be in command of the services of a servant? Were these just gifts dropped unexplained from the sky, part of a pre-existing entitlement that doesn't need to be accounted for? With this looser notion of one's labour—to include labour done by others inexplicably under one's command—Locke's invocation of the transformative power of labour loses some of its intuitive appeal.

However, Locke's words were a godsend to those favouring a more market-oriented arrangement of society. Indeed, they have become a cornerstone argument used to justify capitalism. By suggesting that human labour is the basis for private property, Locke gave private ownership an apparently compelling moral legitimacy rooted in the human realm, no longer reliant on the authority of God. And the fact that Locke deftly expanded the definition of labour to include work done by one's servant and horse meant that private property accumulations weren't limited to work that one could physically carry out oneself. Without this limitation, the possibilities seemed endless: one could hire a legion of servants (or factory workers) and use dozens of horses (or machines), and then lay claim to the product of the collective sweats of all of their brows! There was no limit to the private fortune one could accumulate—all within the umbrella of moral legitimacy set out by Locke. It was clearly no more than a hop, skip, and a jump to the world of Bill Gates.

It's not hard to see why Locke has been celebrated as a seminal thinker by those keen on capitalism and its inequalities. However, in reality, Locke didn't simply ignore the fact that allowing individuals to accumulate private property has repercussions for others and possibly compromises their rights. In fact, he included a caveat to the effect that someone could claim property as his own—*only provided that there was "enough and as good" left over for others*. Needless to say, this changes things significantly; it makes the acquisition of private property conditional on the availability of comparable resources and opportunities for others. What about land and non-renewable resources? Clearly, eventually, there wouldn't be "enough and as good" of these vital commodities left over for others; certainly all the available arable land would quickly be claimed, and that eventuality would come all the quicker under the expanded definition of labour, in which an individual could employ a large workforce and modern machinery to use up a finite resource. If Locke's caveat is to be taken seriously, his justification for private ownership turns out to be rather limited in scope and does not provide much of a moral basis for the amassing of huge private fortunes. This probably explains why pro-market theorists, citing Locke to justify the legitimacy of large property accumulations, have mostly just ignored the caveat.

LIKE LOCKE, most of the major theorists who have contemplated issues of distributive justice have insisted on caveats when it comes to the rights of individuals to accumulate large fortunes. As we saw in the last chapter, John Stuart Mill, Thomas Paine, Leonard T. Hobhouse, and Jacques Turgot all argued that much of an individual's wealth is actually owed back to the community. John Rawls, the leading theorist of political liberalism, only condones the accumulation of great fortunes if it can be shown that this benefits the poorest members of society. (It's often argued, for instance, that big rewards are necessary to encourage those at the top to be productive, thereby stimulating economic growth, which benefits all members of society; we'll explore the merits of this argument later.) Rawls, along with other liberal as well as progressive thinkers, clearly has some serious reservations about extreme inequality, refusing to accept its moral legitimacy unless it can be shown to provide benefits throughout society, particularly to those most excluded from the bounty. Indeed, virtually all the major theorists in the field of distributive justice have been unenthusiastic about large inequalities.

The only exceptions are modern conservative thinkers, sometimes loosely called neo-conservatives, who began to rise to prominence in the late 1970s. Whereas other theorists from Locke through to modern liberals and progressives offer only conditional support for extreme inequality, neo-conservatives treat wealth accumulation— in unlimited amounts—as a natural human right, essentially free of conditions or qualification. In their formulation, society and its entitlements all but disappear as the individual moves front and centre and is endowed with huge natural entitlement to the fruits of the earth.

The leading theorist of this modern conservative school is libertarian Robert Nozick, whose influential 1974 book *Anarchy, State, and Utopia* became the intellectual underpinning of the recent conservative movement. Nozick discards the Lockean notion that an individual only becomes entitled to property by applying her labour to it. Nozick's disinterest in the centrality of labour is striking. For most people, this is the aspect of Locke's concept of property rights that is the most appealing, since it suggests that human toil and effort should be the grounds for entitlement—a principle that seems eminently fair. Instead, Nozick assumes that an individual has some sort of natural right to claim property, as long as no one else has a prior entitlement to it. (This seems to beg the question of where the original entitlement comes from. Nozick simply insists that the property must be fairly acquired. But how so?)

But it is in his treatment of the rights of others and the broader society that Nozick and other modern conservatives really move away from traditional theories of distributive justice. Recall Locke's important caveat that an individual can only appropriate a piece of property if that leaves "enough and as good" for others. Nozick reduces this standard to insist only that others not be left worse off by someone gaining title to a piece of property. Of course, even this lesser standard would seem to impose some constraints. If an individual claims a piece of land, for instance, he is clearly leaving others worse off, since they can no longer claim that same piece of land. However, Nozick insists that, except in very unusual circumstances—such as someone owning the only water hole in a desert—an individual's appropriation of property does not leave others worse off. He reaches this odd conclusion by assuming that the property appropriated would otherwise simply remain unused.[14]

What a strange assumption! Why not consider the possibility that someone else would use it—either by assuming ownership of it himself or by assuming joint ownership of it with others, such as through public ownership? The notion that the property would otherwise simply remain unused and that it would attract no interest from others is bizarre and seems based on a peculiar conception of human behaviour. Of course, if the goal is to come up with a moral justification for unlimited personal acquisition, it is necessary to assume such acquisition is harmless to others, and that's what Nozick does, even though it obliges him to make some odd assumptions.

Nozick goes on to further justify inequality by arguing that, whatever the gap between the fortunes of those at the top and the bottom, as long as these different holdings are the result of arrangements freely entered into on both sides, without coercion, there isn't a problem. In other words, workers may earn a fraction of what their boss earns, but as long as they freely agreed to that situation—by accepting their jobs—then all is fine. But just because there is no overt coercion doesn't mean there aren't subtle but very real forms of compulsion. For instance, the workers may have had little choice but to accept the jobs offered because they were hungry and there was no other work available. Or more broadly, they may have had little choice because of the power wielded by employers and the ability this gives them to shape the economic rules in their favour, such as keeping minimum wages low or placing restrictions on the right to unionize. Similarly, consumers may have no choice but to pay an exorbitantly high price for a product—say, a vital prescription drug—because a company holds an exclusive patent on it. Power, discrimination, and monopoly are huge, largely hidden factors that oblige people to "freely" accept terms that may amount to coercion in all but name.

The neo-conservatives' intense focus on the right to private property is, in itself, revealing. It allegedly springs from a deep respect for the rights of the individual. But why limit the notion of the individual's natural rights to that of property ownership and economic entitlements in the marketplace? Why not assume the individual also has a natural right to the fulfillment of basic social needs—such as, say, access to a decent education or adequate health services? When it comes to defining natural rights, neo-conservatives seem to care fiercely—but exclusively—about the individual's entitlement to property, and his right to accumulate unlimited amounts of wealth.

OUR WINNER-TAKE-ALL reward system is based on the idea that there are uniquely gifted or talented individuals whose social contribution is so great that they deserve infinite financial rewards. But this formulation ignores the reality that wealth generation is only possible because of the massive contribution of society, stretching all the way back to the beginning of the Stone Age. Since billionaires are now deemed to have made it on their own, they are also said to owe little back to society. Indeed, the whole notion of responsibility to society has been so denigrated that billionaires are considered deserving of their fortunes when they contribute absolutely nothing to society—or even when they directly imperil the public interest.

The notion that a billionaire can deserve her fortune is severely flawed. It grossly exaggerates the contribution that any one individual is capable of making, even in the best of cases, like that of billionaire poster boy Bill Gates. In non-poster-boy cases like John Paulson, the claim to greatness and the accompanying financial rewards become, well, farcical.

7

HANK AARON AND THE MYTHS ABOUT MOTIVATION

On a warm evening in April 1974, Hank Aaron thrilled a packed Atlanta baseball stadium when he slugged a massive home run deep into left field, beating Babe Ruth's long-standing lifetime record of 714 home runs. Over the next few years, Aaron would go on to hit another 40 home runs, earning him the title Home Run King, as well as setting career records for runs batted in, total bases, and extra base hits, and establishing him as one of the greatest baseball players of all time.

For his dazzling efforts, Aaron was paid $200,000 a year, making him the highest-paid baseball player of the early 1970s.

Today, the king of baseball is Alex Rodriguez of the New York Yankees. Rodriguez has his own set of impressive statistics, leading the major leagues for home runs, runs scored, and runs batted in, as well as total bases and extra base hits. For this, Rodriguez earned $27.7 million in 2008. Adjusting for inflation (but not for drugs), that makes Rodriguez's pay more than thirty times higher than Aaron's. Yet it would be hard to argue that his performance is more than thirty times better.

Certainly, it's clear that Hank Aaron was a thoroughly motivated player who achieved spectacular results. The fact that his salary was a mere fraction of what equivalent players earn today suggests that the extra pay may be unnecessary as a motivating factor.

In fact, there's little evidence that today's phenomenal pay packages—in sports, entertainment, business, and finance—are more effective in motivating today's players, performers, or executives than the more modest packages were a few decades ago. For that matter, there's precious little evidence that today's performances are even any better. Any marginal difference between the performance level of Hank Aaron and Alex Rodriguez can almost certainly be attributed to drugs that weren't available in Aaron's day. Can anyone seriously make the case that today's top entertainment superstars—Lady Gaga, Michael Bublé, George Clooney—are noticeably superior (or superior at all) to Judy Garland, Frank Sinatra, Gregory Peck? (Or if so, that today's higher salaries are responsible for the difference?)

And when we look at the world of business, the case for today's supersized pay at the top seems even more tenuous, if not preposterous. In 1950, for instance, General Motors paid CEO Charlie Wilson $586,000 (the highest CEO salary at the time, worth about $5 million in today's dollars) for managing what was then a thriving, highly profitable company, widely considered America's leading corporation. In 2007, General Motors paid CEO Rick Wagoner $15.7 million— even as the company he headed suffered a *$39 billion loss.* So GM paid roughly three times as much in 2007 to get results that were infinitely worse.

Examples like this abound in business and the financial world. Indeed, the 2008 Wall Street meltdown has brought the disconnect between executive performance and executive pay into sharp, tragicomic relief. Wall Street firms paid out a staggering $18.4 billion in executive bonuses in the early months of 2008, even as many of those firms collapsed in bankruptcy or were only saved by government bailouts. Merrill Lynch, for instance, earned no profit in the 2007 and 2008 financial years, yet paid out $30 billion in bonuses for those years.

The winner-take-all phenomenon of gigantic pay packages at the top has become the norm in a wide range of fields today, in a way that it wasn't a few decades ago. While the results may seem bizarre or even ludicrous, the skewing of income sharply toward the top has been a key factor contributing to the rise of a new class of multimillionaires and billionaires. The rationale behind it has been central to the neo-conservative case justifying today's extreme inequality. Indeed, it's the fallback position when the first part of the argument—that the rich *deserve* their fortunes—turns out to be riddled with holes, as we saw in the last chapter. Okay, so even if the rich don't deserve their fortunes, these huge rewards are necessary, we're told, to create the motivation for the most talented individuals to perform at exceptional levels, so that the economy will function at optimal efficiency and we'll all gain.

This then is the economic case for extreme inequality. Let's see if it's any more convincing than the moral one.

IT IS ALMOST an article of faith among conservative economists and commentators that anything which diminishes the size of the financial rewards for society's most talented members—such as high taxes—saps them of their motivation to work at full capacity, thereby impeding the overall growth of the economy. The proposition that high taxes are detrimental to growth and prosperity is so widely accepted that it is put forward as if it's self-evident.

This near-certainty is particularly odd since there is almost no evidence to back up such a contention, and much evidence that contradicts it. By looking at recent American history, we can compare what happened under two very different scenarios. In the early postwar period (from the end of World War II until 1980), high marginal tax rates at the upper end effectively limited the amount of income that an individual could receive. After 1980, there was little restraint on large incomes. If the neo-conservatives were correct about the important motivational effect that financial incentives have on performance, then the high-tax period would presumably discourage top performance and result in lower economic growth. Yet, if we look at the evidence, no such thing happened.

Tax rates on high-income earners were extremely high in the early postwar years, with the top marginal rate consistently above 80 percent (and above 90 percent most of the time) during the first two decades, from 1944 to 1964. After that, the top rate dropped to 70 percent, then down to 50 percent in 1980.[1] It plunged farther in the Reagan years, falling all the way down to 28 percent in 1988. During the Clinton administration, it was pushed back up to 39 percent, but then eased back down to 35 percent under George W. Bush.

If high taxes act as a disincentive to work, then presumably the very high taxes on high-income people in those early postwar decades would have had a stifling effect on economic growth. But exactly the opposite happened. Productivity—the true measure of economic progress—grew at an annual rate of 3.1 percent in the 1950s, '60s, and early '70s. And it has grown at a significantly slower rate since then. Economists Joel Slemrod and Jon Bakija draw attention to this apparent paradox: "The strong growth periods were the periods when the top tax rates were the *highest*."[2]

The same pattern has been true in Canada, where marginal tax rates were also above 90 percent in the early postwar period and declined in tandem with U.S. rates. As in the United States, Canadian productivity growth was significantly higher in the high-tax period and much lower in the lower-tax period.[3]

We're not trying to make the case that high marginal tax rates *encourage* economic growth, but simply that the evidence doesn't support the assertion that they *discourage* it. Indeed, the evidence seems to contradict the widely held notion that high taxes on top earners lessen their motivation to work and therefore have a detrimental effect on the country's economic performance. (Another possibility is that the contribution of the top earners isn't as important as it's chalked up to be and really doesn't have much impact on overall economic growth—in which case there may not be any economic reason not to tax these people more heavily.)

If we look at the contemporary international evidence, we find a similar picture. It's widely believed that America's relatively low tax rates are key to its success in the global economy, and that countries with high tax rates have more trouble competing and therefore experience slower growth. But once again, the evidence doesn't bear this out.

The ability to make meaningful cross-country comparisons has improved significantly in the last decade due to the increased availability of data. And as this improved data from OECD countries shows, there is no clear correlation between high tax levels and economic growth. It's true that some of the world's most prosperous nations, such as the United States and Japan, have low tax levels. But other nations, most notably the Scandinavian ones, have had stellar economic performances with much higher tax ratios. As Slemrod and Bakija point out: "That Sweden could maintain a 2000 GDP per capita of $24,779—6 percent above the OECD average, in the face of a whopping 54.2 percent tax-to-income ratio—challenges the hypothesis that high taxes are a sure cause of economic decline."[4] Other leading public finance scholars reviewing the international data have come to similar conclusions.[5]

So the data doesn't support the argument that large incentives at the top are necessary to encourage economic growth. It should also be noted that, even if it could be shown that such incentives do promote growth, there is a further prong to the argument that would need to be proved—that overall economic growth benefits society as a whole, as opposed to simply rewarding those at the top. But the evidence for any broadly shared benefits is even weaker. During the most recent U.S. business cycle, from 1989 to 2006, a staggering 91 percent of all income growth went to the top-earning 10 percent of households, with a hefty 59 percent going to just the top 1 percent. The bottom

90 percent of households received a meagre 9 percent of all the income growth. Indeed, from 1979 to 2006, the bottom 90 percent saw their share of the national income decline, while the share enjoyed by the top 1 percent increased by 204 percent, and that of the top .01 percent went up by a phenomenal 425 percent.[6]

The most thorough recent empirical study on this issue found little evidence to support the notion that a rising tide lifts all boats. The study, by Harvard's Dan Andrews and Christopher Jencks and Australia National University's Andrew Leigh, looked at almost a century of data for twelve industrialized countries and found that while higher gains at the top appear to lead to a small increase in growth, "it is difficult to be sure from our estimates whether the bottom 90 percent will really be better off or not."[7] The authors concluded that the bottom 90 percent are likely to be much better off if growth is slow and equal, rather than rapid and unequal. Their findings were perhaps best summarized in the headline reporting their study in *The Wall Street Journal*: "Trickle-down economics fails to deliver as promised."[8]

So rather than supporting the "trickle-down theory," the evidence leads to the common-sense conclusion that policies aimed at benefiting the rich do precisely that, and no more.

IF THERE'S LITTLE hard evidence to bolster the economic case for large incentives at the top, this isn't really surprising, once the theoretical arguments are examined. According to the neo-conservatives—and indeed to most mainstream economists—high marginal tax rates have the effect of discouraging those in the top income brackets from working harder to earn more income, since this income will be taxed at higher rates. For example, if a corporate lawyer can earn $1,000 for an extra hour of work, and faces a tax rate of 30 percent, that will leave her with $700 after tax, making it worth her while to work the extra hour. If the tax rate is instead, say, 60 percent, leaving her with only $400 after tax, she might well decide to go home and watch TV instead.

It's easy to see how this argument gains traction. At face value, it seems intuitively correct. *The lawyer works to earn income; the more she is paid, the more she is motivated to work. If taxes reduce her pay significantly, she is going to be less motivated to work.* That's certainly logical. On that other hand, it seems just as likely that high taxes could have exactly the opposite effect. *The lawyer works to earn income. If that income is reduced significantly by taxes, she will work longer to make up for the loss because she wants to maintain an elevated standard of living.* Both explanations make sense, and both fit with observations of human behaviour.

And yet the first argument—the one that justifies low taxes—is the one that is widely accepted. Indeed, it is considered a truism in our society that cutting taxes will encourage work effort. By this logic, then, a tax cut would inspire the corporate lawyer to work harder. But why? Wouldn't it be equally plausible that, since she'd be richer, she would use the extra money to relax more, take a longer vacation, plan to retire earlier, or spend more time golfing or internet dating? In many ways, a windfall due to a tax reduction is similar to any other windfall, such as winning a lottery or inheriting money. Do most people respond to winning a lottery or inheriting money by working longer hours?

The truth is, human motivation and behaviour are infinitely more complicated, nuanced, and variable than the straightforward version presented in economic arguments. In the formulation of standard neo-classical economics, the prototypical human, *homo economicus,* is deeply motivated to satisfy his appetite for material goods. Although he would rather avoid work, he can be enticed into doing it if he is rewarded with income, since that allows him to increase his consumption of material goods.

One can understand why economists have chosen such a one-dimensional, mechanistic character as *homo economicus* as their central player. Clearly, they need to simplify human behaviour into predictable and knowable patterns in order to present economics as a hard science—rather than just another social science, where findings are acknowledged to be somewhat subjective and arbitrary. But while it's understandable that economists want their findings to be treated as authoritative, it's doubtful whether human behaviour really fits into the paradigm they offer. Yes, the human appetite for consumption is real, and potentially huge. But it's clearly not the only thing that motivates humans to do the things they do. Many critics have charged that such a simplistic human prototype as *homo economicus*—which has become the model on which our entire economic system is based—is nothing more than a convenient but fairly meaningless cartoon character.

There's a mountain of evidence in the fields of psychology and other social sciences to suggest that the actual motives and behaviour of real-life people are quite different from those of *homo economicus*. Robert E. Lane, a political scientist at Yale University, reviewed more than a thousand studies of human behaviour related to the economy for his book *The Market Experience*. Lane concluded that the way people actually behave bears little resemblance to the greedy, consumption-oriented conduct assumed by standard economic theory. Indeed, a vast array of studies show that, once people achieve a basic material standard of living, economic factors greatly decline as important sources of happiness and satisfaction and are superseded in importance by factors such as family, friendship, self-esteem, and a sense of personal and intellectual development.[9] Or as economist Robert H. Frank put it in his book *Luxury Fever:* "Behavioural scientists find that once a threshold level of affluence is reached, the average level of human well-being in a country is almost completely independent of its stock of material consumption goods."[10]

Before we move on to what really *does* matter to people who live comfortably above the breadline, it's worth pausing here to briefly note what goes on below the breadline. As Frank observes: "Most careful studies find a clear relationship over time between subjective well-being and absolute income at extremely low levels of absolute income."[11] In other words, while human wants and desires may become more varied and complex once basic needs are secured, until this happens, people are primarily motivated to meet their basic material needs, without which they enjoy little life comfort or satisfaction. Perhaps the crude *homo economicus* model, if it has any validity, is most useful as a model of behaviour for those at the bottom of the economic heap. This raises the question of whether the argument about higher pay leading to greater work effort might be most applicable to very low-income workers, who, after all, are typically stuck doing work that is dull, routine, and offers little opportunity for creativity. In such cases, the amount of pay looms particularly large. Such workers don't just badly need money to meet the most basic human needs, but also to compensate for the lack of other job-related satisfactions. For a hotel chambermaid earning $10 an hour, for instance, an extra $1.75 an hour would make a significant difference, and would probably induce him to give up a chance to attend a local choir service or surf pornography on the web in order to spend a particularly profitable extra hour cleaning up the mess left behind by hotel guests.

Interestingly, however, the argument about higher pay being necessary for greater motivation is primarily used to justify lower taxes on the rich, not on the poor—even though the arguments seem to apply better to the poor. Indeed, in the case of the poor, the opposite argument is often made—that too much income will cause them to slack off. Hence the need to keep welfare and unemployment insurance benefits low, lest those at the lower end be encouraged to remain idle.

But let's get back to the rich. If we follow the logic mentioned above, we could conclude that higher pay might seem *least* likely to work as a motivator in the case of those with big incomes. First of all, they already have ample income—so ample, in the case of billionaires and near-billionaires, that pay increases or decreases are unlikely to have any effect on how much they consume, since they are already presumably consuming as much as they possibly can (or care to). Secondly, and more importantly, unlike the poor chambermaid, those at the top of their professions enjoy a level of work satisfaction that is, quite simply, immense. While additional pay might induce the chambermaid to spend that extra hour cleaning up after others, there is no shortage of non-monetary benefits that provide additional motivation for the business executive to work late to close a big deal, or for the rock star to do an encore in front of a stadium full of delirious fans, or for the baseball player to hit a home run with bases loaded in the bottom of the ninth.

In fact, the world of work—particularly self-directed, challenging work that one happens to be very good at—offers a stunning array of satisfactions that deliver rewards at the most primal human level. Indeed, research in the field of psychology establishes that the most basic human psychological needs—for a sense of self, a sense of personal competence, and for self-esteem—are very often tied in closely with one's work. "People's favourable attitudes towards themselves are their most treasured property; in many ways, these are the maximand on which all their other values and motives rest," observes Lane.[12] Work is a crucial way in which people achieve favourable attitudes of themselves, since it gives them a sense of their own competence and ability to function in the world. Pay is an important part of this—but primarily as a proxy for these more basic psychological rewards. Notes Lane: "In the end, all economic behaviour is energized and guided by the pursuit of a sense of personal effectiveness, self-esteem and self-consistency"—that is, a sense of an integrated personal identity.

Considering all this, *homo economicus* may amount to a serious misrepresentation, if not an outright distortion, of the human personality. In the *homo economicus* model, work is considered an undesirable activity—a "disutility," in economic parlance—that humans would rather avoid, but perform as a means to earn income so that they can have the pleasure of consuming material goods. This may well be true when the work is cleaning toilets. However, particularly at the upper level, work is often an exceptionally desirable activity in itself—one that offers deeply satisfying rewards that are far more important than consumption. As Lane puts it: "It is often in the sphere of work not consumption, that the greatest subjective well-being lies."[13]

So it seems unlikely that reducing the pay rewards of the very rich would stifle their desire to work. It's obvious that the most talented individuals in any field are motivated by far more than money. Even billionaires readily admit that money isn't their only or even their primary objective. Leo J. Hindery Jr., the sports cable TV entrepreneur, confided to *The New York Times* that he would have worked just as hard for a much smaller payoff. Wall Street banker Sanford Weill also acknowledged that "I worked because I loved what I was doing." Weill said that he didn't even really know how much he'd made until he retired and had "a chance to sit back and count up what was on the table." Similarly, Kenneth C. Griffin, who received more than $1 billion in 2006 as chairman of hedge fund Citadel Investment Group, commented that "wealth is not a particularly satisfying outcome....The money is a byproduct of a passionate endeavour."[14]

Clearly, some of history's most talented individuals who have made some of the greatest contributions to society have had little trouble performing without much in the way of financial incentives. Norman Borlaug, who saved millions of lives by developing methods for improving agricultural productivity, spent most of his life living modestly in Third World villages. Vincent van Gogh somehow found the motivation to produce hundreds of works of great art, even though he managed to sell only one of them in his lifetime, receiving a pittance for it just before he died. And William Shakespeare was inspired to produce the greatest dramas of all time without even the prospect that they'd become Hollywood blockbusters.

NONE OF THIS is meant to imply that financial incentives don't matter. They clearly do—particularly at the lower levels, where workers need powerful inducements to get them to perform work that is often dreary, repetitive, unpleasant, and unrewarding. And they also matter at the upper levels. While the deep psychological satisfactions of work may matter most, money does act as a proxy for these rewards. Earning an income reinforces an individual's sense of personal competency and self-esteem. Earning a large income greatly reinforces an individual's sense of personal competency and self-esteem, leaving him with very pleasantly favourable attitudes toward himself.

So financial incentives matter. They act as powerful motivators that encourage effort, diligence, creativity, and just plain hard work in people at all levels. The question is: how much is *enough* to provide the crucial level of motivation? If even some billionaires are willing to confess that they would have worked just as hard for less, it might be worth considering whether society could pay them less—or tax back significantly more of what they receive—without diminishing their incentive to work.

And here another important psychological factor comes into play: what seems to matter most to people, once they get above the breadline, isn't how big their compensation is, but how it compares to the compensation of others. Karl Marx observed this human characteristic when he pointed out that "A house may be large or small; as long as the surrounding houses are equally small, it satisfies all social demands for a dwelling. But if a palace rises beside the little house, the little house shrinks into a hut."[15] Robert Frank made a similar observation: "The middle-class professional who lives in Manhattan is unlikely to be burdened by dissatisfaction that her apartment has no room for a Ping-Pong table or wine cellar, and she almost certainly entertains no expectation of having a swimming pool. Yet that same woman living in a Westchester county suburb might not even consider a house that lacked these amenities." In other words, it's not the absolute size of the material reward that matters, but how that reward stacks up against the material rewards of others—where it puts the individual in the pecking order. As Frank points out: "Evidence from the large scientific literature on the determinants of subjective well-being consistently suggests that we have strong concerns about relative position."[16]

This emphasis on relative positioning is backed up by centuries of philosophical thought and observation. As early as the fourth century BC, Aristotle noted that humans are, above all, social animals who naturally seek to relate to and engage with other humans. They feel the need to be part of a larger human community in which they enjoy the acceptance and good opinion of others. Receiving pay for work is a key way that people in our society can establish their place in the community, by proving their competence and worthiness. It's also a way to establish how they measure up against others. The amount of financial compensation one receives, particularly in a materialistic society like ours, is important to establishing one's place in the pecking order.

So what matters most about a pay package is not its absolute size but how it measures up against others. This perhaps explains why, in the early postwar years, business executives, entertainers, and sports stars were motivated to perform very well—indeed, just as well, if not better, than today's much higher-paid equivalents do. Although their absolute pay levels were much smaller back then, they were still paid very, very well *relative to others at the time.* It was this gap between them and others in their world—which gave them an elevated status in their community—that served as the stimulant to high performance.

Of course, now that the gap between the top and the bottom is so much bigger today, isn't the stimulus for high performance all the greater? Yes, it probably is. But how much stimulus can productively be harnessed? What if Hank Aaron was performing the very best he possibly could when he broke those major league records? What would have been gained by topping up his salary to thirty times its already extremely high level?

Current thinking in our winner-take-all culture would suggest that the added financial incentive would have driven Aaron all the harder, so that he might have performed even more spectacularly. Possibly. Or perhaps he'd already gone to the bottom of the well of his capabilities. Who knows? But certainly this raises some questions, such as: is the extra bit of performance—if it could be coaxed out of him through massively higher pay—really worth the extra cost? And what are the downsides of doing so (besides the obvious downside of not spreading the extra pay more widely among others)?

Economists Robert Frank and Philip J. Cook make the provocative argument that winner-take-all compensation may actually lead to behaviour that impedes economic growth. They suggest that today's exceptionally high pay levels draw ever-increasing numbers of participants to compete for the few top-paying jobs. Only a tiny fraction of the aspirants can hope to make it into these dream jobs, and those who don't often end up squandering other talents they would have otherwise developed. Imagine, for instance, a teenaged boy with good marks in science and math who also happens to be the star of his high school baseball team. If he goes to university and gets an engineering degree, he will almost certainly end up with a job earning at least $50,000 a year and make a useful contribution to society as an engineer. Not bad, but of course it pales in comparison to the dream of being a professional ballplayer and earning, say, $6 million or more a year. If the ever-mounting pay of major league players encourages the boy to pursue his baseball dream, rather than his studies, that little bit harder, chances are things will turn out badly for him—and for society, to which he'll likely end up contributing less without a major league career or an engineering degree.[17]

The stupendous pay cheques at the very top may indeed be creating serious distortions, not just in some people's lives but more broadly in the economy. If Hank Aaron's 1974 salary was sufficient to push him to perform stunning baseball feats, what is the effect of making that financial incentive thirty times larger? It's possible it makes no difference, that what drives top baseball players to spectacular achievement is the thrill of being regarded the best in the world at something they love, in which case topping up their pay so handsomely is simply a needless and foolish squandering of money. On the other hand, it's possible the increased pay does have an effect, not only attracting more participants to compete for the prize, but also placing ever more pressure on those trying to grab Hank Aaron's crown. Could this additional pressure perhaps explain why so many professional athletes, unable to do any better on their own, turn to steroids? Is there really any other way to continually improve upon the performances of the equally talented players who went before them? Are top athletes on a treadmill where they can't possibly go any faster, but are willing to try anything—including cheating—to reach new heights, goaded on by the sheer enormity of the stimulus dangled in front of them?

In the age of winner-take-all compensation, a similar propensity for cheating seems to have infected the upper levels of the business and financial worlds. It's worth considering whether the mindset that led Wall Street types to abandon all sanity and morality—mixing together toxic brews of junk mortgages, car loans, and credit card debts and then selling pieces of these sickly concoctions to unknowing "investors"—is partly the result of the overstimulation of their greed impulses.

When the broader public first became aware of collateral debt obligations and credit default swaps during the financial meltdown in the fall of 2008, the most common reaction was bewilderment. The hyper-charged Wall Street world was so removed from the regular world most people inhabit—where pay bears some relationship to hours worked, effort, and results, and where it provides the means for living a normal life in a normal reality—that it seemed baffling and indecipherable. How did grown men and women, apparently in full control of their faculties, make decisions that were not just over-the-top greedy but were so evidently irresponsible and threatening to the well-being of so many others, including themselves? One possibility was that the billion-dollar compensation packages on view all around them had simply stimulated their hypothalamuses to the point of mental, physical, and moral exhaustion, encouraging them to risk everything for the billion-dollar prize, without which life had become almost meaningless. Like laboratory rats getting a rewarding food pellet for performing a task, Wall Street bankers were being fed such an onslaught of pellets for doing high-risk deals that they'd lost the ability to function in any normal, rational way.

None of this is meant to evoke sympathy for drug-taking ballplayers or greedy billionaire bankers, who, after all, have been key proponents of large compensation packages for themselves. The point is not to excuse their behaviour, but rather to raise questions about what role excessive financial rewards may have played in encouraging it. If the effect of extreme financial stimulation is to encourage greedy-bordering-on-dysfunctional behaviour, then the large financial rewards of our winner-take-all compensation system may not just be unnecessary, but actually destructive.

IT'S COMMONLY ARGUED, of course, that companies need to pay high salaries to attract the most talented individuals and keep them from going to competitors. So while it may be true that a lower-paid ballplayer would be just as motivated to hit that bases-loaded home run in the bottom of the ninth, he would probably be enticed by an offer to move to another team that would pay him more. In a competitive free market, then, high pay is necessary to ensure that companies and organizations can attract the best talent so that they can function optimally.

It should immediately be noted that this argument in no way refutes the desirability of imposing high taxes on large incomes. High taxes would not, for instance, prevent teams from attracting the best players by offering gigantic pay packages. Teams could pay as much as they wanted to—and the players could still go to the highest bidder. Only after all this is resolved, and everyone is out playing ball, would taxes kick in. The high marginal rates would not interfere at all in the selection process, since they would only apply after the fact and would apply the same to all (this is the beauty of tax rates; they are neutral, applying the same set of rules to everyone).

It should also be noted that, while high pay in sports and entertainment may be the result of highly competitive markets, this is less true in the world of business and finance. Of course, businesspeople and financiers make similar arguments—that huge rewards are necessary to attract the best talent. Indeed, this has been Wall Street's main justification for continuing to lavishly reward CEOs and top executives: top talent can command top dollar; that's just the way the free market works.

But on closer examination, it turns out that CEO pay is determined less by the workings of the free market (a misleading concept at the best of times) and more by the power wielded by those at the top of the business and financial world. One of the ways this plutocracy has exercised the extraordinary power it's achieved in recent years has been to drive up its own pay to astronomical heights. This has been easy to accomplish because executive pay is determined by corporate boards of directors, which are typically made up mostly of other, similarly positioned executives—people who are often friends, colleagues, former classmates from MBA courses, or simply associates who frequent the same golf clubs or art auctions as those whose pay is being judged. As a vehicle for determining pay, these corporate boards are more like cozy clubs than bodies likely to render meaningful, arm's-length market assessments.

Ostensibly, of course, corporate boards represent shareholders. So they theoretically represent a large number of people and interests. In reality, however, shareholder elections are pretty much insider events, particularly in cases where there are large numbers of shareholders who are unlikely to be sufficiently organized to challenge the dominant management group. Indeed, it is rare even to have a competing slate in a shareholder election. One notable critic of the compensation system is Richard Posner, a U.S. Court of Appeals judge and senior lecturer at the University of Chicago Law School. As Posner bluntly puts it: "Shareholder election of directors resembles the system of voting in the Soviet Union and other totalitarian nations."[18]

Even leaving aside actual friendships and close associations between members of the board and those they are assessing, there is an additional potential conflict of interest. "A board of directors is likely to be dominated by highly paid business executives, including CEOs of other companies," writes Posner. "They have a conflict of interest, since they have a financial stake in high corporate salaries, their own salaries being determined in part by the salaries paid to persons in comparable positions in other companies." Added to that personal conflict of interest is the likelihood that these executives will regard the high level of compensation going to themselves and those they are judging as an appropriate reflection of the intrinsic worthiness of corporate executives.

The problem becomes circular, since the CEO of a company influences the selection of its directors, who then determine the CEO's compensation. If the directors authorize a large compensation package for the CEO who has put them in place, that CEO is likely to appreciate the important contribution the directors are making and support generous directors' fees. The CEO and his team also select the company's auditors, who certify the company's financial statements. If the CEO is pleased by the auditors' report, he might well retain these same auditors to provide consulting services, under which the auditors might steer underwriting contracts to investment banks, whose securities analysts give the company very positive reports. Altogether, Posner suggests that the relationship between the CEO, the members of the board of directors, and the firm's auditors typically involves a great deal of "mutual back-scratching."[19]

All this suggests that the exorbitant pay CEOs and other top executives enjoy has less to do with the operation of the free market (whatever that is) and more to do with the extraordinary power they exert over their own pay. If the wages of a company's clerical or janitorial staff were set by boards controlled by clerks and janitors, would you be surprised to see the salary of a good filer or floor-mopper shoot up?

IN ADDITION TO CONTROLLING corporate boards, top executives have been able to use their clout on the political front to win legislative changes that allowed them to push their own pay ever higher. This can be seen in the case of "executive stock options," which in recent decades have become key vehicles for raising CEO compensation in both the United States and Canada. (Stock options were only used by one-third of Canada's top one hundred public corporations in 1991, but by the end of the decade, all of them were using this method of executive compensation. The value of stock options for Canadian CEOs in the 1990s exceeded their salaries by 300 percent.)

It's worth taking a moment to review how stock options work, and how that's changed in recent decades. A stock option is simply an arrangement that allows an executive to buy a certain amount of the company's stock at a point in the future—at a prearranged price. Say, for instance, the executive has an option to buy stock for $10 a share.

If the stock rises in value, the executive would exercise his option, paying only $10 for shares that are now worth perhaps $20, $40, or even $100 a share, allowing him to profit enormously. On the other hand, if the stock fails to rise—or falls in value—the executive would simply not exercise his option, making the stock option a no-lose proposition for him.

Stock options were developed in the 1930s and have been used for a long time. But they became wildly popular after 1980, largely as a result of changes in tax laws won by the business community through extensive lobbying efforts. Essentially, the changes allowed the profits that executives received through stock options to be taxed as capital gains—and therefore at a lower rate—instead of being taxed at full rates as regular employment income. Executives were also permitted to avoid paying tax on the gains until they actually sold the stock.

Among other things, this created a perverse incentive for CEOs. Stock options encouraged executives to focus on pushing up the stock price in the short term, often inducing them to take huge risks to produce enormous spikes in the stock price. The increased stock price was generally unsustainable and was typically achieved at the expense of other actions that would have served the company better in the long term. By giving CEOs a short-term horizon, the stock option provided an incentive for them to behave in ways that were often at cross-purposes to the best interests of the company and its shareholders.

But the important thing to note here is that the changes that made stock options so wildly profitable were part of a deliberate set of policy changes whose implications were well understood by those who pushed for them and by those who passed them into law. If lawmakers had wanted to prevent stock options from becoming vehicles for short-term windfall gains, they could have easily imposed mandatory holding periods before the stock could be cashed in.

All this suggests that the huge pay increases at the top have been largely the product of deliberate moves by CEOs, through their control of corporate boards and their influence over governments and legislators. This may seem obvious, but it contradicts the view typically offered by economists and commentators, who insist that today's higher incomes are the product of technological change and globalization. These factors have undoubtedly had some impact; the technological advance of television, for instance, has allowed professional athletes and entertainers to be marketed to much larger audiences, vastly increasing the potential rewards. But television has been around since the early 1950s and was widely developed by the early 1970s—well before the phenomenal rise in incomes at the top. Furthermore, while technology and globalization may account for the higher incomes of sports and entertainment stars, they don't explain the spectacular rise in the pay of CEOs. Even if we assume that technology and globalization have made corporations more profitable, this still doesn't explain why such a large share of the profits has drifted to the very top jobs in the corporations.

The technological factor is also often cited to explain why so many workers today are earning such low incomes. We're told that skills have become more important than ever in this technological age, leaving unskilled workers highly disadvantaged. But many highly skilled workers have also experienced minimal income growth. As noted earlier, there's been almost no real income growth for the bottom 90 percent of income earners—a group that includes millions of highly skilled workers and well-educated professionals, such as engineers, teachers, and nurses. Income growth has been almost entirely restricted to the top 10 percent, with the growth getting proportionately bigger as income rises. It is hard to explain this clear pattern of income gravitating higher and higher up the income ladder exclusively by reference to skill or education levels.

It is also worth noting that the increased concentration of income at the very top is a phenomenon that's really only occurred in the Anglo-American countries—the United States, Britain, and Canada.

But if globalization is a key factor in explaining increasing inequality, why isn't the same trend visible around the globe, or at least in other countries that are competing successfully in the global economy, such as Germany, France, or Japan?

The reason is that technology and globalization are only partly responsible for the huge increase in incomes at the top. Those who are pleased with the current trend toward increased inequality have seized upon these two factors to explain it, perhaps because they appear to be neutral forces beyond human control. If technology and globalization are responsible, then there's no point in trying to do anything about this strange new inequality. The emergence of a new class of billionaires is just the natural outcome of modernity, and attempting to limit it would only hold back the tides of progress, ultimately hurting us all.

But the evidence suggests that the increase in inequality has not been an inevitable development caused by neutral forces beyond our control. Rather, it's been largely the product of a concerted campaign by a powerful elite determined to enrich itself.

IT SEEMS THAT the economic case for extreme pay at the top is just as flawed as the moral one. Yet when both cases are exposed as full of holes, there's still another fallback position for those seeking to justify extreme pay at the top. In fact, it's their *real* fallback position.

The rich may not deserve their vast incomes, and there may be no real economic reason for paying them so handsomely. (As we've seen, some of them admit they'd work just as hard for less.) But that doesn't mean they'd willingly get by with less. Certainly, any attempt to take more of their income away through taxation is invariably met with the threat that they'll move their money out of the country. So, overall, their argument really goes like this: *We deserve our huge incomes. And we need to keep receiving these immense sums in order for the economy to keep growing. But, even if neither of these statements is really true, don't think your pawns have our king in check. If you raise our taxes, we'll simply move our money offshore.*

With this threat, they take control of the chessboard.

Or do they?

8

TAKING THE FUN OUT OF TAX HAVENS

At an exclusive luncheon in midtown Manhattan, about six dozen wealthy Americans sipped very rare wines and mingled with special Parisian guest Henri Loyrette, the director of the Louvre. One could say that the room was full of HNWIs, which sounds like a polite word for swine flu, but is actually the acronym the financial community uses for High Net Worth Individuals—people with investable assets worth more than $1 million, the point at which an individual becomes of serious interest to a banker.

The elegant gathering, in April 2008, was hosted by the giant Swiss bank UBS, the world's largest manager of private wealth. It was just one of many such events organized by the bank as part of its strategy of reaching out to America's multimillionaires and billionaires. In recent years, UBS has stepped up its efforts to become the banker of choice of HNWIs by opening posh offices in New York, Chicago, Houston, and other U.S. cities with pockets of significant wealth. Its bankers also court the wealthy with lavish private events at the America's Cup, Art Basel, Boston Symphony Orchestra concerts, and other sporting and cultural events frequented by the very rich.

This is the highly exclusive and discreet world of "wealth management," that is, the arranging of personal or corporate financial affairs to maximize investment returns and minimize (or avoid altogether) tax payments. Managing one's wealth is a task that looms huge in the lives of a select few, while being utterly beyond the experience of the vast majority of the population. Like everything else that caters to the rich, the offices and reception halls where "wealth managers" conduct their business are elegant and opulent. The fine trappings distract attention from the fact that a significant part of what goes on here amounts to criminal activity.

Tax avoidance by the rich is a massive industry that includes both legal and illegal aspects. The legal part is made up of a huge array of think-tanks, lobbyists, and public relations firms pitching the case for low taxes on the rich to government officials, lawmakers, and the public. In addition, an army of tax lawyers and accountants serve wealthy clients by handling their financial affairs in ways that minimize their tax burdens. All this, which undoubtedly saves the rich—and thus deprives our governments of—billions of dollars a year, is done within the limits of the law.

But there's another massive part of the business that veers into the illegal. It focuses on hiding money from tax authorities by moving it into offshore bank accounts.

While there's nothing illegal about having a foreign bank account, it is illegal to fail to report income to tax authorities, including by hiding it offshore to avoid detection. Estimates suggest that more than one-third of the wealth of HNWIs, or somewhere between $8 trillion and $10 trillion, is stored offshore in countries—including such well-known tax havens as the Cayman Islands, the Channel Islands, Switzerland, and Liechtenstein—where lax banking laws have allowed the internationally wealthy to keep their fortunes secret.[1] Banks in tax haven countries don't offer anything—besides complete secrecy—that isn't offered by domestic banks. So there's no conceivable reason to go to the trouble of putting one's money in an offshore account other than to hide it, presumably from tax authorities—a federal offence in both Canada and the United States. If the size of the tax haven banking industry and the money stored in it is any indication, there are a great many crooks among the wealthy, almost none of whom have ever been charged.

It is striking how slow-moving authorities in both countries have traditionally been in clamping down on this huge area of criminal activity. This sluggishness is curious since more vigorous prosecution would inevitably lead to substantial inflow into government coffers— much more so than in the case of other property-related crimes. But while governments vigorously go after low-income individuals who defraud social assistance programs, they have been notoriously lax in pursuing high rollers who commit tax fraud.

This has recently changed somewhat in the United States, partly because tax haven banks are believed to have contributed to the destabilization of the international financial system and ultimately to the 2008 financial meltdown. The sudden U.S. government interest is also driven by the fact that, in two separate cases, employees of tax haven banks came forward on their own with information, providing rare and revealing glimpses into the incredibly secretive world of offshore banking. In the most important of the two cases, Bradley Birkenfeld, a high-level, Geneva-based banking official at UBS, provided information to U.S. authorities that ended up sparking government and congressional investigations and brought considerable heat down on UBS, which was accused of operating a covert tax-evasion scheme for Americans. In the other case, Heinrich Kieber, an employee of LGT, a bank owned by the royal family of Liechtenstein, provided data on more than 1,400 bank clients to authorities in Germany, Britain, the United States, and several other countries.

At U.S. trials and congressional hearings in the spring and summer of 2008, the long-secret world of tax haven banking was at least partly unveiled. Birkenfeld, who grew up in the Boston area, admitted to a U.S. federal court judge that he had participated in elaborate schemes to help wealthy U.S. clients evade taxes, by creating fictitious trusts and corporations to conceal offshore ownership and helping clients file false tax returns. "I was employed by UBS," he said when asked why he had done these things. "I was incentivized to do this business." Pleading guilty to conspiracy, Birkenfeld explained that he and other UBS bankers trolled for wealthy clients at art shows, golf and tennis tournaments, yachting regattas, musical performances, or any other events "where rich people hang out." The forty-three-year-old, who also admitted to smuggling diamonds into the United States for a wealthy client, described how Swiss bankers communicated with their clients with encrypted messages to avoid detection by authorities. A UBS manual, presented as evidence at a Senate sub-committee hearing, instructed bank employees on how to hide client information from police and immigration authorities while passing through customs. With mounting evidence that the bank conspired with U.S. citizens to hide their incomes, UBS was obliged to pay a fine of $780 million and, more importantly, agreed to hand over the names of some seventeen thousand Americans holding undeclared accounts in its bank.

The world of tax havens had been dealt a considerable blow. Bank secrecy—which the Swiss had elevated to a national principle—had been seriously compromised. All this coincided with the international financial meltdown in the fall of 2008, bringing additional attention to tax haven banks for their role in augmenting the volume of footloose funds available for financial speculation. One of the few international reforms the G20 had little difficulty agreeing on at its London summit in April 2009 was a ramping up of pressure on countries that failed to comply with international tax-compliance standards—something bureaucrats inside the OECD had been recommending for a long time. A united stand by the world's most powerful economies prompted a number of long-resistant tax haven countries to agree to fall into line. With only a few holdouts—Costa Rica, Malaysia, Philippines, and Uruguay—more than a dozen such countries, including a considerably chastised Switzerland, committed to the higher standard.

All that is encouraging, but falls considerably short of what's actually needed to stem the extensive use of tax havens and the considerable damage they do to national treasuries. In fact, the solution is quite simple and easy to implement. What's needed is not just a promise from tax haven countries to adhere to international standards, but a requirement that all financial institutions, whenever they make a payment to a client, report that payment to the tax authorities of the country where the client resides. The report would be automatic, in electronic form, and include a unique number to identify the client. That way, all governments around the world would be notified of all payments made to their wealthy citizens, and be able to tax them accordingly—in the same way that governments receive notification from domestic banks about payments to citizens within the country, and use that information to verify their tax returns. Such a system could be enforced by an existing body like the World Trade Organization, the Bank of International Settlements, or the United Nations. It would be particularly beneficial to Third World nations, which badly need the money parked overseas and have few resources to track down wealthy drug lords and other rich people determined not to share their resources with their abjectly poor fellow citizens.

Perhaps this scheme sounds too ambitious, but in fact it's no more complex than the international system of passports, which works well and with few compliance problems. Each passport has a unique identification number. Every time a person crosses a border, her number is swiped into a computer, which instantly discloses information about her. Transmitting an electronic record of all payments made by tax haven banks would be no more complicated than that. It turns out that, among the benefits of the computer age are not only video games, but the easy tracking and taxation of the gigantic hidden fortunes of the world's billionaires.

BUT IF THE MAJOR Western countries, led by the United States, seemed to have new energy for clamping down on tax havens for facilitating out-and-out tax evasion, there has been less interest in restricting the use of tax havens for practices that are less overtly illegal but still drain billions each year from the U.S. and Canadian treasuries. Typically, companies set up dummy corporations in tax haven countries, then juggle their books so that their profits are shifted to these dummy corporations, which are subject to extremely low rates of tax. In the spring of 2009, the Obama administration promised to go after this long-time and highly lucrative tax avoidance scheme in an effort to collect an extra $200 billion a year in taxes from U.S. corporations. But after a deluge of corporate lobbyists descended on Capitol Hill, the White House backed off a few months later, saying that the promised reform would have to wait. As *The Wall Street Journal* explained: "The Obama administration has shelved a plan to raise more than $200 billion in new taxes on multinational companies following a blitz of complaints from businesses."[2]

If the Obama administration was at least showing some (limited) willingness to go after the tax evasion and avoidance schemes that were stripping billions out of the U.S. Treasury each year, north of the border, the same old sluggish indifference to the tricky, offshore tax schemes of the rich prevailed.

FOR ANYONE who has ever had their financial affairs probed by the relentless, no-stone-left-unturned auditors of Canada's tax department, the testimony of former prime minister Brian Mulroney must have seemed mystifying.

Of course, Mulroney's entire testimony was mystifying, as he tried to explain why, shortly after leaving office in 1993, he had met with German businessman Karlheinz Schreiber in hotel rooms and accepted cash payments of more than $200,000. Mulroney's explanation—that he was providing international consulting services for Schreiber—

was vague, undocumented, and mostly involved dead people who couldn't corroborate it. But in 2009, it was almost impossible for the commission investigating the payments to make any sense of them, since the commission's terms of reference restricted it from probing what might seem like a highly salient factor—Schreiber's earlier role as a lobbyist for a $1.8 billion airplane deal that a German consortium signed with Crown corporation Air Canada while Mulroney was in office. (Mulroney denies any connection at all to the airplane deal and he won a $2.1 million settlement and an apology from the Canadian government after it launched a 1995 investigation implicating him in alleged kickbacks.)

But almost as fascinating was a subplot involving Mulroney's dealings with Canadian tax authorities over the payments, which is the focus of our interest here. According to his testimony, Mulroney had accepted $225,000 in one-thousand-dollar bills from Schreiber during meetings in hotel rooms in Montreal and New York City, storing the cash in a safe in his Montreal home and a safety deposit box in a New York bank. He did not make any note of receiving the money, in his personal records or in information provided to his accountants, nor did he report the payments on his annual Canadian tax returns—until six years after receiving them. At that time, Schreiber was being aggressively investigated in Germany for corruption, fraud, and tax evasion, and his relations with Mulroney had soured. Mulroney would have had reason to fear that his payments from Schreiber might become public, leaving him vulnerable to prosecution for tax evasion.

In any event, Mulroney arranged to make a "voluntary disclosure" to Canadian tax authorities about his past unreported income. His tax lawyers were able to negotiate a deal with the Canada Revenue Agency that allowed Mulroney to pay tax on only half of the belatedly reported income, without any penalties. This raises all sorts of interesting questions. Canadians are led to believe that fully disclosing their incomes in annual tax returns is compulsory under Canadian law, and failure to do so will result in serious penalties and even criminal prosecution. How, then, was Mulroney able to get such a sweet deal—taxed at half rates, no penalties, no prosecution?

In reality, penalties are never imposed on individuals making voluntary disclosures. These tax laggards are permitted to simply pay the tax owing, plus interest. What made the Mulroney settlement unusual—and even more generous than the norm—was that he was permitted to pay tax on just 50 percent of the income he'd failed to report, rather than on the entire amount.

One is tempted to conclude that the tax authorities were showing favouritism to a former prime minister. But voluntary disclosures are made anonymously, with tax lawyers submitting the returns to authorities for assessment without disclosing the name of their client. If the rules were followed, officials at the Canada Revenue Agency presumably didn't know they were dealing with a former prime minister when they offered him exceptionally favourable terms for resolving his overdue taxes—what might appear on face value to be a serious case of tax evasion. (Interestingly, under Canadian tax laws, the privileges of the voluntary disclosure program are denied to individuals who are already under investigation for possible tax evasion, or who have failed to report income received from individuals already under investigation. When Mulroney filed his voluntary disclosure in 1999, Schreiber was already being scrutinized for tax evasion in Germany, seemingly disqualifying Mulroney from taking advantage of the program.)

So perhaps the kid-glove treatment wasn't a courtesy extended to Mulroney as a former prime minister, but rather a typical example of the way Canadian authorities deal with rich people who don't fully disclose their incomes each year, as the law requires. Although Mulroney's identity was not disclosed, it would have been clear to revenue officials, from the amounts involved and the high-priced lawyers handling the case, that he was a well-to-do individual. So the tax subplot in the Mulroney saga appears to offer a rare glimpse into how lenient the Canadian government is with rich people trying to avoid paying taxes.

UNDER BOTH Liberal and Conservative prime ministers, the Canadian government has, to put it mildly, shown little interest in tracking down the offshore accounts of wealthy Canadians.[3] Some of this reluctance can be attributed to the sheer difficulty of penetrating the wall of secrecy that surrounds tax haven banks. But how to explain Ottawa's sluggish response when, in the winter of 2008, Canadian authorities were unexpectedly handed secret bank documents providing the details of offshore accounts held by more than a hundred Canadians hiding funds in the LGT bank in Liechtenstein? This lucky break happened because, as mentioned above, LGT employee Heinrich Kieber had handed over bank documents to German authorities, who had in turn passed the information on to a number of countries, including Canada.

The Kieber revelations, like those of UBS's Bradley Birkenfeld, were a dramatic breech of the usually impenetrable world of tax haven banking. Kieber's data sparked an uproar in Germany and led to the conviction of one of the nation's leading businessmen as well as 450 other tax-evasion investigations and the resignation of some high-ranking officials. In Italy, the case grabbed headlines when the names of the wealthy tax evaders were released to the media. But things were much more subdued in Canada. A year and a half after receiving the data, the Canada Revenue Agency responded to a question from the media[4] by announcing it had reassessed the wealthy Canadians involved and concluded they owed some $17 million in taxes, interest, and penalties. By July 2010, a total of $5.2 million of that had been collected. But no one has been charged with tax evasion—a criminal offence that would have signalled that the government considered hiding money in offshore accounts to be a serious matter.

Even more lackadaisical was the government's approach to tracking down wealthy Canadians who had stashed billions of dollars in UBS bank accounts in Switzerland. Once again, its slow-motion actions were striking given the fact that so much of the legwork had already been done. The case began to unfold in the spring of 2007, when Birkenfeld approached U.S. tax authorities with information about how the Swiss bank assisted rich Americans in evading tax. In the course of the subsequent investigation, U.S. authorities unearthed documents that showed UBS also operated a "Canada Desk," which, as of October 2005, was managing some *$5.6 billion* in offshore money. This startling revelation, which got some limited attention in the media, suggested wealthy Canadians were hiding vast fortunes overseas. The story became more serious still in January 2009, when senior UBS official Raoul Weil was declared a fugitive by a U.S. court for fleeing in the face of charges that he conspired to help U.S. citizens evade taxes. As head of global wealth management for UBS, Weil had also been in charge of the Canada Desk.

Despite these stunning developments, Canadian tax authorities didn't even get around to doing a preliminary interview with UBS Canada officials until September 2009, more than a year after the documents were unearthed and reports appeared in the media.

What makes the UBS case particularly intriguing is the fact that UBS Canada was headed up by the influential Conservative politician Michael Wilson, who served as a powerful finance minister in the Mulroney government from 1984 to 1991 and as Canada's ambassador in Washington from 2006 to 2009. Wilson has turned down requests for interviews, saying through officials that it "wouldn't be appropriate" for him to comment.[5]

We're not suggesting that Michael Wilson was involved in assisting tax evasion. UBS Canada, which he headed, is a licensed subsidiary of Swiss-based UBS, and the two entities are separate operations. According to UBS Canada, it had nothing to do with the team of private bankers who came from Switzerland to court rich Canadians as part of the Canada Desk. (Foreign bankers are not supposed to come to Canada to conduct business, according to Canada's Bank Act.) While the Canada Desk team handled some $5.6 billion in assets from Canadians, UBS Canada separately managed an additional $2.6 billion right here in Canada.

What we're drawing attention to is the lack of importance the Canadian government seems to attach to ensuring that rich Canadians pay the taxes they owe. Apart from obvious considerations of fairness, Ottawa is blithely allowing a huge revenue loss by not more aggressively tracking down tax cheats who park their money overseas.

And here Michael Wilson's role does get interesting. Assuming that he was not in any way aiding tax evasion, there is still the question of how much he knew about the activities of the Canada Desk. As chairman of UBS Canada, Wilson "oversaw all UBS operations in Canada, which included the Investment Bank, pension fund management, and Wealth Management businesses," according to his official biography on the Canadian government's website. Are we to believe that UBS Canada—and its overseeing chairman—knew absolutely nothing about the activities that a related company was conducting in Canada, in a closely related field? Both UBS and UBS Canada are in the "wealth management business"—that is, the business of providing banking services for wealthy individuals and companies. This is a tiny world involving a relatively small number of players. It is difficult to imagine that $5.6 billion of Canadian wealth was being handled by UBS bankers flying in from Switzerland, and yet officials at the licensed UBS subsidiary here—presumably looking for business from within the same elite circles—knew nothing about it.

If Wilson did know what was going on, did he not have an obligation to intervene to stop it or report it—or at least to come forward after the fact and provide Canadian authorities with all the information he had about the apparently unlawful business practices going on in a company related to the one he headed? Is that too much to expect from him? After all, he has occupied some very high-ranking positions of public trust in this country, and was serving as Canada's ambassador to the United States at the time the revelations about the Canada Desk were coming to light. It is not even clear that the Canadian government ever bothered to approach Michael Wilson to ask him what he might know about significant illegal activities apparently defrauding Canada of hundreds of millions of dollars in revenue. In July 2010, Caitlin Workman, a spokesperson for Canada Revenue Agency, refused to divulge whether the agency has had any contact with Wilson at all on the matter, citing confidentiality concerns—even though Wilson's personal tax information was presumably not involved.

For that matter, what does the whole episode say about Wilson's own views about the rich and what their appropriate share of the tax burden should be? Here we are delving into the role Wilson has played over the years in helping reduce taxes on the rich—which is perfectly legal, but raises some moral questions. At the risk of digressing a bit, it could be noted that Wilson has never been particularly worried about the rich getting off lightly when it comes to paying taxes. Outside of politics, he has had a highly successful career advising wealthy clients at RBC Financial Group and as vice-chairman of RBC Dominion Securities, where he was responsible for senior client relationships and gave advice to both Canadian and international companies. As finance minister in Mulroney's Conservative government, Wilson oversaw a major overhaul of the federal tax system in 1987 that considerably eased the tax burden on Canada's well-to-do. Earlier tax reform efforts, by Liberal finance ministers Edgar Benson in 1972 and Allan MacEachen in 1981, had attempted to make the tax system more progressive, with higher taxes on the rich, but they were ultimately blocked by massive opposition from Canada's business community. This progressive tax reform tradition, dating back to the Carter Royal Commission on Taxation in the 1960s, was turned on its head by Wilson, who easily pushed his tax "reform" measures through, with the support of grateful business leaders.[6]

During Wilson's long stint as finance minister, some of Canada's wealthiest families received very significant breaks on the tax front. In 1986, the Reichmanns were saved $500 million after they received the privilege of an advanced ruling permitting them to take advantage of a questionable tax scheme that Bay Street had dubbed "the Little Egypt Bump"—just before the Finance department changed the rules so that the scheme could never be used again.[7] In 1991, a wealthy family (believed to be the Bronfmans) was spared an estimated $700 million in taxes when it was permitted to move more than $2 billion worth of assets to the United States tax-free—again, just before that particular barn door was slammed shut forever.[8] A year later Wilson, in the guise of "closing a loophole," changed the rules governing the taxation of family trusts, thereby saving a number of wealthy Canadian families untold billions.[9]

All this was perfectly legal, of course. Indeed, in all these cases, Wilson was using his power as finance minister to make changes that benefited the wealthy. Our point here is simply that, had the issue of taxing the rich been treated with any seriousness, his predilection for reducing the tax burden on the rich—given the negative impact the measures have had on the country's finances and on the fairness of the tax system—would have made him a highly controversial political figure.

THE ECONOMIC CASE justifying extreme inequality is just as weak as the moral case. As we've seen, it boils down to a threat—either explicit or implicit—that if the government imposes significant taxes on the rich, they'll move their money elsewhere.

The rich clearly believe this threat gives them leverage to push for lower taxes for themselves. And governments often acquiesce in the face of this threat, lowering taxes on the high-income crowd on the grounds that they'll be less likely to engage in tax avoidance and evasion schemes.

This is an odd way to deal with the problem.

When people of modest means break the law by stealing—perhaps because they don't have enough income—the government's response isn't to make sure they have more income, but rather to punish them, even to strengthen the penalties so that others will be discouraged from considering such activity. But when the rich break the law by hiding income offshore, the government often responds by lowering tax rates so the rich will have less incentive to engage in such behaviour.

The real solution would be to get tough on tax havens and the people who use them. As noted above, this would be very simple to do, by using basic computer technology to put in place an international system for reporting all bank payments. People wanting to hide income from authorities would then find it no easier to move money undetected around the world than to travel without a passport.

Checkmate.

9

WHY BILLIONAIRES ARE
BAD FOR YOUR HEALTH

Many adjectives come to mind when thinking of how to describe Americans, but "short" probably isn't one of them.

We're used to the notion of the United States as the world's dominant power—a land of untold resources, wealth, and consumption. And one reflection of this abundance is the fact that for most of the past two and a half centuries, Americans have been literally the tallest people on earth. Feeding off the abundant wild game and rich agriculture of their vast new land, colonial Americans measured a full three inches taller than Europeans.

The mythological American is the towering figure of John Wayne. He's the tall, muscular sheriff in the Wild West or the strapping Marine rushing in to win the day in World War II. Potent and appealing as these images may be, they're more nostalgia than reality today. The truth is—compared to Europeans—Americans have effectively shrunk. In the movie remakes, John Wayne should be Dutch.

The reality is that the inhabitants of the Netherlands are now the tallest people in the world. They're almost three inches taller on average than Americans, and continuing to grow. Dutch males average six foot one—seven inches taller than they were just over a century ago. And crowded around the towering Dutch at the top end of the height scale are other northern Europeans—Norwegians, Swedes, Danes, Belgians, and Germans.

For that matter, in the movie remakes, John Wayne could be French, Italian, Spanish, Japanese, Greek, Canadian, Singaporean, Swiss, Brazilian—almost any nationality in the developed world but American. Among advanced industrial nations, Americans are now at the very bottom end of the height scale (except of course for a few extraordinary giants like John Paulson). And no, it's not the influx of short Hispanics that's brought down the average. The height pattern is the same even when the sample is limited to non-Hispanic, native-born Americans.

Height is a potent symbol. But it also appears to be a useful measure of the well-being of a nation's citizens. Economic historians John Kormos and Benjamin Lauderdale, who have conducted an extensive investigation of the changing height patterns among nations, conclude that it is a telling indicator of something very basic about a society: "Height is indicative of how well the human organism thrives in its socioeconomic environment."[1] It is a particularly good indicator of how well societies care for their young, since height is set early in life, notes Thorvaldur Gylfason, a professor of economics at the University of Iceland. Unlike body weight, which can fluctuate significantly over a lifetime, tallness is determined during certain growth spurts in infancy and adolescence. It is heavily influenced by nutrition, which generally reflects the broader social and economic conditions of a child's life.[2] Height, then, is a good indicator of how well a society is creating conditions that allow its citizens to develop and thrive.

Height may be most useful for its simple, provocative quality. It is a concept we can all relate to, and one we instinctively, at a gut level, associate with a certain primitive superiority. It captures our attention better than other, more familiar measuring sticks, like life expectancy or infant mortality. The "shrinking American" is a powerful way to highlight how dramatically the United States has failed in the last few decades to keep pace with other advanced nations in creating conditions that allow its own citizens to develop and flourish. This

American decline has been profound and relentless, so that the United States is now the outlier among industrial nations, having fallen significantly behind the rest of the pack—particularly the northern Europeans—in a wide range of areas of social well-being.

And the reason, it turns out, is integrally tied up with the rise of billionaires.

THE NOTION THAT POVERTY is bad for human well-being is easily grasped. We can all readily appreciate how people with inadequate access to food, shelter, and the basic amenities of life end up suffering from a wide range of problems, with detrimental effects on their health and welfare. We can also easily understand how such material deprivation leads to personal distress that manifests itself in dysfunctional behaviour, such as higher crime rates and more violence, teen pregnancy, and drug addiction. The link between poverty and many forms of personal suffering and social breakdown is not only thoroughly documented but intuitively obvious.

What is not so obvious is that extreme levels of inequality in society have an effect similar to poverty. This has become clear in a growing body of research. As epidemiologists Richard Wilkinson and Kate Pickett put it in *The Spirit Level*: "all problems which are more common at the bottom end of the social ladder are more common in more unequal societies."[3] This explains why even rich countries with high material living standards often have significant social problems. And it is not just the poor in these countries who suffer from them. Countries with higher levels of inequality have higher levels of social problems—*at all levels of income*. Typically, the incidence of such problems is highest at the bottom end, but it continues through all income levels, becoming gradually weaker with each step up the financial ladder. Simply living in an unequal society puts one at greater risk of experiencing a wide range of health problems and social dysfunctions.

This may sound unlikely, but the evidence is powerful. Wilkinson and Pickett have assembled data on all the advanced industrial nations in an attempt to determine the relationship between their level of income inequality and their performance in a number of key health and social areas, including life expectancy, infant mortality, obesity, mental illness, children's educational attainment, teenage births, and rates of homicide and imprisonment. In chart after chart, the same picture emerges: the greater the level of inequality in a country, the higher the rate of the particular health or social problem being measured. To provide a good overview in one chart, Wilkinson and Pickett have created an Index of Health and Social Problems, which captures each country's overall social performance and then correlates the index with the country's level of inequality. The picture is striking. The countries with the least inequality—Japan and the Scandinavian nations—are at the bottom left-hand corner, while the ones with the most inequality—the United States, Portugal, and the United Kingdom—are in the top right. In between, the other countries fall around a straight line between the two extremes, their level of inequality correlating almost exactly with the size of their social problems. The chart reveals a relationship between inequality and social problems that is so pronounced it cannot be accidental.

It's also clear that it isn't the overall "richness" of the country that determines its level of social problems. The United States and Norway are both very rich countries; they have almost identically high per capita national incomes. But the distribution of income within the two countries is very different—highly equitable in Norway, highly inequitable in the United States. The U.S. national income level is very high, despite the large number of poor Americans, because a small number of fabulously rich citizens hauls up the average. But the striking thing is that the two countries experience vastly different levels of social dysfunction. Norway has extremely low levels of health and social problems, while the United States has a record that is way worse than every other Western nation, almost off the chart. The dramatically different social situations appear to be attributable to the dramatically different levels of inequality in the two countries.

This whole area of research was launched in the late 1960s with a massive investigation into the health of British civil servants known as the Whitehall study. The highly stratified British civil service, located mostly in buildings on a road called Whitehall in central London, provided an almost laboratory test case for British epidemiologist Michael Marmot to examine the impact of status levels on health. At the time it was widely believed that those at the top of an organization experienced tremendous stress because of their demanding jobs, and that this explained why they dropped dead of heart attacks at an alarmingly high rate. But as Marmot assembled the data on some eighteen thousand civil servants, it quickly became clear that this popular notion wasn't just wrong, it was actually upside down. Those at the top were not actually dying of heart attacks at a faster rate than those in lower-ranking jobs. Just the opposite was happening. A subsequent follow-up study, Whitehall II, confirmed the same clear trend: the lower down the status scale within the hierarchy, the higher the rate of heart attacks—as well as a host of other diseases. Notes Marmot, who now teaches at University College in London and the Harvard School of Public Health: "the men at the bottom of the office hierarchy have, at ages forty to sixty-four, four times the risk of death of the administrators at the top of the hierarchy."[4]

Marmot's remarkable findings have since been reinforced in dozens of other studies. There is now a large body of evidence showing that, as one moves lower down the hierarchy, one has a greater risk of poor outcomes in a number of areas, including life expectancy; infant mortality; stroke; diseases related to the heart, lung, kidney, and digestive tract; tuberculosis; HIV-related disease; suicide; and violent death. One intriguing study, for instance, compared the longevity of Oscar-winning film stars to another group of film stars with slightly lower status—those who had co-starred in winning films and those who were nominated but didn't end up winning the ultimate prize. The researchers, Donald Redelmeir and Sheldon Singh, postulated that actors who actually win an Oscar experience a huge boost in status and prestige as they move to the very top of the Hollywood hierarchy, well above even otherwise successful actors who have not won the coveted prize. Strikingly, the researchers found that the actual Oscar winners lived four years longer than the slightly lower-status Hollywood stars.[5] Indeed, the findings of a wide range of studies looking at the impact of status have been so consistent that, as Marmot notes, one's status can be considered an excellent indicator of one's likely health outcome: "Where you stand in the social hierarchy—on the social ladder—is intimately related to your chances of getting ill, and your length of life.... The higher the status in the pecking order the healthier [people] are likely to be."[6]

This doesn't mean that high-status people don't sometimes die young or that low-status people don't ever live long lives. Both happen. But when the broad picture is surveyed, strong patterns emerge, and these patterns consistently show earlier deaths at lower status levels. Perhaps this simply reflects the tendency of people in lower-status positions to smoke more, exercise less, and have bad diets? Perhaps— but even when these known behavioural health risks are taken into account, there is still a clear gradient showing better health related to one's status in the social hierarchy. It's interesting that the gradient is evident even in countries, like Britain, with a public health care system. While overall health results are better in countries with public health care systems (as opposed to countries without them), health care for all doesn't eliminate the significantly poorer health outcomes at lower levels in the social hierarchy.

Health researchers have found that status-related conditions are actually the key determinants of a person's health. Dennis Raphael, a professor of health policy and management at Toronto's York

University, maintains that, contrary to popular perception, the primary factors shaping the health of Canadians are not medical treatment or lifestyle choices (like smoking, exercise, or high-fat diets). Rather, he says, research establishes that one's health outcome is determined above all by factors like one's income level, employment and housing situation, and degree of acceptance in the community.[7]

This may seem puzzling. It's easy to understand how social status or a person's position in the pecking order would affect something subjective like their mood, level of happiness, or sense of well-being. But it's harder to understand how it would affect something as tangible as actual bodily disease. Yet this is precisely what the evidence suggests. The connector that explains the link between status considerations and actual physical health outcomes is stress and the body's response to it.

We can see how this works by looking at animals. In the wilds, animals respond to stressful situations—being cornered by a large, hungry predator, for instance—by immediately mobilizing energy in the bloodstream and directing it to the muscles. At the same time, bodily functions that aren't immediately necessary (digestion, waste disposal, grooming, ovulation, storing energy for the future) are shut down by the inhibition of insulin secretions and of parasympathetic tone, as well as by the activation of the nervous system, glucocorticoids, and glucagon. All these responses mobilize the animal's resources to maximize its performance in escaping or perhaps taking on the predator. In the process, they alter the body in a number of ways, including increasing the animal's heart rate and blood pressure.[8]

Humans respond to stress in much the same way, when we, for instance, find ourselves suddenly confronted with an assailant or the car we are driving hits an ice patch and swerves out of control. We may also respond to more subtle threats to our well-being when we are, say, obliged to speak in public, appear at a job interview, or report to a demanding boss. Then there are other sorts of personally threatening situations that may be long-term or chronic—fear of becoming unemployed or being unable to meet a mortgage or credit card payment, worrying about being considered inadequate—that can trigger sustained activation of the body's stress mechanisms.

Stress levels can actually be measured, since humans under stress release the hormone cortisol (also called hydrocortisone), which shows up in saliva and blood. Two psychologists at the University of California, Sally Dickerson and Margaret Kemeny, examined the results of more than two hundred published reports of experiments measuring cortisol levels in human volunteers exposed to various stressful situations. Dickerson and Kemeny found that stress levels were particularly pronounced when individuals felt they were being negatively assessed or looked down upon; "tasks that included a social evaluative threat (such as threats to self-esteem or social status) in which others could negatively judge their performance, particularly when the outcome of the performance was uncontrollable, provided larger and more reliable cortisol changes that stressors without these particular threats." Highly stressful, for instance, were experiments in which volunteers had to perform tasks in front of an audience that would score them. The stress proved most acute when the tasks were impossible, leaving the individual feeling helpless to spare herself the embarrassment or humiliation of performing poorly in front of others. Dickerson and Kemeny concluded: "Human beings are driven to preserve the social self and are vigilant to threats that may jeopardize their social esteem or status."[9]

Of course, stress can take many different forms, and not all of it involves threats to our social status. Getting up to give an Oscar-accepting speech no doubt gives the actor a wildly thumping heart. Similarly, corporate CEOs and high-ranking political figures are under a great deal of pressure to perform. But with that stress comes prestige, power, and control over their situations. Wall Street players undoubtedly feel the pressure of handling billions of dollars, but they also get the thrill of being able to manipulate markets and juggle—and earn—huge fortunes. All this makes them feel important and in control, as if they've got the world by the tail. No wonder dowdy, middle-aged bankers wake up in the morning and (as Matt Taibbi put it) see Brad Pitt in the mirror.

It seems to be far more stressful to wake up and see the Hunchback of Notre Dame in the mirror. Indeed, the worst stress seems to come from situations in which the individual feels humiliated or low in status compared to others. Marmot identifies feelings of lack of control or autonomy as the key to triggering an unhealthy stressful situation. In extensive interviews with the civil servants in his Whitehall studies, Marmot found that lower status was inevitably tied up with less control and autonomy in the workplace. Clerical jobs were not only boring and poorly paid but gave workers no control over their situation; at this lowly level, typists were even subject to rules restricting them from talking to each other on the job. They certainly weren't valued or viewed as significant contributors to the organization. Marmot notes that, try as he might, he simply couldn't conceive of a situation in which Marjorie, from the typing pool, saunters over one morning to Nigel, an administrator eleven ranks above her, and says, "I've been thinking, Nige. We could save a lot of money if we ordered our supplies over the internet. What do you think?" So low is Marjorie's status that the notion of her feeling comfortable bringing even a potentially good idea to the attention of someone far above her in the work hierarchy is no more likely than the possibility that she would approach a member of the royal family with an idea on how to strengthen the appeal of the monarchy.

IT'S NOT HARD to see how income levels are associated with social status. The income we receive is an important indicator of where we stand in the social hierarchy—particularly in our highly materialistic society. As noted earlier, neo-classical economic theory assumes that capitalism correctly rewards the individual for her contribution to society, suggesting that one's income properly reflects one's worth and therefore one's status in the community. Whether this is true or not—and, as we argue in this book, it isn't—these are the values and ideas that dominate modern North American thought. Furthermore, income levels are closely tied up with levels of autonomy and control in the workplace. In general, the high-paying jobs are also the ones with the most freedom and power. The toilet cleaner cannot decide to reward himself with an extra-long lunch hour or choose to delegate the scrubbing part of his job to others so that he can concentrate on developing big-picture strategies for redesigning washrooms. As one descends the pay scale, the desirable features associated with work—status, control, autonomy, opportunity for creativity, pride in one's product—recede a little farther on each downward rung.

There are sometimes offsetting factors that reduce the stress of a low income. A struggling artist, for instance, might accept minimal pay as a deliberate trade-off that allows her to do work she loves. She may even enjoy considerable social status among her peers, who admire her talent and her willingness to starve for her craft, and who may consciously reject income as a meaningful measure of value. But for the most part, our incomes are the single most important indicator positioning us in the broad social hierarchy, regardless of what field we are in. Indeed, in our society, income is the closest thing we have to a universally recognized measure of what we are deemed to be "worth."

In relatively equal societies, there is less of a gap between the incomes of individuals at different levels in the social hierarchy, and therefore less emotional and psychological stress about being positioned lower down. Equal societies also tend to have higher taxes, with tax revenues directed toward the population's broad social needs—health care, education, family support, unemployment insurance. This not only helps provide a level of basic support for all, it also promotes a more co-operative, less individualistic approach, with emphasis on goals like equal opportunity and fairness rather than ever-greater material accumulation. The result is less focus on income status and fewer social divisions. When everyone uses the public health care system and sends their children to public schools, status distinctions tend to be less acute, and the stress accompanying them diminishes.

In unequal societies, just the opposite happens. The very rich tend to withdraw into their own rarified world, travelling by limousines and private planes, entertaining themselves at exclusive clubs and resorts, and living physically apart from the rest of the population, often behind gates or even walls. They come to see themselves as essentially independent of society, purchasing their own health care and education and relying on their own security systems. This leads to resentment that their tax dollars are paying for costly public services that they don't much use, leaving them determined to reduce these costs to keep their taxes from rising. Given their political clout, they're able to maintain enormous pressure on politicians to keep taxes low, thereby starving the public system of the funds needed to maintain shared services and programs that are basic to the well-being of the broader community. The deterioration of key public services and programs increases the vulnerability of most members of society, as well as exacerbating social divisions and stress levels.

All this appears to lead to a deterioration in social relations and a breakdown in trust. As society becomes more stratified, with more noticeable differentiation between income levels, people tend to identify and associate more closely with the people at their own level, making it more difficult to relate to or empathize with those at other levels. The resulting breakdown in trust can be seen in the results of the European and World Values Survey, in which random people in different countries were asked whether they agreed with the statement "Most people can be trusted." Those in more equal countries were much more likely to agree; in egalitarian Sweden, 66 percent agreed, while in the United States, only 38 percent did.[10] This lack of trust in others can be seen in the large number of gated communities in the United States and the popularity of SUVs. That these bulky, high-off-the-ground, fortress-like vehicles have replaced snappy little convertibles as the car of choice suggests that Americans have come to value looking sporty and sexy below meeting their perceived needs for a high level of physical security.

Not surprisingly, perhaps, there also appears to be higher levels of mental illness in highly unequal societies. Some mental illnesses are considered genetic, but recent decades have seen a dramatic rise in rates of other, stress-related illnesses, notably anxiety and depression, particularly in highly unequal countries like the United States, Britain, and Australia (closely followed by New Zealand and Canada). Meanwhile, rates for these syndromes remain relatively low in more equal societies like the Netherlands, Belgium, and Japan. Wilkerson and Puckett note that, to a large extent, mental health is rooted in self-worth. "People who don't value themselves become frightened of rejection; they keep others at a distance, and get trapped in a vicious circle of loneliness."[11] It is easy to see how conditions of extreme inequality feed such feelings, reinforcing anxiety about status. We are back again in the terrain of the "social evaluative threat."

In some, these feelings lead to violent actions. Feeling socially threatened and humiliated is the key cause of violence, according to James Gilligan, a psychiatrist at Harvard Medical School and director of the Center for the Study of Violence. Gilligan notes that violent behaviour is a response to threats or perceived threats to an individual's pride, threats that leave him feeling ashamed, put down, or humiliated. This is particularly potent in young men who lack other sources of pride in their lives—typically, men with no jobs, income, or education who come from socially broken families in which they were inculcated with little in the way of self-esteem or a sense of their own worthiness. When such individuals are insulted or humiliated, they have nothing to fall back on, no other part of their lives to escape into. The challenge to their pride is all there is, and it must be met. Gilligan insists that, in more than thirty years of working with violent offenders, he has "yet to see a serious act of violence that was not provoked by the experience of feeling shamed and humiliated ... and that did not represent the attempt to ... undo this 'loss of face.'"[12]

Once again, such threats seem to be enhanced in countries with extreme income inequality. Documentation of international homicide rates by the United Nations shows the United States at the far extreme, almost off the chart, with a murder rate dramatically higher than any other industrialized nation. The U.S. rate, for instance, is 64 murders per million people, more than four times higher than Britain's (15 murders per million) and more than twelve times above that of highly egalitarian Japan (just 5.2 murders per million).[13] Health analyst Danny Dorling notes that growing income inequality in Britain in the 1980s was reflected in the rising homicide rate: "There is no natural rate for murder.... For murder rates to rise in particular places ... people have to be made to feel more worthless. Then there are more fights, more brawls, more scuffles, more bottles and more knifes and more young men die."[14]

Even for people who don't resort to violence or end up with health problems, extreme income inequality appears to have other negative consequences. Among the "healthy" responses to the rise of billionaires in our midst is a greater focus on keeping up with the very high material standards they set. Economist Robert Frank has dubbed this "luxury fever," a disease he insists infects the whole society.[15] He notes that the proliferation of luxury goods for the wealthy has the effect of making the regular goods consumed by the rest of us seem inadequate in comparison. This leads to a general inflation of expectations. Gas barbecues or wristwatches that seemed perfectly satisfactory a couple of decades ago have now been replaced with much more exotic versions—barbecues that can cook ten breasts of chicken while keeping warm an additional twelve steaks and thirty ears of corn, and wristwatches that glow in the dark fifty metres underwater. After a while, it starts to seem normal to have these more exotic items; it's all just part of keeping up with the flow of modern life.

Advertising and the media constantly remind us of the high material standard enjoyed by those at the top of the hierarchy. TV sitcoms and advertisements typically depict very wealthy suburban families as the norm in society, leaving viewers quietly aware of how shabby their own houses, cars, and clothing are in comparison. These messages are absorbed by children and teenagers, putting additional pressure on parents by having their own children reinforce the idea that they must emulate these impossibly rich lifestyles.

With billionaires constantly pushing up the public's notion of what's materially possible, the standard just keeps rising, subtly and not so subtly imprinting itself on our brains. These greater expectations creep into every corner of our lives. Take children's birthday parties. They used to be modest affairs revolving around pin-the-tail-on-the-donkey games and the presentation of a homemade cake. Today they're more likely to involve a real donkey—or perhaps a more upscale pony—or a live clown or pottery instructor, as well as the presentation of a professionally made cake elaborately decorated with models of the child's favourite cartoon characters. If nothing else, the simple addition of "loot bags"—purchased at specialty stores and presented to every child exiting the party—can add hundreds of dollars to the cost of the event. Parents under financial strain may strongly wish to revert to the old type of party, but they fear looking inadequate by failing to live up to their child's expectations of what is now considered normal in many middle-class circles.

Needless to say, the proliferation of useless trinkets inside the loot bag doesn't seem to make children today happier than children were back in the 1950s, '60s, or '70s. Indeed, studies have shown that all the extra gadgetry and bells-and-whistles now available haven't improved the overall happiness level of North Americans. What they have done is create an enormous pressure to keep up, simply to maintain one's position in the social hierarchy. This requires us to work more. So, rather than taking more time off as our society gets richer, we're working longer hours, increasing our consumption levels in tandem with the material standards set by those higher up the food chain. Instead of spending more time with family or pursuing satisfying activities and interests (as the more egalitarian Europeans have tended to do), we've opted for longer hours on the job (Americans work an average of 274 more hours—about six more weeks—per year than Scandinavians),[16] enabling Americans to buy more of the generally useless things that are the markers of status and position in a highly stratified society.

OF ALL THE NEGATIVE social consequences of extreme inequality, perhaps the most striking is its impact on social mobility. Central to the modern democratic ideal is the notion of equal opportunity. Even those who don't seem to care about income inequality tend to support the idea that everyone should have an equal chance to better herself in life. The hugely different realities in the lives of the poor and the rich and the resources they have available to them might seem to make this impossible, but it nonetheless remains an ideal almost universally subscribed to in Western societies, particularly the United States.

In reality, however, social mobility is significantly lower in countries with high levels of income inequality, such as the United States. A group of researchers at the London School of Economics demonstrated this by accumulating data from eight countries, recording the incomes of fathers at the time of the birth of their sons and the incomes of those sons at the age of thirty. The results clearly showed that the sons were far more likely to advance beyond the income levels of their fathers in more egalitarian countries. The most equal countries in the survey—Norway, Sweden, Denmark, and Finland—all showed high rates of social mobility. Canada was high as well, and Germany fairly high. At the other end, with much lower social mobility, was Britain, and then even further back was the United States, with the least social mobility of the eight countries studied.[17] So they aren't just shrinking—Americans are also increasingly immobile, trapped in the circumstances of their birth. So much for the American Dream.

It's interesting to note that America's poor performance in social mobility is a relatively new phenomenon. The United States used to come much closer to its own ideal of offering economic opportunity and a chance to climb the social ladder. Another set of data, for instance, shows that social mobility actually improved in the United States from 1950 to 1980—the early postwar years, when high tax rates and more equal pay resulted in a more equal distribution of income. But after 1980, when the Reagan revolution brought about a sharp increase in income inequality, social mobility dropped off suddenly and dramatically. The pattern is similar for Britain.[18]

The explanation for this may be fairly simple. The key to social mobility seems to lie in public education. The more educated people are, the more opportunities they have for advancement and earning. In the eight countries in the study mentioned above, the ones with higher levels of equality also all had higher levels of public spending on education. (This is not surprising, since public education is one of the key priorities of government, so countries that collect a lot of tax tend to spend a lot on it.) In Norway, the most equal of the eight countries in the study, fully 97 percent of all education spending was devoted to public education, compared to only 68 percent in the United States.

This brings us back to the important role played by public spending. High levels of public spending can be found in almost all the positive health and social outcomes that we've been discussing in this chapter. If we look, for instance, at the incidence of child poverty—a clear indicator of social distress—we see that it is almost ten times higher in the United States than in the Scandinavian countries. A staggering

21.7 percent of American children live in poverty, compared to a mere 2.4 percent in Denmark, 3.4 percent in Finland, and 3.6 percent in Sweden (the Scandinavian average is 3.3 percent). Similarly, there are striking differences in levels of public support for other vulnerable groups. In the United States, the elderly live on incomes that are 51 percent of their pre-retirement incomes, compared to 66.5 percent for the elderly in Scandinavian countries. People with disabilities are even more disadvantaged. In the United States, their incomes are 58.7 percent relative to the general population; in Scandinavian countries, those with disabilities are much closer to the norm, with incomes that are 86 percent of the national average. Countries with higher public spending have also been far more effective at closing the gender gap. In a gender gap index developed by the World Economic Forum, the Scandinavian countries score consistently higher.[19]

The most important ingredient in determining social well-being, however, is the level of equality, not the amount of public spending. Indeed, public spending is just one way of achieving equality. Japan, which has very low levels of public spending, is a highly equal society, mostly because Japanese companies have more equal pay rates, with much smaller differences between executives and lower-level workers than in other Western countries (particularly the United States). As a result of this more equitable market distribution of income, Japan scores impressively in all the measures of health and social well-being. This suggests that high levels of public spending are important in Western countries simply to compensate for the very unequal distribution of market incomes.

The impressive social results in the Scandinavian countries have long been noted by those arguing for a stronger government role in correcting the inequality generated by the marketplace in North America. At the same time, there's been a tendency to see the superior social benefits in Scandinavia—or even broadly in Europe—as some sort of trade-off for economic prosperity. It's been widely believed that high taxes and social spending may help lots of people, but they destroy the work incentive and thereby reduce everyone's material well-being. But as noted in Chapter 7, there's actually little evidence to support this contention and a lot of evidence to refute it. Indeed, it's becoming increasingly clear that it's not necessary to choose between social benefits and prosperity—it's possible to have both. This is important, since the alleged greater economic vitality of unequal countries has been a key prong in the argument justifying extreme inequality.

In the wake of the 2008 financial collapse, the economic results for the United States (and Britain, another highly unequal country) have of course been very poor. But in case that's just a weird aberration, let's look at what was going on before the Wall Street meltdown. The data show that, on a number of important economic measures, countries with more equal distributions of income were doing just as well or better than more unequal ones. Let's take two extremes—the highly unequal United States and the highly equal nations of Scandinavia (which we'll lump together and consider as one entity).

If we look at GDP per capita in 2004, the U.S. was out in front, with $39,700 compared to $32,825 for the Scandinavian countries. But GDP per capita doesn't really tell us much about how ordinary Americans are doing economically since, as noted before, it is simply an average of all incomes and is therefore greatly elevated in the U.S. by the presence of a small number of extremely rich people. Moreover, the U.S. GDP per capita is high partly because so many Americans have to work long hours simply to make ends meet. Besides, income alone hardly tells a complete story of the economic situation of a nation's citizens. Another important measure is the degree of economic security those citizens enjoy—what economic supports are available in unemployment and retirement. On an economic security index developed by the International Labour Office, and on which a lower score indicates that a country is providing less economic security to workers, the United States scores a poor 0.61, compared to 0.94 for Scandinavia.

Defenders of the U.S. economic model often point to economic growth rates, noting that the U.S. experienced higher growth from the late 1990s until the 2008 financial collapse. This is true; the average growth in GDP per capita was 3.1 percent in the United States, compared to 2.3 percent in Scandinavia (and 2.0 percent in continental Europe). But when it came to other important economic measures, the Scandinavian countries did as well or slightly better than the United States. Despite their extensive social programs, the Scandinavian countries managed to avoid deficits. While the U.S. deficit in 2004 was 4.7 percent of its GDP, the Scandinavians were running a *surplus* of 4.1 percent. Furthermore, on an "innovation" index developed by the United Nations Conference on Trade and Development, the U.S. scored 0.927, while Scandinavia scored a more impressive 0.951.

And when it came to competitiveness, as measured by the business-financed World Economic Forum in Geneva, the U.S. and the Scandinavian countries were typically in a tight race for the laurels. Indeed, Finland hogged the top spot for a number of years in the 2000s, and all the Scandinavian nations always hover around the top of the chart. On an index of growth in competitiveness, based on the World Economic Forum measurements, and on a Global Creativity Index, the Scandinavians slightly outstripped the United States. And when it came to spending on research and development as a percentage of GDP, the Scandinavians were again ahead, spending 3.4 percent, while the U.S. spent 2.7 percent.

All in all, there's little to support the case that the United States was the stronger economic performer. If it was, its superiority was fairly marginal. And that was then. The financial crisis and subsequent economic downturn has played havoc with America's economy, leaving it with persistently high unemployment and a massive trillion-dollar deficit. Then there's the fact that the financial collapse was rooted in American free-market ideology and the willingness of U.S. authorities to allow their banking sector to be essentially unregulated. That lack of regulation was (and continues to be) the product of intense lobbying by Wall Street bankers and the dominance of this overly rich and powerful group. However the U.S. economic model may have stacked up against the more egalitarian Scandinavian model in recent years, any possible superiority has been more than wiped out by the devastating impact of the Wall Street–generated financial collapse.

More broadly, there's some intriguing evidence that suggests inequality may discourage innovation. Three German economists recently made the case that egalitarian societies create strong incentives for manufacturers to invest in the kinds of technological innovations that enable products to be more widely dispersed among the population, contributing to overall improvements in the standard of living. The economists, Reto Foellmi, Tobias Wuergler, and Josef Zweimüller, argued that while new products are often first developed as luxury items for the wealthy, the subsequent innovations that enable these items to be produced on a larger scale only happen when there is a larger market of people able to afford a more efficiently produced (and therefore cheaper) version.[20] The automobile, for instance, was originally produced for sale to the very rich, but the kind of innovation that led to the mass production of the Model T Ford at cheaper prices was encouraged by the presence of an American middle class. This suggests that a more equal income distribution may actually lead to higher levels of investment in technological innovation and, therefore, greater economic prosperity.

So extreme inequality is not only directly linked to a wide range of health and social problems, it also appears to be bad for the economy—ultimately, extremely bad for the economy, as the 2008 financial crash shows.

Indeed, the role of a wealthy super-class in bringing about the collapse points to what is perhaps the most basic trouble with extreme inequality: that the concentration of money in so few hands inevitably affects how power is exercised. When a tiny faction controls such a large proportion of the nation's wealth, it will also likely control the nation—the particular trouble with billionaires to which we now turn.

10

WHY BILLIONAIRES ARE
BAD FOR DEMOCRACY

There's an intriguing old photo in the office of Montreal businessman
Leo Kolber. It captures Kolber as a young man, jumping in the air
with his arm around another young man who is also jumping in the
air. The two young men are smiling, particularly Kolber. No wonder
he is smiling. Although living with his widowed mother in a modest
Montreal neighbourhood, here he is jumping playfully in the air, arm
in arm with one of the richest men in the world: Charles Bronfman,
an heir to the massive Bronfman fortune. The photo was taken in the
1950s on the grounds of Montreal's Elm Ridge Golf Club, in the early
days of a college friendship that would last a lifetime—and would
catapult Kolber himself into the ranks of the super-rich. Looking at
the photo now, one senses that the smiling young Leo Kolber already
had a pretty good hunch he'd lucked into something big.

The photo is displayed on a table of special personal pictures in
Kolber's lovely, spacious office inside the sprawling complex of the
Bronfman holding company, Claridge Inc. Still fit in his early eighties,
Kolber springs around the room showing off photos of himself with
prime ministers, foreign dignitaries, and wealthy business figures.
"I'm always the guy in the background," he notes. True. Kolber *is*
always in the background—the fixer who makes things happen,
moving seamlessly through the interconnecting worlds of money and
politics. We'd like to move him briefly into the forefront here because

he provides a nice illustration of how the very rich exercise political power—how they're able to set the agenda in key areas, and in the process block the interests of the broader public and undermine the functioning of democracy.

The young Leo Kolber not only became Charles Bronfman's best friend, but he soon won the trust of Charles's father, the legendary liquor baron Samuel Bronfman, who put the smart, ambitious young Kolber in charge of managing the family fortune, as president of the family holding company. Kolber ended up running the Bronfman's Cadillac Fairview real estate company and sitting on the board of a number of other Bronfman-related businesses. He was instrumental in key Bronfman business deals, including the eventual sale of Cadillac Fairview, in which he personally earned $100 million. While Kolber brought brains and talent to the job, it's fair to say that his success and his influence in political circles were integrally tied up with the Bronfmans and the fact that he was, in his own words, "the Bronfmans' boy."[1]

As the Bronfmans' trusted insider and advisor, Kolber also became their connection to the political world. The Bronfman affiliation opened doors for Kolber in Ottawa, allowing him to cultivate close personal relationships with the most senior political figures, including prime ministers Pierre Trudeau, Jean Chrétien, and Brian Mulroney. Although Kolber and the Bronfmans provided financial support to Mulroney, their main connections have been with the Liberals. Kolber proudly called himself chief bagman for the Liberal Party, raising millions of dollars for its coffers, including large amounts of Bronfman money and his own. In appreciation, Trudeau appointed Kolber to the Senate in 1983.

Among other things, Kolber ended up as chair of the Senate banking committee—a role that interests us here. Soon after assuming that position in 1999, Kolber got the committee to launch an investigation into Canada's capital gains taxes. In May 2000, the committee released a report recommending that capital gains taxes be significantly reduced—a recommendation that would do little to help the vast majority of Canadians who don't own much in the way of stocks, but would greatly help rich investors and business executives with stock options. (In the year before the Senate committee released its report, the average capital gain received by someone earning between $20,000 and $40,000 a year was about $150, while the average for a person earning more than $250,000 was $74,000.) High-income earners receive about five hundred times more in capital gains than middle- or low-income earners.

As a key facilitator and advisor in the Bronfman world, Kolber was well versed in the ways of lessening taxes on the rich. Of course, elaborate tax avoidance is a skill widely practised in the business community, but the Bronfmans had elevated it to something of an art form. Indeed, the family had a history of near-wizardry when it came to making their own taxes disappear. In the 1940s, their long-time family retainer, Lazarus Phillips, one of the sharpest legal minds in the country, had designed a series of investment trusts that allowed the Bronfmans to maintain control of the family fortune while avoiding all taxation on the income flowing into these trusts. The complex web of trusts even allowed the Bronfmans to avoid taxation upon the death of any of the trust's beneficiaries, allowing control to pass tax-free from generation to generation—in apparent defiance of Canadian tax law.[2] In recognition of this public service, Lazarus Phillips was awarded a seat in the Senate and, interestingly, ended up on the Senate banking committee—which played a key role in 1970 in opposing taxes on capital gains—blazing the trail for another Bronfman fixer, Leo Kolber, a couple of decades later.

The Bronfmans are also believed to have been responsible for a particularly aggressive tax-avoidance ploy in 1991. The scheme only came to light five years later, when it was unearthed by the auditor general of Canada. Although the identity of the wealthy family involved has never been confirmed, it was widely reported to be the Bronfmans. (The Bronfmans initially denied this, but their denials stopped after a while, even though they continued to be named as the family in media reports.)

Here's what happened. At least $2 billion in stocks (believed to be Seagram shares) were moved from a trust resident in Canada to a trust resident in the United States—a transfer that would typically trigger a tax payment of about $700 million to the Canadian treasury. In this case, however, the family involved approached Revenue Canada for an "advance ruling"—that is, a ruling from the government assuring them they could move the money out of the country without owing any tax. Without such a ruling, family members would be unsure of whether they could avoid paying the tax. They could go ahead and transfer the stocks and see if Revenue Canada allowed the transaction to be tax-free. But it would be risky; they might end up facing that $700 million tax bill. Indeed, under Canadian tax law, it certainly appeared that they would owe the $700 million—which is why they pleaded their case in advance.

But Revenue Canada was not convinced by their pleading. In December 1991, nine months after the original request, a rulings review committee decided that no advance ruling should be given. The family was informed that its request had been declined. But they didn't take no for an answer and kept pushing for a ruling. There was a flurry of high-level meetings within the department, and others involving senior officials in the Finance department. (Despite its considerable powers, the office of the auditor general was unable to find minutes for some of the key meetings.) Finally, two days before Christmas, Revenue Canada abruptly reversed itself and granted the advance ruling, assuring the family that it could move the money to the United States without paying any taxes.

Was there political interference? Did senior officials—possibly acting on the authority of cabinet ministers or even the prime minister—overrule the Revenue Canada officials who were charged with making the decision? It certainly seems possible, especially if the family involved was the Bronfmans. After all, the Bronfmans, through Leo Kolber, were exceptionally well-connected politically, not just to the Liberals but also to Brian Mulroney, who was prime minister at the time the advance ruling was granted.

Kolber himself reveals that he and the Bronfmans had given $100,000 to Mulroney's 1983 leadership bid—one of the biggest donations to that campaign, which became the turning point in Mulroney's political career. "I discussed [the donation] with Charles," Kolber explains, "and we agreed it was not only a smart move, but the right thing to do. We liked Brian…"[3] But that ample contribution was only part of what Kolber had done to help Mulroney push aside Joe Clark and capture the Conservative leadership. Perhaps even more important was Kolber's role in winning over a faction inside the Conservative Party that threatened to block Mulroney's power grab. It's worth telling the story briefly here, if only because it so nicely captures the extent of the often invisible power wielded by the truly wealthy.

The story involves the late Eddie Goodman, a powerful Conservative fundraiser and backroom player, particularly in Ontario. As Mulroney tried to line up support in his bid to unseat Joe Clark, he was encountering resistance within the party from the important Red Tory bloc loyal to Bill Davis, who was then Ontario premier. Goodman, a kingpin in that bloc, was particularly resistant to Mulroney.

At Mulroney's request, Kolber intervened to smooth things over with Goodman. As the Bronfman family *consigliere*, he was in an excellent position to do just that. After all, Goodman was the Toronto lawyer for the Bronfmans' Cadillac Fairview Corporation, and he was accustomed to jumping to their requests. As Kolber put it: "When I was running Cadillac Fairview and we had an issue with

Queen's Park, I could be inside Davis' office in five minutes if Eddie was handling it."[4]

So Kolber simply picked up the phone and called Goodman to ask him to come onside with Mulroney or at least stop resisting Mulroney's leadership bid. Over the phone, Goodman gave Kolber an earful of complaints about Mulroney, but when Kolber suggested that he meet the politician himself, Goodman immediately acquiesced. Kolber then arranged to fly Mulroney to Toronto in the company plane, and had Goodman and Mulroney meet for lunch in Kolber's private dining room at Cadillac Fairview. By the time Kolber joined them for coffee two hours later, Goodman had abandoned his resistance, paving the way for Mulroney to go on to win the Conservative leadership. "That was my other contribution to his leadership campaign," notes Kolber, "helping to get Fast Eddie Goodman onside."

A contribution like that doesn't go unnoticed, particularly by someone like Brian Mulroney, who famously said, "Ya dance with the one who brung ya." If the Bronfmans had had a difficulty with the tax department (potentially costing them $700 million) during Mulroney's tenure as prime minister, wouldn't Leo Kolber have been tempted to pick up the phone—just the way he did when he needed to talk to Bill Davis about something affecting Cadillac Fairview? Would Mulroney have completely forgotten about the role Kolber (and ultimately the Bronfmans) had played—financial and otherwise—in cinching his leadership bid? Could that explain why, after Revenue Canada had clearly ruled against the family request for an advance ruling, the government's position was suddenly reversed for no apparent reason and the ruling granted?

Almost a decade later, in 2000, here was Kolber in another capacity, as chairman of the Senate banking committee, trying to use his influence to push the Chrétien government to reduce taxes on capital gains. It was Kolber who initiated the move. "I put it on the table," said Kolber, acknowledging that a cut in the capital gains tax rate had not been a priority for Chrétien, that it was actually "the furthest thing from his mind."[5] At Kolber's direction, the Senate committee plunged into the issue, calling as expert witnesses a number of businessmen and economists, who were mostly supportive of the tax cut and argued that it would increase investment in the country and make Canada more competitive in global financial markets. After several months of hearings, the committee recommended that capital gains be taxed at only half-rates.[6]

One might be tempted to dismiss the significance of a recommendation made by a committee of the unelected Senate. But while the Senate banking committee has no real power, it has considerable influence with the government. It is one of the more prestigious committees of Parliament, partly because its members are often respected figures from the world of business and finance.

Meanwhile, in addition to the advocacy of the Senate banking committee, Kolber was working behind the scenes, using his considerable personal influence with the Chrétien government to further the cause of capital gains tax reduction. Again, it's worth spending a moment to point out Kolber's deep connections with those who wielded power.

Kolber's links to Chrétien and the Liberal Party are long and deep and, as always, spring from his close affiliation with the Bronfmans. He had had a very close relationship with Chrétien's mentor, Pierre Trudeau, for whom Kolber had organized lavish fundraising dinners in his home involving the Montreal elite; after Trudeau's retirement, Kolber and his wife, Sandra, continued to entertain Trudeau at their home and even travelled extensively with him to China, Russia, and Central America.

In addition to his strong relationship with Trudeau, Kolber had been cultivating a relationship with Chrétien for at least a decade before he tried to influence Prime Minister Chrétien to reduce capital gains taxes. Kolber knew the Liberal leader personally from his involvement with party fundraising and also from sitting with him on the board of the Toronto Dominion Bank in the late 1980s, when Chrétien was practising law after losing his first Liberal leadership bid. Kolber recalls being in his own Montreal office one day when he received a phone call from Chrétien, who was in Montreal on other business. Chrétien asked if he could drop by for fifteen minutes. The visit stretched to three hours, during which time Kolber and Chrétien discussed taxes, agreeing that they were too high at the upper end. Later, when Chrétien was in the early stages of organizing his second (and successful) leadership bid in 1989, Kolber was one of the first people approached by Johnny Rae, the Power Corporation executive who was trying to get Chrétien's campaign off the ground. Rae asked Kolber for $10,000 in seed money. Kolber immediately pulled out his chequebook.[7]

Chrétien was one of three prime ministers (along with Trudeau and Mulroney) whom Kolber considered among his "good friends." Kolber had golfed with Chrétien and arranged to have him stay overnight as his guest in the clubhouse of the posh Elm Ridge club (where a young Kolber had jumped in the air, arm in arm, with Charles Bronfman). And as chief fundraiser for the Liberal Party, Kolber had raised millions of dollars for Chrétien and his party. As a token of his appreciation, Chrétien had elevated Kolber (at Kolber's request) to the chairmanship of the Senate banking committee.

So when Kolber used that position to push for a reduction in the capital gains tax rate, he was doing so as someone with a well-established, close relationship with a prime minister who undoubtedly felt some gratitude—if not indebtedness—toward him. In the lead-up to the budget in October 2000, Kolber addressed the Liberal caucus (of which he was a member), urging the MPs and senators to support a cut in the capital gains tax rate, as his committee was recommending. Kolber recalled that, after he spoke, Chrétien advised the caucus to "listen to Leo on this, because he is right."

Kolber also recalled that at that caucus meeting Finance Minister Paul Martin expressed reservations about the proposal, arguing that the tax cut would be a tough sell because it would be seen by the public as being "a sop to the fat cats." But despite these objections from the finance minister himself, when the October 2000 budget was unveiled, it included a reduction in the capital gains tax rate—just as Leo and his committee had recommended. Kolber believes that it was Chrétien, not Martin, who made sure the cut was in the budget. "Without Chrétien, this doesn't get done," said Kolber.[8]

That tax cut has proved to be particularly beneficial to Canada's wealthiest citizens. In 2009 alone, it cost Canadian governments $1.7 billion in lost revenue. Since about half of all capital gains are enjoyed by the richest 1 percent of Canadians, their tax savings in that year alone amounted to a stunning $875 million. In the decade from 2000 to 2010, they saved $7.93 billion in taxes—thanks to the efforts of Leo Kolber.

Indeed, largely as a result of the capital gains tax change, Canada's wealthiest families experienced a decline in their effective tax rates—that is, the rates of tax they actually paid. Between 1992 and 2004, the effective tax rates paid by the highest earning one thousand Canadians—including presumably Charles Bronfman, who ranks eighteenth on Canada's billionaire list—dropped from 42 to 31 percent, a decline in their tax burdens of roughly one-quarter.[9]

What all this suggests is that Kolber played a central role in bringing about a major reduction in taxes for Canada's wealthiest citizens, benefiting the Bronfmans, many of his own friends and colleagues, and, for that matter, himself. Kolber was able to bring about this major change—even though there had been no momentum for it and some resistance from a finance minister fearing a public backlash—largely because of the extraordinary access he had to the very top levels of political power, due to his role as the "Bronfmans' boy."

FEW PEOPLE IN THE LOBBY of Toronto's Hilton Hotel noticed when the CEOs of Canada's five big banks and the country's leading insurance companies arrived early in the evening of May 17, 2010. These men aren't particularly famous or recognizable—even though together they oversee trillions of dollars in assets and could be described as a sort of executive committee of Canada's ruling elite.

They were at the Hilton that evening to host a dinner to raise funds from the broader corporate community for a new monetary policy research centre, connected to the business-funded C.D. Howe Institute. While monetary policy may sound dull, it is a subject close to the hearts of those with large amounts of lucre, because it deals with preserving the value of money, particularly against the scourge of inflation.

That might not seem very controversial. After all, nobody wants to see the value of money eroded through inflation. It's just that, to prevent inflation, it's sometimes necessary for the nation's central bank to raise interest rates. And while high interest rates do cool inflation, they also raise the cost of borrowing money, thereby making it harder for consumers to afford purchases, for homeowners to pay their mortgages, and for businesses to employ workers. So for the vast majority of Canadians, high interest rates usually pose a greater threat than inflation. Most workers would prefer to risk a little inflation rather than face the more devastating consequence of unemployment.

This trade-off between fighting inflation and fighting unemployment lies at the centre of the monetary policy debate. But it's a debate that's been almost entirely dominated by the financial elite, which has largely managed to shape this vital area of public policy in its own interests.

The elite's dominance over monetary policy was firmly established in the late 1980s, when Bay Street blueblood Michael Wilson, finance minister in the Mulroney cabinet, appointed anti-inflation zealot John Crow as governor of the Bank of Canada. Crow had developed his hardline approach to inflation while working as an economist for the IMF, specializing in Latin America during the inflationary 1960s. As governor of Canada's central bank, he launched an aggressive campaign to eliminate inflation, pushing interest rates higher and higher in the name of achieving "zero inflation" or "price stability." This plunged the Canadian economy into a deep recession in the early 1990s, with hundreds of thousands of Canadians losing their jobs and the official unemployment rate rising to 12 percent. As opposition mounted, the financial community—operating through the C.D. Howe Institute, or the "Howe" as it's known—provided crucial intellectual justification for a high interest rate policy that was becoming increasingly controversial and unpopular with Canadians.

Indeed, what happened with that anti-inflation battle in the early 1990s is a good example of how the wealthy are able to prevail even when the policies they favour have a directly negative effect on the vast majority of citizens.

The goal of "zero inflation" was an extreme one. In fact, it had never before been tried in any major country in the world, and there didn't appear to be any pressing need for it in Canada. Inflation can be a serious problem when it reaches the sort of hyper-inflation levels of Germany in the 1920s or postwar Latin America. But Canada in the late 1980s and early 1990s had only very moderate inflation, in the 4 to 5 percent range. Furthermore, since there'd been almost no international experience with a zero inflation policy, there was little evidence of any broad benefit to society. But there was lots of evidence that the mechanism for achieving zero inflation—high interest rates— would lead to high levels of unemployment.

All this suggested that adopting a zero inflation policy in Canada would amount to a dangerous experiment, with no clear upside for the public but a very clear downside. For this reason, the policy was rejected as too extreme by some of Canada's leading economists, including Pierre Fortin of the Université du Québec à Montréal and Lars Osberg of Dalhousie University—both past presidents of the Canadian Economics Association. Indeed, a zero inflation policy effectively repudiated the goals set out in the original mandate establishing the Bank of Canada in the 1930s, which required the bank to seek a balance between preventing fluctuations in price levels and employment levels. Considerations about employment were now shunted aside and the focus put exclusively on stopping prices from rising.

The financial community favoured this radical policy, and the Howe played a crucial role in making the case for it. This was no easy task, since there was virtually no evidence to support it. Nevertheless, with the help of some conservative economists, the Howe pushed the case for zero inflation in a series of quasi-academic conferences, press releases, and books. Probably the most important of these was *Zero Inflation: The Goal of Price Stability*, a paperback published by the Howe in 1990,[10] in which Peter Howitt, a well-regarded economist from the University of Western Ontario, made a stunning prediction about the benefits of zero inflation—that a permanent reduction in inflation of just one percentage point would be worth the equivalent of sixteen times the current GNP, *or roughly $11 trillion!*

That certainly put some meat on the slender bones of the zero inflation argument. Here was an apparently serious academic from a reputable university making the case that zero inflation could offer some truly spectacular economic benefits—apparently more than enough to compensate for the negative economic effects of higher unemployment.

But on closer examination, Howitt's prediction is built on sand. It's worth a quick review here, if only to show how the financial elite was able to influence the debate and shape an important area of public policy, even though there was no real evidence to support the case it was putting forward, as even Howitt himself acknowledged.

Howitt's dramatic prediction about the potential gains of reducing inflation was based on a mathematical model constructed by two economists inside the Bank of Canada's research department, which purported to show that every percentage point of inflation reduced productivity growth by 0.38 percent. Howitt admitted that he considered this finding purely speculative. Even so, he went on to use it as the basis for some calculations of his own, and quickly came up with the striking conclusion that reducing inflation by one percentage point would be worth sixteen times the GNP. Having lobbed out this fantastic number, he quickly distanced himself from it. "Of course, there is no assurance that this estimate is correct," he wrote, "accordingly this conclusion must be treated tentatively."

But Howitt then proceeded to ignore his own sensible advice, continuing: "Nevertheless, in the absence of any other empirical estimates, *one must take seriously* the possibility that this is the order of magnitude of the long-term gain to society from having a lower rate of inflation [italics added]." But why must we take any of this seriously? Perhaps the reason no one had come up with a different estimate was that there was no accurate way to do so. If there was no assurance that the original estimate was correct (as Howitt himself noted), then wouldn't basic logic—not to mention academic prudence—lead us to conclude that we simply don't know what the benefits of reducing inflation might be?

Howitt again urged caution, noting that the number he had come up with "is so large that one hesitates to put too much weight on it in the absence of corroborating evidence." Good point. But rather than simply concluding that there wasn't enough evidence to make any meaningful prediction, Howitt decided to come up with a more "conservative" prediction. Still using the original, questionable estimate, he postulated that the benefits of a one-point inflation reduction amounted to merely $1 trillion. "Thus, *even under these conservative assumptions*," he wrote, "the current discounted value of the gain to society from reducing inflation further below the current 5 percent level is far greater than the estimate of the cost [italics added]."

But isn't something amiss here? Both these numbers—the extreme and the "conservative"—were based on an estimate that Howitt himself cautioned might not be correct. So why should we take either of them seriously? As economists Brian MacLean and Mark Setterfield commented: "We are not convinced. If two people claim to have seen a UFO, with one person claiming that it is large, and the other person claiming that it was small, should we assume that the UFO was medium-sized?"[11]

Despite the weakness of its case, the Howe (and the financial community it represented) managed to provide a veneer of academic respectability for the Bank of Canada's radical war on inflation. The result was continuing high unemployment throughout the first half of the 1990s and, largely as a result of that unemployment, huge government deficits. Indeed, Canada's significant deficit problems of the early to mid-1990s were generated not by an increase in public spending, as is popularly believed, but largely by the zero inflation policy with its high interest rates.[12]

In the spring of 2010, when the bank CEOs gathered at the Hilton, monetary policy was threatening to become a battleground once again. The lingering effects of the Wall Street crisis had left Canada awash in unemployment and deficits. With workers pressuring for continued high levels of public spending to counteract the recession, the financial community argued that all that spending was driving up the deficit and threatening to set off a serious round of inflation.

The monetary policy research centre being launched by the Howe would provide a new vehicle for pushing the case for extreme vigilance against inflation and for continuing the Bank of Canada's exclusive focus on inflation control. The centre was being presented to the public as an "independent" voice—one that would provide policy advice to the bank and the federal government based on apparently neutral research, even though it was clear that it would simply parrot the anti-inflation views of the financial elite that was paying for it. That was the point of the dinner at the Hilton Hotel. At $1,250 a ticket, the event would raise considerable funds from the corporate sector for the new centre, adding to the $1.7 million already contributed by leading financial firms. (Absurdly, the new monetary policy centre qualified as a "charitable" organization, so bankers attending the Hilton event got a tax receipt to deduct part of the cost of their tickets.)

The centre was really just another way for the elite to further consolidate its control over this crucial area of public policy, from which the broader public was essentially excluded. And if there was any doubt about whether the Bank of Canada would pay attention to this new centre and its "independent" research, one clue was the presence of the bank's governor, Mark Carney, at the Hilton shindig as the guest speaker. While Carney was in a position of authority over the bankers, he was also from their community, having learned about the banking world during thirteen years' working for Wall Street powerhouse Goldman Sachs.

Clearly, the executive committee of Canada's ruling elite was hard at work, making sure that the ongoing impact of the Wall Street–induced recession would fall hardest on working people, not on the wealthy.

BUT NOTHING BETTER ILLUSTRATES the capacity of the rich to get their way in politics than the sheer power heist carried out by Wall Street banks in the last few decades. This immensely powerful clique has managed to essentially capture control of Washington and dismantle the entire U.S. financial regulatory apparatus put in place after the 1929 crash. The extent of the bankers' political clout is most vividly demonstrated by their continued dominance in the aftermath of the 2008 crash. Public outrage over Wall Street's role in triggering the near-collapse of the financial system has been enormous. This should have given the U.S. government enough leverage to bring the big banks to heel and to reimpose a regulatory regime to protect the public from such recklessness in the future. But this hasn't happened. Instead, as Simon Johnson and James Kwak observe, the White House extended "a blank check to the largest, most powerful banks in their moment of greatest need....When Wall Street was on its knees, Washington came to its rescue."[13]

The political muscle of the very rich may be most evident in issues like financial deregulation, taxation, and monetary policy. But it extends well beyond the purely economic sphere. Wealthy interests have also been a key stumbling block—indeed, the only real stumbling block—in efforts to organize a global campaign to tackle climate change. In fact, the climate change battle illustrates the immensity of the danger in allowing so much political power to be concentrated in the hands of the few. Apart from the proliferation of nuclear weapons, it is hard to imagine an issue that is more threatening to human life on the planet.

Since the greenhouse gas phenomenon became properly appreciated in the scientific community in the 1980s, international efforts to mobilize to correct the problem have been truly extraordinary. Virtually all the world's scientists with expertise in this area have come together, through the UN's Intergovernmental Panel on Climate Change, and spoken with one voice about the urgent need to reduce carbon emissions. Although doing so involves significant changes, polls show that the public, particularly young people, are willing to begin the process and fault the government for not providing more leadership. A Harris-Decima poll released during the Copenhagen conference in December 2009 found that 84 percent of Canadians think their government is failing in its handling of the environment.

For years now, the real obstacle has been the immense political clout of the oil lobby, which, among other things, has conducted extensive campaigns to deny the validity of the science of climate change. In Canada, for instance, climate change denial efforts have been spearheaded by the amply funded business think-tank the

Fraser Institute, which, in the weeks leading up to Copenhagen, hosted screenings across the country of the anti-Kyoto film *Not Evil Just Wrong*. The Fraser's relentless campaign over the past decade, buttressed by media attention to climate change deniers, has succeeded in creating enough apparent controversy around the issue for the Canadian government to get away with taking no action— despite the enormity of Canada's carbon footprint and the growing condemnation of the world.

IT IS PERHAPS SELF-EVIDENT that wealthy interests exert disproportionate influence over the political agenda and in the process undermine democracy. As Aristotle noted some three hundred years before the birth of Christ, "where the possession of political power is due to the possession of economic power or wealth ... that is oligarchy, and when the unpropertied class has power, that is democracy." A few hundred years later, the Greek historian Plutarch already considered the subversive role of money in politics as one of those self-evident truths that one grows weary of observing: "An imbalance between rich and poor is the oldest and most fatal ailment of all republics." In the early twentieth century, U.S. Supreme Court Justice Louis Brandeis put it bluntly and memorably: "We can have democracy in this country or we can have great wealth concentrated in the hands of a few. We cannot have both."

Yet despite the great inequality in our midst today, the notion persists that our modern Western nations are democratic, that they are controlled by the will of the majority. While most people would probably agree that the rich have more weight in politics, elections are nevertheless taken seriously in our mainstream culture and public discourse. People talk about the importance of citizens voting, and see voter turnout as an indication of the health of the democracy. Presumably this reflects the widespread belief that our democracies work, that the will of ordinary citizens will prevail, that any party which strays too far from popular sentiment will be tossed out by the voters and replaced by another party that better responds to the public's needs and desires. According to this view, despite the importance of money in politics and the dominance of the backroom boys, the interests of ordinary citizens are broadly protected because fear of alienating the majority will keep the most cynical politician in line.

This analysis is bolstered by the presence in our democracies of large numbers of organizations promoting all sorts of different interests and viewpoints. With varying degrees of effectiveness, these groups manage to get their voices heard in the public debate. Even groups defending clearly marginalized people—such as the homeless or refugees—succeed in getting some media attention and in presenting their concerns to elected representatives. All this helps contribute to a general sense that power is widely distributed, that multiple voices are heard, that competing groups balance each other out, and that social policy councils, associations of injured workers, and environmental activists somehow counter the power of billionaires and business associations.

Although many on the left have always dismissed this comforting view of a functioning democracy as naive, it was accepted by mainstream political scientists throughout the 1950s and '60s. But as business became increasingly assertive and successful in achieving its goals, political scientists began questioning their own confidence in "pluralism"—the notion that power is widely distributed, that no one group exercises dominance. By the mid-'70s, two of the world's most pre-eminent political scientists, Robert Dahl and Charles Lindblom, began to reassess the pluralist views they themselves had long subscribed to.

In 1976, in a jointly authored new introduction to their classic text *Politics, Economics and Welfare*, Dahl and Lindblom distanced themselves from their pluralist views: "Interpretations that depict the American or any other market-oriented system as a competition among interest groups are seriously in error for their failure to take account of the distinctive privileged position of businessmen in politics.... In the United States, more money, energy, and organizational strength is thrown into obstructing equality than achieving it." The two political scientists concluded that "to democratize the American polyarchy further will require a redistribution of wealth and income."[14] By 1982—as the Reagan revolution moved into full gear—Dahl recanted any previous pluralist tendencies: "It is perfectly obvious that one of the most influential structures in any society is the distribution of income and wealth. Disparities of income and wealth confer extraordinary advantages and disadvantages. The distribution of advantages and disadvantages is often arbitrary, capricious, unmerited, and unjust, and in virtually all advanced countries no longer tolerable."[15]

With the arrival of George W. Bush in the White House in 2001, the political dominance of the wealthy became so pronounced that the 14,000-member American Political Science Association (APSA) took the unusual step of setting up a task force to study the impact of rising inequality on the nation's democracy. The fifteen members were carefully chosen so that the group not only included leading political scientists but also represented a diverse array of ideological viewpoints as well as varying methodological approaches and specialties. The task force then spent two years reviewing the best available scholarship as well as conducting new empirical studies and submitting its work to rigorous peer review. In its report, released in 2004, it delivered a forceful indictment of the current state of American democracy: "Citizens with lower or moderate incomes speak with a whisper that is lost on the ears of inattentive government officials, while the advantaged roar with a clarity and consistency that policy-makers readily hear and routinely follow. The scourge of overt discrimination against African-Americans and women has been replaced by a more subtle but potent threat—the growing concentration of the country's wealth and income in the hands of the few."[16]

As the task force report suggests, the threat posed by the concentration of wealth is becoming graver. In the past thirty years, as the rich have become vastly richer, they've devoted far more resources and become much more adept at influencing all aspects of the political process in their favour. Political scientists Jacob S. Hacker and Paul Pierson have identified the mechanics of how this influence is exercised in examining the case of the Republican tax cuts of 2001 and 2003.[17] Those cuts represented dramatic changes that fundamentally altered the nation's fiscal landscape and its distribution of income. They were passed into law even though they provided average citizens with only very modest benefits and considerable long-term risks, while giving the wealthy what can only be described as a massive windfall. Some commentators have suggested that the tax cuts became law because ordinary voters ultimately support favourable treatment of the rich, possibly in the hopes of someday joining their ranks themselves. But Hacker and Pierson, in carefully analyzing the extensive polling data on the issue, show that Americans clearly did not favour the substance of the Bush cuts.

Although some polls suggested that there was broad support for the cuts, Hacker and Pierson note that such polls simply asked whether or not voters favoured "Bush's tax cut proposal," without offering any alternative or pointing out the trade-offs involved. Asking if a voter wants a tax cut is a bit like asking if he wants some chocolate. Of course he does! But when the question became "Do you want a tax cut, or would you like to spend surplus national revenues on something else?" respondents consistently ranked tax cuts below other priorities. As opposed to Social Security, tax cuts lost by a margin of 74 to 21; versus Medicare, they lost 65 to 25; versus a grab bag of "education, the environment, health care, crime-fighting and military defense," the margin was 69 to 22 percent. Voters showed a clear preference for an agenda sharply at odds with the one being offered by the Bush administration.

The rejection of the substance of the Bush tax cuts became even more pronounced on the question of where the benefits should go. In other words, if there was going to be a tax cut, the public consistently and strongly opposed the idea that the benefits should go almost solely to the well-to-do. For instance, a March 2001 survey asked respondents whether federal taxes should be cut across the board, which, the survey noted, would give the largest share of the cut to the wealthiest Americans, or whether cuts should be aimed more at middle-income Americans. When presented with these two options, 73 percent of respondents favoured the plan that skewed benefits toward the middle class. Who would have guessed?

Moreover, it appears that the Bush administration was well aware of the public's preferences. In a now-released internal memo from 2001, a top Treasury official named Michele Davis advised her boss, Treasury Secretary Paul O'Neill, to push the president's tax-cut plan at an upcoming event, while cautioning him to keep in mind that "the public prefers spending on things like health care and education over cutting taxes." Davis, who served as O'Neill's press secretary, clearly understood that her government's plan was at odds with what the public wanted. So what did she do—suggest changes to the plan, propose a rethinking of the policy? If governments really were responsive to the public's desires, and voters really did call the shots, Davis would have been concerned about letting her boss—and the Bush administration that ultimately employed her—get too offside with popular aspirations. But rather than feeling reined in by public opinion, the Bush administration and its officials appeared to see the popular preference as merely a problem that had to be carefully handled. "It's crucial that you make clear that there are no trade-offs here," Davis wrote matter-of-factly to the Treasury secretary, even though there clearly were trade-offs. "Roll-out events like this are the clearest examples of when staying on message is absolutely crucial. Any deviation … will change the way coverage plays out from tomorrow forward."[18]

Davis obviously never intended the public to see her note, which was directed solely at those who presumably shared the administration's determination to put the tax cut in place despite the public's strong reservations. Hacker and Pierson went on to explore how it was that a political party, which must face the electorate fairly regularly, seemed unconcerned about satisfying that electorate. An important element seemed to be the increasing importance of small but exceptionally well-funded conservative pressure groups. For instance, the Club for Growth, with only ten thousand members, might seem like a bit player in U.S. federal politics, but with a bankroll of $10 million, it had become a force to be reckoned with in congressional races, funnelling money to candidates on the basis of their zeal in tax-cutting. The club was particularly effective in weeding out, early on, any Republicans who dared to deviate from the party's central tax-cuts-for-the-rich agenda. Club president Stephen Moore noted that when he approaches wealthy donors for money to use against such candidates in primary contests, "they start wetting their pants."[19]

Another well-heeled pressure group, Americans for Tax Reform, has focused its efforts on keeping potentially independent-thinking Republicans from wandering too far from the tax-cutting agenda. The group seeks written pledges from politicians and political candidates that they will oppose all efforts aimed at raising tax rates at the upper end. Although some moderate Republicans originally resisted, increasingly they succumbed; by July 2009, 172 congressmen and 34 senators had signed the pledge. Such is the power of highly focused, well-financed pressure groups to keep Republican politicians from going off message.

With this sort of discipline enforced by the party's wealthy donors, Republicans fell into line, unanimously backing a tax-cut package that would have infuriated a properly informed electorate. Of course, the administration had gone to great lengths to make sure that the public had little sense of what was actually going on; this included the Treasury department releasing some highly misleading statistical information and Bush himself stating barefaced lies, like insisting that "by far the vast majority of my tax cuts go to the bottom end of the spectrum." The public was further confused by the actual design of the tax cuts, in which the meagre benefits going to the middle class were provided quickly upfront while the really massive benefits directed toward the upper end kicked in a few years later, when public and media attention would inevitably have moved on.

The result was a stupendously large redistribution of resources to the very affluent. The richest 0.1 percent of Americans saved *284 times more* from the Bush tax cuts between 2001 and 2010 than people in the middle 20 percent of the U.S. income distribution[20]—a result that, as the polling data show, the American public did not want and that will, sadly, make even larger sums available to conservative pressure groups seeking further tax reductions.

BUILDINGS ON THE CAMPUS of the University of Toronto bear the names of some notable Canadians, including literary giant Northrop Frye, public health pioneer John FitzGerald, and inventor Sir Sandford Fleming, who introduced the concept of standard time. But the edifices named in honour of distinguished individuals typically date back more than three decades. In recent years, campus buildings and auditoriums have been named almost exclusively after people whose distinctive characteristic is the possession of lots of money.

There's a reason for this. As universities have lost government funding in the last few decades, they've turned more and more to private donors. Universities are now heavily in the business of fundraising, devoting huge effort to wooing wealthy alumni. And the effort has paid off. In the past five years, U of T has collected an average of $120 million a year from benefactors. In exchange for all that money, donors get their names on plaques, programs, rooms, wings—even whole buildings, if they donate enough. The result is that affluent businessmen are now honoured and commemorated throughout the university. Particularly prominent at U of T for instance are merchant banker Joseph Rotman, pharmaceutical entrepreneur Leslie Dan, and businessman Peter Munk, chairman and founder of Barrick Gold, the world's largest gold mining company.

But if the campus has become a showcase for the wealthy, there's apparently no room to honour a man who is as close as the country comes to a genuine hero. A group of U of T professors found this out when they approached the university in 2007 with the idea of naming the Health Studies Program after Tommy Douglas, considered the father of Canada's public health care system. In 2004, Douglas was selected the Greatest Canadian of all time, following a nationwide contest organized by CBC -TV in which people cast more than 1.2 million votes over a six-week period (the runners-up were Terry Fox and Pierre Trudeau). But other than being the most respected Canadian ever, what does Tommy Douglas have to offer the University of Toronto? Not enough to justify having a program named after him, apparently.

Paul Hamel, a biologist in the U of T Faculty of Medicine and one of the professors who pushed for the Tommy Douglas naming, says that the university simply wasn't interested in the idea because they saw little potential in it for fundraising. Apparently university administrators believe the rich are more enthusiastic about seeing their own names carved on plaques than in honouring the man who brought public health care to Canada. Hamel and his group were informed that they'd have to raise $2 million to get the program named after Tommy Douglas. Hamel criticizes the university for adopting this attitude, which he sees as a function of the growing power exerted by its fundraising arm, known as the Office of Advancement. "As a result, the priorities of the university have been skewed toward areas that interest the elites," says Hamel, "rather than toward the priorities of faculty, staff, and students who are engaged in critical analysis, research, and teaching."

This aspect of philanthropy is rarely mentioned in the public feting of wealthy benefactors. On the contrary, the role of philanthropy in funding universities—as well as hospitals, museums, art galleries, concert halls, and opera houses—is typically advanced as one of the reasons we shouldn't be alarmed by the rise of billionaires. Their generosity is helping to maintain healthy funding for many of our key public facilities and institutions, we're told. Furthermore, wealthy benefactors are credited with contributing to pluralism, by providing funds for activities, organizations, and viewpoints overlooked or underfunded by government.

In truth, our public institutions' growing reliance on wealthy donors highlights another aspect of the problem of the power wielded by the elite and the negative impact this has on democracy. As public institutions become more dependent on the rich, they inevitably end up catering to the rich, either directly or indirectly. Indeed, fundraising procedures seem to encourage donors to become involved in reshaping the university. Here's how Dezso Harvath, dean of York University's Schulich School of Business, describes the process: "You set up a steering committee with two or three major banks, insurances companies, and trust companies, and ask: 'How is the field changing, what are the new requirements, what kind of graduates would you like to see? ... From there, it was a short distance to saying, 'We need some financial support to make it happen.'"[21]

This approach has led to increasingly large corporate donations. Notes Harvath: "When you make programs relevant, when you are responsive, the business community is very responsive." Clearly, Harvath means relevant and responsive to people who have funds to donate—like Toronto financier Seymour Schulich, who donated $15 million to York in 1995 in exchange for having the administrative studies school named after him. But being relevant and responsive to wealthy donors means the university is likely to encourage activities and approaches that the wealthy like and to underfund or discourage ones they don't. This reliance on wealthy business interests seems certain to undermine the role of universities and colleges as places of critical thought, where the prevailing policies and dogmas— championed by those wealthy business interests—are carefully scrutinized and debated.

All this has been justified on the grounds that our public institutions need money, following the cutbacks of the 1990s. Of course, the problem is circular. If governments hadn't cut tax levels so deeply—particularly for corporations and high-income individuals— they would have sufficient revenue to sustain our public institutions, as they did in the early postwar years. For that matter, if the charitable deduction were to be removed from the tax code, governments could collect a great deal more revenue from the wealthy and be better able to fund important public priorities. Of course, the wealthy would strongly resist such a change. As Wall Street billionaire Sanford I. Weill told *The New York Times*: "I want to give away my money rather than have someone take it away."[22] Philanthropy provides the rich with some very significant benefits that they would be reluctant to relinquish. The benefits to the public are less clear, once the lost tax revenues are factored into the equation.

Indeed, the practice of naming a building after an affluent donor creates a false sense of how much financing the donor actually provided. For instance, there was much celebrating in April 2010 when it was announced that a new $35 million donation from Peter Munk would enable the University of Toronto to establish a school for global studies. The new Munk School of Global Affairs (not to be confused with the existing Munk Centre for International Studies, based on an earlier Munk donation to the university)[23] is to be housed in a century-old stone building on fashionable Bloor Street West and features an elevated pixel board flashing the latest world news headlines. But what wasn't mentioned in the press announcement is that Munk will receive a $16 million tax reduction for his

$35-million contribution, reducing his actual personal contribution to $19 million. So he will really be paying just a little more than half the cost of his contribution, while the government (that is, Canadian taxpayers) will pay just under half. For that matter, if Munk made his donation in the form of shares in publicly traded companies—as most donors do—then his tax savings will be considerably larger (possibly by millions of dollars) and his personal contribution far smaller than $19 million.[24]

The Ontario and federal governments also announced that they would each contribute $25 million to the new school, bringing the total contribution of Canadian taxpayers to at least $66 million. But when it came to naming the building, the taxpayers' $66 million simply disappeared; only Munk's $19 million (or less) counted. Accordingly, the new school, with its handsome building on Bloor Street, has been named after Munk, ensuring that the thousands of people who pass by every day will not only be confronted with news headlines but also a constant reminder of Peter Munk's generosity and commitment to higher education and global understanding. Few of them will realize that Munk's contribution only amounts to about one-fifth of the overall cost of establishing the new school, or that they, as taxpayers, contributed the other four-fifths. Indeed, since there will also be ongoing costs for running the school—which taxpayers will cover—Munk's share of the overall cost of the school will be well below one-fifth. It would be more accurate to call it the Canadian Taxpayers' School of Global Affairs, with Some Help from Peter Munk.

Rather than contributing to pluralism, the charitable donations of the rich enhance the dominance of billionaires—to the point where we as a society have even surrendered to these wealthy titans the power to determine who will be honoured by having their names on our public buildings. Philanthropy also gives wealthy donors the power to direct large sums of public money to the causes of their choice. (It's striking to note that the rich direct very little to helping the poor.[25] While the well-to-do seem motivated to have their names prominently displayed at educational, cultural, and medical facilities, where their largesse will presumably be noted by their peers, they show almost no interest in contributing to community centres, recreation halls, or swimming pools in poorer parts of town.)

So, for $19 million (or less) of his own money, Peter Munk has managed to direct at least $66 million of public money toward a project he favours: a global affairs school. And it's likely to be a global affairs school that will fit with the political views and sensitivities of Peter Munk. U of T administrator Tad Brown insists that there will be no compromise of the university's academic freedom. Brown says that Munk will have no influence over what goes on at the school he is helping establish. But is the school likely to engage in research on issues that might offend Munk—such as, say, taking a critical look at mining ventures in developing countries and their impact on the environment and local populations? While there may be nothing technically prohibiting Munk's new school from carrying out this kind of academic inquiry, it seems unlikely that the university would appoint faculty members whose research might annoy this generous benefactor and therefore discourage others like him from trusting the university with their money in the future.

Philanthropy offers the wealthy an appealing option. Rather than simply handing money over to tax authorities, as all of us are obliged to do, the fabulously rich can afford to donate large sums in ways that allow them to increase their public influence, even as they're honoured in the community for their virtue and generosity. Honorary university degrees and other public tributes are frequently bestowed on philanthropists; Peter Munk, Joseph Rotman, and Leslie Dan, for example, have all been awarded the Order of Canada, the country's highest civilian honour. And philanthropists receive highly flattering media attention for their largesse.

Munk's 2010 donation to the University of Toronto, for instance, merited a fawning front page news story in *The Globe and Mail*, which heralded the gift as the largest in U of T's history, and celebrated his new school as a "vision of a global plaza reconfiguring Toronto's downtown Bloor Street West and becoming the hub of Canada's conversation with the world."[26] It's impossible to buy publicity any better than that. Whatever controversies may follow Munk abroad—his company has come under attack from environmental and indigenous groups, who've held annual demonstrations in Chile, Argentina, Peru, the Philippines, and Tanzania as part of a Global Day of Action Against Barrick Gold Corporation—back home, Munk is associated with loftier things. His name is indelibly linked with good works and emblazoned on important public buildings (to which he has contributed a relatively small portion of the costs).

Given the perks, it's debatable whether this should even qualify as philanthropy at all. Individuals receive a tax credit when they make a gift to a charitable organization, but in cases like this, the donor gets something very valuable in return—his name publicly commemorated for all to see. This should be treated for what it is: not a gift to the community, but rather a business transaction in which an individual purchases that most treasured of items—a personal legacy.

THE CAPACITY OF THE RICH to undermine democracy—so obvious and yet so strangely invisible—is surely the most serious negative effect of extreme inequality. Even if we were somehow able to deal with all the other negative consequences, such as the myriad ill effects on health and social well-being, we would still be left with the impact of extreme inequality on the very functioning of democracy.

And the consequences of rendering democracy dysfunctional are simply huge. It means not only that we are disempowered as citizens— which would be bad enough—but that we are effectively blocked from enacting policies that protect our own vital interests, and may even be necessary for our survival as a species. This capacity of billionaires to imperil the public interest becomes ever more menacing as the human capacity for destruction grows ever larger. If wealthy interests use their clout to prevent us from taking collective action on climate change or other environmental disasters, then the negative effects of extreme inequality are beyond calculation.

As a society, we have largely sidestepped the whole issue of the connection between wealth and political power, ignoring the obvious truth in Louis Brandeis's observation that "we can have democracy ... or we can have great wealth concentrated in the hands of a few. We cannot have both." Pluralism may be a fairly accurate way to describe the political situation that prevailed in North America in the 1950s and '60s, or that exists today in the Scandinavian countries. But it seems to have little to do with the current reality in the United States or Canada. Yet we continue to subscribe to the comforting notion that we live in a pluralistic society, where political power is widely distributed—even though we probably don't really believe it's true any more.

Perhaps there are a few people who still believe that folks like Peter Munk, Leo Kolber, and the CEOs of our major banks are just some of the voices out there—voices that are no more heeded in the political process than those of workers, students, the unemployed, and the poor.

11

THE TRUE BADGE OF CITIZENSHIP

Vernon Hunter, an employee of the U.S. Internal Revenue Service, was at work in his office in Austin, Texas, one afternoon in February 2010, when his life was abruptly brought to a bloody and horrific end. An airplane driven by a man enraged by the American tax system had just slammed into the side of Hunter's building, killing himself and Hunter and injuring a number of other IRS employees. With memories of 9/11 still haunting the nation, the fiery killing of Vernon Hunter by a suicide bomber seemed certain to stir anger and outrage. Yet oddly, it passed almost without notice.

It wasn't that fears of terrorism no longer stirred passions in America. Six weeks earlier, a foiled attempt by a Nigerian student to blow up an airliner approaching Detroit with a bomb hidden in his underwear had sparked mountains of outrage over the apparent breakdown in security. Both the Nigerian would-be attacker and the Texas pilot bomber were motivated by political rage, so their actions were clearly acts of political terrorism—the subject that had consumed America since September 2001.

The Nigerian was said to be a Muslim extremist who was protesting America's military interventions in Islamic countries. The Texan, Joe Stack, left behind a long manifesto expressing anger and frustration, primarily against government and the tax system, and concluding "violence is the only answer." Yet while the Nigerian student was quickly branded a terrorist, with commentators complaining that U.S. authorities had respected his legal rights in the process of detaining him, there was hardly any criticism—let alone full-blown outrage—directed toward the Texas killer.

Indeed, Stack's grotesque act of violence was treated almost with kid gloves, with politicians and public figures holding back condemnation. Both the local Texas prosecutor and a White House spokesman went out of their way to deny that Stack was a terrorist. Media anchors and commentators were surprisingly restrained, with ABC's *Good Morning America* asking the adult daughter of the Texas bomber whether she considered her father a hero. *A hero?* What an odd question. "Yes, because now maybe people will listen," replied Samantha Dawn Bell, adding merely that she acknowledged that her father's action had been "inappropriate." (In a later interview, she retracted her suggestion that her father was a hero, but continued to defend his views.)

Republican congressman Steve King of Iowa tried to shift the blame for the Texas attack onto the IRS. "I think if we'd abolished the IRS back when I first advocated it, [Joe Stack] wouldn't have a target for his plane.... It's sad the incident in Texas happened, but by the same token, it's an agency that is unnecessary and when the day comes when that is over and we abolish the IRS, it's going to be a happy day for America."[1] In the context of almost a decade of near-hysteria over terrorism in America, these comments about "the incident" by an elected member of Congress were stunning in their mildness, and in their apparent tolerance for terrorism and murder. Yet there were no calls for Congressman King's resignation, nor even any condemnation from the Republican caucus.

Among other things, the quasi-tolerance for the Texas suicide bomber highlights the hypocrisy of the U.S. campaign against terror. The entire American political and media establishment reject the Nigerian underwear bomber's cause—forcing the U.S. military to withdraw from Muslim countries—and so the young man's willingness to use violence to advance his cause is roundly and forcefully condemned. But some of the most powerful forces in America support the anti-tax cause of the Texas suicide bomber, so his willingness to use violence to advance his cause is judged less harshly, almost sympathetically.

The IRS reported that there were 1,014 threats made against its employees in 2009 (up from 834 in 2005), suggesting that while the Texas bomber may be unusual in actually resorting to violence against tax officials, he is not the only one out there thinking about it. Given this climate of extreme anti-tax hostility, it would seem all the more important for public figures to firmly condemn the attack on the IRS building. But while condemning acts of terrorism is the bread and butter of U.S. politics, there were few voices lambasting Joe Stack, or even lamenting the tragic and horrific passing of Vernon Hunter, who, in addition to being a father of six, was a military veteran who had served his country in Vietnam.

Politicians and media figures seemed reluctant to wade in, no doubt fearful of ending up on the wrong side of a faction that has grown extraordinarily powerful. The anti-tax movement is now so established, its message so deeply embedded in U.S. political culture, that it largely goes unchallenged. Very few are willing to take it on— to the point that even when an act of terrorism is committed in its name, it is largely given a free pass.

ON THE SURFACE, it seems simply obvious that people would hate taxes. After all, taxes require people to hand over money. But then, there doesn't appear to be similar antipathy toward other things that require people to hand over money—like grocery bills or the cheque that arrives at the end of a restaurant meal. Of course, in these situations people are paying for goods and services that they receive. But taxes also pay for goods and services that people receive, and that are at least as essential to their well-being: an education, pensions, police and fire protection, national security, roads, highways, bridges, canals, libraries, museums, parks, sewer systems, garbage pickup, snow removal, water purification, food inspection, disease control, and so on. The success of the anti-tax lobby lies in its ability to separate taxes in the public's mind from these many services and necessities that taxes pay for, and that the public truly values.

These efforts, exemplified by the invention of Tax Freedom Day, simply omit the reality that citizens get things in return for taxes, and instead focus exclusively on the amount of taxes citizens pay. Tax Freedom Day—developed by the Tax Foundation in the United States and by the Fraser Institute in Canada, and popularized with the active help of the media—is designated as the day of the year when the average family has earned enough to pay off its annual tax bill. Only then is the family considered to have stopped "working for the government." (Does it follow then that, for the rest of the year, Canadians will be working for Loblaws, Canadian Tire, Shoppers Drug Mart, and other places they'll spend money?)

Of course, it should be acknowledged that there is one important difference—we choose to shop at Loblaws, Canadian Tire, and Shoppers Drug Mart, while taxes are not optional. But the attempt by anti-tax lobbyists to present taxes as coercive obscures their essentially democratic nature. Taxes result from decisions made through our democratic system, which we all have an opportunity to participate in. Through the democratic process, we have decided to pay collectively for certain goods and services because we consider them important, and because if we paid for them individually on the open market, they'd cost a lot more and be much more difficult to provide. Rather than seeing them as a denial of freedom, we should regard taxes as an essential part of citizenship in a free and democratic society.

Indeed, they have traditionally been regarded as a cornerstone of democracy. The slogan "no taxation without representation" became the rallying cry of the American Revolutionary War, reflecting the connection the colonial rebels made between taxation and democracy. That connection also figured prominently in the late-nineteenth-century political battle over the introduction of an income tax in the United States. One congressman who opposed the income tax argued that, since the poor would be exempt, it would undermine democracy, because the poor would have no legitimate claim to control a government to whose treasury they had not contributed. In a passionate counterattack in Congress, the famed orator William Jennings Bryan pointed to the enormous tax burden the poor shouldered due to the tariff: "If taxation is a badge of free men, let me assure my friend that the poor people of this country are covered all over with the insignia of free men." While there was debate about which class was shouldering the bulk of the tax burden, there was a general recognition that taxes and democracy were integrally connected.

In Canada too, arguments about the importance of taxation in a democracy became central in the debate over the introduction of an income tax during World War I. Those arguing for an income tax insisted that the rich had to contribute financially to the nation's war effort just as the poor were contributing to it on the battlefield. While the Conservative government of Robert Borden toyed with the idea of imposing conscription to meet the country's expanding military involvement, a rallying cry rose from the ranks of labour and farm organizations across the country: "No conscription of men without conscription of wealth!" Conservative Finance Minister Thomas White tried to head off demands for the income tax, insisting that the rich people who would be affected by it had already made generous contributions to the Red Cross. But the public wasn't convinced. Facing a deeply divided country and keen to win Liberal support for its conscription bill, the unpopular Borden government indicated that it would be willing to support an income tax. On July 24, 1917, the conscription bill passed in the House of Commons, with the support of many Liberals. The next day, White announced that the government would introduce an income tax. The government understood that the public had come to regard conscription of wealth through taxation as a basic duty of citizenship, not unlike that other most basic duty of citizenship: defending the country in battle.

It's striking to see how far we've moved from these early notions of taxation as central to democracy to the point where taxation is considered an evil so great that it prompts thousands of U.S. citizens to threaten the physical safety of government tax collectors and makes mainstream politicians cautious in condemning a terrorist attack on tax authorities. This momentous change in public attitudes can be traced back to the aggressive neo-conservatism that appeared in the Anglo-American countries in the late 1970s and really took hold in the 1980s. Key to the development and promotion of this conservatism and its fierce anti-tax ideology was the emergence of a new school of thought in the U.S. known as "public choice theory."

In essence, public choice theorists, borrowing from modern economic thought, take as their central premise that humans are motivated exclusively by personal self-interest, greed, and material acquisitiveness. They basically extend the assumptions of modern economic theory to the political sphere, insisting that all participants in the political process (voters, politicians, civil servants) are only interested in and capable of acting on their own self-interest. As critics Hugh Stretton and Lionel Orchard note, the public choice theorists have attempted "to persuade people that material greed is, and will inescapably remain the single, natural dominant motive of their political, economic and social behaviour."[2] So the notion that a government could represent some sort of broad "public interest" is deemed to be naive, even fraudulent. According to the public choice theorists, there is no overarching public interest, just a collection of individual desires and preferences. In their formulation, government comes across as little more than a public trough that everyone is trying to get their face into.

With any concept of a broader public interest set aside like this, public choice theorists turn to simply maximizing the rights of the individual and limiting the power of government to interfere with this individual, particularly through taxation. They argue that government shouldn't be allowed to use the tax system for redistribution, since this enables the majority to unfairly pursue its own self-interest at the expense of the wealthy few. To prevent this, some public choice theorists have argued for actual constitutional protections against majority rule in the field of taxation. Needless to say, many in the elite see much merit in this idea of effectively outlawing the masses from exercising their democratic power in this crucial area.

The impact of the public choice theorists has been huge. Although their writings are largely technical and remain obscure outside the academic world, they have provided apparent intellectual backing to bolster the conservative case for smaller government and lower taxes.

In reality, however, the intellectual merits of their arguments are slight. Their case rests on the assertion that humans are purely motivated by narrow self-interest and a desire to accumulate material possessions. But while humans clearly do pursue their own self-interest, the rigid *homo economicus* character implied in public choice theory seems to be only a partially satisfactory depiction of the scope of human behaviour. The Nobel Prize–winning economist Amartya Sen provided a nice retort to it with the following scenario: "'Can you direct me to the railway station,' asks the stranger. 'Certainly,' says the local, pointing in the opposite direction, toward the post office, 'and would you post this letter for me on your way?' 'Certainly,' says the stranger, resolving to open it and see if it contains anything worth stealing."[3]

The impulse that comes to most of us when a stranger asks directions is probably not to mislead him, nor is a relentless determination to rob trusting strangers likely the norm (although there would certainly be some individuals who would do so). A lot of what goes on in our day-to-day lives has little to do with conniving to steal from others in order to gain more for ourselves and a lot to do with simply getting along with them. (For that matter, at times human behaviour appears to be downright altruistic, as evidenced by the fact that billions of dollars were raised almost overnight for victims of the South Asian tsunami and Haitian earthquake, from thousands of individual donors who received no public adulation or even recognition for their contributions.)

The point here is not to present a softer or more benign view of people, who are clearly capable of horrendous greed and aggression. It is rather to suggest that human needs are more complex and varied than public choice theory implies. Specifically, the theory fails to take into account our intensely social nature—an aspect of human behaviour that has been identified in decades of research in the social sciences, particularly psychology, anthropology, and sociology. As noted in Chapter 7, this highly social nature explains the tendency of humans to measure their success against others, to be acutely conscious of their stature and rank in the social hierarchy. It also suggests that humans have a deep need for community. They naturally seek to relate to and be accepted by other people. They desire to belong to a larger community—whether family, clan, gang, club, social network, or society at large—and as part of the group will generally participate and contribute willingly.

The late economic historian and anthropologist Karl Polanyi argued that this social aspect is the most consistent feature of human behaviour and is clearly visible in all social organizations across continents and through time. By emphasizing the social aspect, Polanyi did not mean that people are unselfish. Humans are primarily concerned with their own welfare, just not exclusively so. But this focus on their own welfare doesn't mean that their motivation is mainly materialistic. On the contrary, Polanyi argued that the welfare of individual humans depends largely on their social relationships and on the preservation and viability of their communities. This suggests that sustaining and strengthening those communities—by improving their social cohesion, maintaining their physical infrastructures, and protecting them against threats that can only be addressed collectively, like global warming and other environmental disasters—is ultimately as important to humans as their individual material accumulations.

Under the neo-conservative dogma that has dominated North American society for several decades, these social and collective needs have been given short shrift, forced to take a back seat to the supposed dictates of the marketplace and the facilitation of individual wealth accumulation. But if social needs and the desire for viable communities are as deeply ingrained in humans as Polanyi and others suggest, this intense focus on personal material acquisitiveness may not be the great liberator it's purported to be. On the contrary, it may well be depriving humans of something very basic to their hard wiring as social beings.

While focusing on material acquisition seems utterly natural and normal to us, Polanyi noted that earlier societies throughout history typically gave top priority to other goals, like worshipping religious figures, celebrating cultural icons, or honouring bravery on the battlefield. Until the emergence of capitalism in parts of the Western world in the early sixteenth century, the so-called "economic motive" of material acquisition was simply one of many aspects of community life, and not one singled out for special attention. Indeed, until the eighteenth century, there wasn't even a separate word for "the economy;" the material well-being of the community was simply treated as part of its overall well-being.

In traditional societies, the bonds of the community involved some sense of responsibility to others, a willingness to share to prevent members of the group from going hungry. While there were frequent periods of scarcity—caused by external threats like war, pestilence, or drought—the principle that everyone in the community should be free from hunger prevailed in traditional societies, according to Polanyi, "under almost every and any type of social organization."[4] Even in feudal societies, where peasants toiled on vast estates controlled by wealthy nobles, the peasants were entitled to certain "common rights" that gave them access to sufficient land and resources to cover their basic needs (albeit at a very modest level).

This suggests that co-operation and sharing of resources— something that can be accomplished efficiently through a tax system— may be a natural tendency in humans, connected to our nature as social animals. The tendency to share appears to be instinctual in other highly social primates. Marc Hauser, an evolutionary biologist at Harvard, notes that the rhesus monkey will send out a special call to others in his group if he happens upon a particularly high-quality batch of food while foraging. A monkey who doesn't send out an alert will be punished. If other monkeys catch an individual gorging on a batch of ripe coconuts, he will be beaten by the dominant male in the group.

Similar behavioural patterns can be seen in humans. "There's not a human society in the world that doesn't redistribute food to nonrelatives," notes Samuel Bowles, director of the behavioural science program at the Santa Fe Institute. "Whether it's through the state, or the chief, or a rural collective, or some other mechanism, food sharing of large nutritional packages is quite extensive and has been going on for at least a hundred thousand years of human history."[5] Bowles points to the Ache of Paraguay, hunters who bring their bounty back to be split among the tribe. "The majority of calories are redistributed," he points out. "It ends up being something like a 60 percent income tax." The social requirement of sharing is even more evident in the case of the Tandroy of southern Madagascar, where the death of a rich tribe member leads to ritual acts of sharing. "The rich person's stock is killed and eaten by everyone," often to the last head of cattle, notes Bowles. "That's a 100 percent inheritance tax."

Polanyi argued that, with the emergence of capitalism, there was a deliberate attempt to eliminate these long-established practices of sharing and replace them with behaviour based on personal acquisitiveness. Whereas traditional and feudal societies had discouraged greed and materialism on the grounds that they posed a threat to the common good, capitalism actively encouraged these traits, massaging them and cheering them on, indeed elevating them to the centrepiece and guiding principle of society. At the same time, the new capitalist system abandoned the traditional imperative of the social bond, to the point of actually allowing members of the community to go hungry. In fact, the threat of hunger became a deliberate strategy under capitalism, a means to prod peasants to work, even under the horrific conditions in the new mines and factories (today we might call it a "work incentive"). Breaking with centuries of history, capitalism introduced the concept of using scarcity and deprivation as a deliberate tool of social engineering and control.

Of course, capitalism is generally regarded in the West today as key in our evolution as a species toward a more advanced way of life. But Polanyi reminds us that capitalism, which was put in place by the rising merchant class in seventeenth-century England, was especially brutal in its early stages and was not appreciated nor widely accepted for a long time. On the contrary, it was so devastating and disruptive to the lives of the vast majority of people that they attempted to resist it with whatever means they could, often tearing down hedges around the newly enclosed fields with pitchforks and hoes. Among the early resisters was a group known as the Diggers, who fought for the common people to regain the right to dig and forage on lands that were now being claimed as private property. Digger leader Gerrard Winstanley accused the members of the new elite of a kind of theft that permitted them to "lock up the treasures of the earth from the poor."[6]

Resistance to unbridled capitalism went on in various forms for centuries, and still continues. Without this resistance, in which members of the public seek "the protection of society," there would have been nothing to stop the most appalling abuses of the early days of capitalism, when young children were obliged to work all night in factories and mines or were stuffed up blackened chimneys to serve as human cleaning utensils. Polanyi describes the process that's taken place over the last few centuries as a "double movement" in which each step implementing capitalist reforms was met by a determined effort by large numbers of people to protect themselves from the potential damage of these reforms.

While it didn't stop the entrenchment of capitalism, the resistance did lead to the development of the modern welfare state, with its labour and social protections. This has certainly helped mitigate capitalism's worst excesses, with some countries allowing more mitigation than others. The progressive tax system has been a central feature of this welfare state, funding its programs and distributing income in a more equitable manner than the market systems installed under capitalism typically allow. The welfare state and progressive taxation have gone a long way toward restoring the social dimension that raw capitalism shunts aside.

It is this bulwark of progressive taxation and welfare state protections that the neo-conservatives have moved aggressively to tear down. But their case rests on a flimsy premise—that human behaviour boils down to individual greed and acquisitiveness. Such a formulation flies in the face of overwhelming evidence that humans are intensely social animals. As such, their desire to protect themselves and their communities from the full force of unleashed greed is at least as natural—and historically evident in the resistance to unbridled capitalism—as their desire to endlessly accumulate material possessions. Rather than elevating greed to a hallowed, iconic stature, as the neo-conservative movement does, it would seem more in keeping with human needs to treat the impulse toward material acquisitiveness as simply one aspect of human behaviour—one that can release useful energy but that, unchecked, can cause great damage to the social fabric upon which so much human well-being relies. As the late British historian R. H. Tawney eloquently put it: "So merciless is the tyranny of economic appetites, so prone to self-aggrandizement the empire of economic interest, that a doctrine which confines them to their proper sphere, as the servant, not the master of civilization may reasonably be regarded as … a permanent element in any sane philosophy."[7]

PERHAPS THE MOST POTENT argument put forward by the anti-tax movement in recent years has been the notion that taxes are unduly coercive, that they amount to an assault on freedom. Among those who played a role in popularizing this idea was Robert Nozick, whose widely celebrated *Anarchy, State, and Utopia* won the U.S. National Book Prize in 1975 and was selected as one of the hundred most influential books since World War II by the *Times Literary Supplement.* Nozick set the tone for the anti-tax militancy to follow when he wrote that "taxation of earnings from labour is on a par with forced labour."[8]

This is a stunning assertion. Equating it with forced labour turns the traditional concept of taxation as integrally connected to democracy upside down. Democracy is about empowerment; forced labour is a form of slavery—the exact opposite of empowerment. But does Nozick's claim make any sense? Are individuals really disempowered by taxation?

In truth, taxing the income that individuals earn from their labour leaves them free to determine almost every significant aspect of their self-development: whether to labour, which labouring activities to pursue, how long and under what conditions to labour—all aspects that are denied by forced labour. Taxation only reduces the reward that they receive from their work—a reduction that, as members of society, they have a role in determining. Under slavery, there is no pay and no say over conditions.

Indeed, it was the lack of coercion involved in taxation that led the late tax scholar Henry Simons to endorse the progressive income tax system. Simons's arguments on the subject have largely been ignored in recent years, but they are worth considering briefly here. Simons, who considered himself a libertarian and is still revered in conservative circles, defended progressive taxation as part of his strong belief in the merits of capitalism. He recognized that capitalism could only survive in a democracy if the general public benefited from it, and this involved redistributing its bounty, which otherwise ends up concentrated in the hands of the few (as anyone who has played the board game Monopoly knows).

Simons argued that progressive taxation was the best way to achieve the necessary redistribution—since it involved the least amount of government intrusion in the market. Taxes, after all, don't interfere in the market's ability to determine prices and to allocate resources through the price mechanism—key features of the market economy. They don't involve a government bureaucrat imposing measures that interfere with the basic elements of supply and demand. "No fundamental disturbance of the whole system is involved,"[9] noted Simons in his classic 1938 text *Personal Income Tax*. He elaborated on this theme later in *Economic Policy for a Free Society*, emphasizing how progressive taxation achieves redistribution without impinging on freedom: "What is important for libertarians is that we preserve the basic processes of free exchange and that egalitarian measures be superimposed on those processes, effecting redistribution *afterward* and not in the immediate course of production and commercial transactions [italics added]."[10]

It could be added here that taxation—and even heavy taxation of the rich—was supported by no less a conservative favourite than Adam Smith, the eighteenth-century founder of the classical school of economics. This might come as a surprise since Smith's legacy has been largely appropriated in recent years by neo-conservatives.

While they've managed to tear snippets out of context to present his *The Wealth of Nations* as a manifesto for unbridled capitalism, in fact Smith was wary of the social consequences of the emerging industrial capitalist system and in particular the dangers of inequality. Throughout *The Wealth of Nations,* Smith consistently championed the rights of workers against the rights of merchants and industrialists. And he showed his cynicism toward business interests when he famously noted that "people in the same trade seldom meet together, even for merriment and diversion, but that conversation ends in a conspiracy against the public."

Far from rejecting the legitimacy of taxing earnings, Smith devoted much of *The Wealth of Nations* to a discussion of the best means of collecting taxes, and repeatedly indicated a preference for shifting the burden off the poor and onto the rich. He strenuously objected, for instance, to a particular tax—common in his day—that was based on the number of windows in a house. "The principal objection to all such taxes is their inequality, and inequality of the worst kind, as they must frequently fall much heavier upon the poor than upon the rich. A house of ten pounds rent in a country town may sometimes have more windows than a house of five hundred pounds rent in London; and though the inhabitant of the former is likely to be a much poorer man than that of the latter."[11] Smith called for heavier highway tolls on luxury carriages than on freight wagons so that "the indolence and vanity of the rich [can be] made to contribute in a very easy manner to the relief of the poor." Indeed, although he wrote before the introduction of income taxes, Smith clearly anticipated and supported the idea of progressive taxation: "It is not very unreasonable that the rich should contribute to the publick expence, not only in proportion to their revenues, but something more than in proportion."[12]

Certainly it's hard to imagine Smith having any sympathy for Nozick's charge that taxes on earnings are akin to forced labour. He rejected suggestions put forward in his day that taxes were "badges of slavery." As he wrote in *The Wealth of Nations*: "Every tax ... is to the person who pays it a badge, not of slavery, but of liberty. It denotes that he is subject to government, indeed, but that, as he has some property, he cannot himself be the property of a master."[13]

THE ATTEMPT BY CONSERVATIVES to present taxes as coercive also conveniently ignores the extensive coercion involved in property rights, which conservatives wholeheartedly endorse.

Indeed, conservatives see property rights as the very basis of freedom. But while property rights do extend freedoms to some, they deny those same freedoms to others. An individual who owns a plot of land is free, for instance, to build a log cabin or create a fish pond on it, but others are not free to do so. Indeed, they are blocked from doing so. Once a piece of land becomes someone's property, all other people are denied access to it; they are prevented from building on it, taking something from it, or transforming it in any way, even from walking across it. Anyone who violates the rules of property will be subject to punishment by the state. Without such coercion there would be no enforceable property rights. The point is: both property rights and taxation involve the exercise of coercive power by the state.

In the case of taxation, however, the coercive power of the state doesn't diminish freedom so much as redistribute it more broadly. Take the case of the owner of the plot of land. If, as a result of taxes levied on his income, he is obliged to sell the land, he would be deprived of his right to build a log cabin and a fish pond on it, limiting his freedom. But if the government, using tax revenues, were to purchase the land and turn it into a public park, the freedom of non-owners would be greatly expanded. Land that they had previously been denied access to would now be available for them to enjoy—to hike through, to play games on, to camp on overnight. The tax did not eliminate the freedom to use the land; it simply redistributed it.

Has the overall amount of freedom been expanded or diminished? It's hard to say. But one thing that can be assumed is that more people benefit as a result of the redistribution. In most industrialized countries, almost two-thirds of taxes collected are simply transferred to recipients of government spending programs in the form of cash. And, in a market economy, "to have money is to have freedom," notes political philosopher G.A. Cohen.[14] Money is equivalent to a series of tickets to do things. The richer you are, the more tickets you have to do the things you want to do, which is to say, the freer you are. Not to have money is not to have freedom. The greatest constraint on freedom in our society is undoubtedly low income. So when the government taxes someone, it restricts that person's freedom, but it greatly enlarges the freedom of those who receive transfer payments and other government benefits. For that matter, taxation can also potentially enlarge the freedom of all, by, say, investing in something that will benefit the whole community—such as a cleaner environment or purified drinking water. The diminishment of freedom experienced by the taxpayer is at least partially compensated for by the benefits achieved through such government investments.

Indeed, the sorts of "public goods" that government alone can provide are essential to personal autonomy, which is the essence of freedom. In other words, freedom is more than simply the absence of coercion—it involves individuals having an array of choices in their lives, and public goods greatly contribute to the value of the choices on offer. As the contemporary political writer John Gray put it: "Autonomy, if it is to be meaningful and valuable, requires not only capacities for choice on the part of the individual but also a span of worthwhile options in his or her cultural environment.... Autonomy is not worth much if exercised in a Hobbesian state of nature."[15]

EVEN AS THE INCOMES of those at the top have risen higher and higher, their tax load has gotten lighter and lighter. The tax cuts introduced by the Bush administration in 2001 and 2003 consolidated those of the Reagan era. But while the result has been a cornucopia of money at the top, there's also been an attempt on the part of the rich and their advocates to deny the charge of favouritism. So, for instance, *The Wall Street Journal* has vigorously opposed Obama's proposed tax hikes on high-income earners, insisting that "it's going to be hard for the rich to pay any more than they already do."[16]

The notion that the rich are shouldering an unduly large share of the tax burden echoes throughout the conservative and business press. Indeed, business commentators frequently argue that the rich pay a disproportionately large share of all tax revenue, suggesting that they are contributing, if anything, more than their fair share to the cost of operating public services. And on first glance, there seems to be some truth in these assertions. As *The Wall Street Journal* correctly notes, the share of income taxes paid by the rich has been rising; the top 1 percent now contribute a hefty 40 percent of all U.S. income tax revenue.

But this simply reflects the fact that income is now so heavily concentrated at the top. In other words, yes, the rich are paying an increasingly large share of all income taxes, but only because they receive an increasingly large share of all income. The *Journal* concedes this fact, but goes on to insist that, even so, the tax burden on the top 1 percent is onerous. After all, while they receive 22 percent of all income, they pay fully 40 percent of all income taxes, making their share of taxes almost double their share of income. "The tax code is already steeply progressive," the *Journal* concludes.

Really?

In fact, if we look at taxes actually paid, we see that the U.S. tax system is only mildly progressive.

By itself, the income tax is progressive—that is, it takes a proportionately bigger bite out of higher incomes. In 2009, the lowest 40 percent of U.S. households actually received a net benefit through the income tax, due to various tax credits. The middle 20 percent of households paid 2.3 percent of their income in income tax, while the top 20 percent paid 13.4 percent and the top 1 percent, 17.9 percent.[17]

However, in addition to the income tax, the U.S. federal government also levies a payroll tax, a corporate income tax, an estate tax, and a few excises taxes. When all these are considered, the tax system is still progressive, although less so.

But these federal taxes are the only progressive part of the system. If we also include state and local taxes, which are generally flat or often regressive, the picture changes considerably,[18] and we see that the burden on the rich is not much heavier than the burden on those much lower down the income ladder. For instance, with state and local taxes included, those in the bottom-earning group—the lowest 40 percent, who obviously have limited financial resources—pay fully 18.7 percent of their paltry incomes in taxes. Those in the middle group, the next 20 percent, pay 27 percent of their incomes in taxes. Those in the top 1 percent pay 30.9 percent.

In fact, if we look closely at the numbers, we notice something bizarre—the effective tax rates paid by those at the very top are actually lower than the rates paid by those who are simply near the top. (This reflects the fact that much of the income received by the top 1 percent is in the form of capital gains, which are taxed at lower rates.) While the top 1 percent has a 30.9 percent effective tax rate, those just below them in the 90 to 99 percent level actually pay slightly higher effective tax rates—between 31 and 33 percent. If the system was truly progressive, effective tax rates would rise as income rises. But that's not what happens. Instead, effective tax rates rise only very gradually as income rises, *and then they actually drop off at the very top.* So rates at the summit are actually regressive. Most citizens would probably be offended by this fact if they knew about it, argues tax analyst Martin A. Sullivan: "My casual impression is that some people favor progressive rates and about an equal number favor flat rates. Very few endorse regressive rates."[19]

The same pattern is true in Canada; indeed, if anything, the regressivity is more pronounced here. When all types of taxes are included, it turns out that the poorest 10 percent of Canadians— those earning $13,500 a year or less—paid fully 30.7 percent of their tiny incomes in taxes! Meanwhile, the top 1 percent—those with incomes above $300,000—had a slightly lighter burden, paying 30.5 percent of their enormous incomes in taxes.[20]

So much for steep progressivity, or progressivity at all.

BUT LET'S GO BACK to *The Wall Street Journal*'s assertion that "it's going to be hard for the rich to pay any more than they already do." The *Journal* is suggesting that the rich are already so heavily burdened by taxes that any more tax would simply be unreasonable, if not unbearable. As we've seen, the newspaper reaches this conclusion by looking at the total amount of tax revenue collected from the top 1 percent and then measuring how large a share this is of the overall tax revenue collected. But as noted, this gross number is very misleading; it simply reflects the degree to which income has become highly concentrated in the hands of those at the top. It tells us nothing about the individual tax burdens of these rich individuals, and therefore about how heavily their taxes weigh on them. Yet surely this is the more meaningful measure. If we are trying to assess the fairness or appropriateness of an individual's tax burden, it hardly matters how much overall tax is collected from all the people in that individual's income group— what matters is how heavy the burden is on the individual. And as we've seen, the personal tax burden of those in the top 1 percent is about the same as it is for most of the rest of the population. How is this unduly onerous on the rich? If anything, it is easier for someone earning $300,000 to give up 30 percent of her income than it is for someone earning $13,500 to give up 30 percent of his.

Furthermore, as we've seen, the rich paid much higher taxes in the past without suffering any damaging consequences. The extent of the drop in taxes on the richest Americans has been powerfully documented—ironically, by a group of wealthy Americans who favour a more progressive tax system. The group, which calls itself Wealth for the Common Good, notes that the share of total federal taxes paid by the top 0.1 percent fell from 60 percent to only 33.6 percent from 1960 to 2004. If these individuals—Americans with annual incomes that averaged more than $7 million—had paid taxes at the 1960 rate, the Treasury would have collected an additional $281 billion in revenue in 2007. Another striking indication of the depth of tax cuts for the rich can be seen by looking at the declining tax burden on the four hundred highest-earning Americans. In 1955, this ultra-high-income group paid taxes at a rate that amounted to 51.2 percent of their incomes. By 2007, that rate had dropped to just 16.6 percent. If these individuals at the very top of the income ladder had paid taxes at the 1955 rate, the U.S. Treasury would have collected an additional $47.7 billion in 2007—from only four hundred individuals.

If there's any lingering doubt about the validity to *The Wall Street Journal*'s characterization of the situation, perhaps we can dispel it by holding another national income parade.

But this time the size of the marchers will reflect their *after-tax* incomes. If the rich are truly paying the heavy rates of tax that *The Wall Street Journal* would have us believe, then this parade should look very different from the ones we saw in Chapter 1, which were based on *pre-tax* incomes. If the tax system is truly progressive—indeed "steeply progressive"—then it would act as an equalizer, producing a more egalitarian distribution of income throughout the country. In terms of the parade, we would expect a levelling of heights, with considerably taller people at the beginning and the middle, and less immense giants at the end.

But once the marchers are all lined up again, both the Canadian and American parades look pretty much the same as their pre-tax versions. Both consist of a vast sea of very short workers, with people of average height only appearing around about the forty-minute mark. Significantly tall people only appear toward the end, with a tiny gaggle of enormous giants in the last few seconds. And John Paulson's face is still only visible from a spaceship. Although everyone is smaller, the proportions are roughly the same. Rather than being the great equalizer, the overall tax system is actually neutral. Its redistribution is effectively nil.

12

REVAMPING THE OVARIAN LOTTERY

So what?

For many on the right and even a surprising number on the left, inequality has become a non-issue, even as it's grown by leaps and bounds. Of course, conservatives have always had a high degree of tolerance for inequality. But in recent years many progressives seem to have joined them, abandoning the left's traditional demand for equality. Today, many influential progressives insist that poverty, not inequality, should be the focus, and that how well the rich are faring is irrelevant. "Let's worry about making sure the circuitry of the American dream isn't shorted, rather than whether some folks draw more current from the grid," wrote sociologist Dalton Conley in the liberal magazine *The American Prospect.* "It's the fate of the middle and lower classes that should concern progressives, not how many private jets the super-rich can afford."[1]

Conley, who heads the sociology department at New York University and has written extensively on the problems of poverty, acknowledges the resurgence of the rich and the extraordinary political power that comes with such economic power. He even notes that this concentrated economic power undermines democracy. But he argues that the way to fix it isn't to go after the rich, but rather to make adjustments to the political system. He advocates, for instance, amplifying the power of small donors on political campaigns by having the government match their donations (such as in New York City, where this is done, at a rate of six to one) or restricting the size of congressional districts, so that political campaigns would be less costly, giving smaller donors more importance. Conley also recognizes the problem extreme inequality creates in the financial realm. "Nowhere is the linkage between inequality and political power starker than in the realm of finance—now one-fifth of the nation's gross domestic product. The so-called regulators have been totally captured by the regulated."

But while Conley acknowledges some of these key problems of extreme inequality, he is strongly opposed to making an issue out of it, calling that a "losing proposition" and an unwise political strategy. He is perhaps more emphatic on this point than others, but he is urging a strategy that many progressives have already been following in recent years. Conley's emphasis on attacking poverty rather than inequality has been largely adopted by the North American political parties that argue for any sort of progressive change. Indeed, attacks on the concentration of wealth—the wellspring of populist politics in earlier times—have largely been shunted to the margins of political debate. They've been discredited as divisive and nasty, as a "politics of envy" that unfairly targets the rich and foments feelings of class warfare. This has amounted to a profound political change. Attacks on concentrated wealth were well within the mainstream when President Franklin Roosevelt railed against the special interests of "financial monopoly, speculation and reckless banking" back in 1936. "Government by organized money is just as dangerous as government by organized mob," FDR told a wildly cheering crowd at Madison Square Garden in a speech fiercely attacking private economic power—a speech it is hard to imagine a political leader delivering today.

President Barack Obama has reopened this front a bit, with promises to raise taxes on those in the top income bracket. But his gesture is a modest one that would only bring the top marginal tax rate back up to 39 percent (from 35 percent)—clearly a long way from the 80 percent (and higher) rate that prevailed through much of the early postwar years. The Obama hike would simply restore the top rate to where it was in the Clinton years, before George W. Bush's additional tax cuts for the rich.

Obama's reluctance to go further, to try to restore the kind of progressive taxation that existed before the Reagan revolution of the 1980s, reveals much about the self-imposed limits of progressive politics today. Conventional wisdom has it that anything beyond a return to the Clinton-era level of taxation at the top would be deeply out of sync with American public opinion. But is that even true? When Obama made an offhand comment during the election campaign that it's good to "spread the wealth around," the Republicans reacted with glee, believing they finally had a line from Obama that they could use against him. But their relentless campaign to use the quote to portray Obama as an anti-American socialist failed to generate much outrage.

This isn't surprising, considering that polls have shown a substantial majority of Americans actually believe their country has become too unequal. As Benjamin Page and Lawrence Jacobs note in *Class War: What Americans Really Think About Inequality*, fully 72 percent of Americans (and even 56 percent of Republicans) agree that differences in incomes in America are too large.[2] Polls also showed strong support in the fall of 2009 for a surtax on high-earning families (with incomes above $1 million) to help pay for expanded health insurance coverage. And in January 2010, a statewide plebiscite in Oregon gave voters a choice between reducing the state deficit through spending cuts or through higher taxes on corporations and high-income earners. The people of Oregon chose the tax increases.[3] All this suggests that a serious campaign by a popular president for actually spreading the wealth around might well resonate with the public.

The decision by left-leaning leaders to abandon attacks on concentrated wealth and inequality has been disastrous for progressive causes and for the common people whose interest these leaders purport to represent. To begin with, attempts to bring about reforms that would help those lower down the ladder are bound to fail as long as the economic power of the wealthy is left intact, since the wealthy will inevitably use their clout to block progressive change. The kinds of reforms Conley proposes are tiny drops in the bucket, even if they were to be widely enacted. Matching political donations six to one—or even sixty to one—won't counter the massive and pervasive power of the wealthy elite, who don't just exert their influence through political donations but through countless other direct and indirect means. There are many stages of the political process, each one with many opportunities for influence to be exercised: the selection of political candidates, the drafting of party platforms, the financing and organizing of political campaigns, the drafting and amending of legislation, the input of interest groups, the shaping of public opinion through media and think-tanks. The wealthy aren't just adept at influencing one stage of this process but each and every stage. Indeed, even when they aren't directly trying to influence the political process, they manage to, because politicians are constantly anticipating their demands, anxious to curry their favour. As one congressional assistant noted: "You can't run for the Senate in Arkansas if the Waltons oppose you."[4]

It might seem logical to assume that when the wealthy are particularly prosperous, they are more likely to support policies that help the poor. But the record shows the opposite, that the poor fare worse when inequality is most pronounced. Economic historian Peter Lindert, who has studied redistributive policies in England and the United States over three centuries, describes a phenomenon he calls the "Robin Hood paradox": the more unequal a society becomes, the less it adopts redistributive policies favouring those at the lower end. Lindert speculates that the answer to the apparent paradox "must lie in the relationship of income distribution to political voice.... Highly skewed societies are ones in which the wealthy elite retains a high share of political power as well as of wealth and income." Evidently, the bigger the share of income the rich enjoy at any given time, the more clout they have to enact policies in their own interests—and the more they do so.

By declining to protest the concentration of wealth, progressives have conceded important ground. At the centre of their case should be a strong moral argument about the illegitimacy of a small number of people gaining control over too large a share of society's resources, and with it, undue control over society. Conservatives have their own moral argument, about the legitimacy of private property and the illegitimacy of taxes imposed on what they regard as justly acquired riches. There is much ground for debate here between the two sides, but progressives have largely folded their tent and gone home. This has allowed the conservative anti-tax argument to dominate, even as the concentration of income and wealth at the top has become ever more extreme. The conservatives' use of a morally charged narrative has enabled them to be effective in making their case—a case that only serves the interests of a very small group and that, without some creative moral embellishment (by a lot of high-priced talent), would be intuitively unappealing to most people.

The disastrous effects of abandoning the moral high ground to conservatives can be seen in the uncertain fate of the estate tax, which has been the backbone of progressive taxation in the United States since 1916. It is the one tax that exclusively hits the very rich. Only about 2 percent of all estates are affected by it; fully 97.7 percent of all the adults who died in 1999 were able to leave all their holdings to their heirs without triggering a penny in estate taxes. The only people who pay the tax are members of the wealthiest and most powerful families in America (in 1999, nearly a quarter of the estate tax revenue came from just 550 estates, all containing wealth exceeding $20 million). Even so, the amounts collected by the tax are substantial: roughly

$25 billion a year, more than twice the annual size of the federal grants given to help American students attend college.[5] Furthermore, the tax has little negative effect on economic activity in the country, and is considered largely benign by public finance economists. In other words, it is a levy that appears to do little damage while doing much good; economist Robert H. Frank describes it as "the closest thing to a perfect tax that we have."[6]

And yet, astonishingly, over the course of the past decade, the U.S. estate tax has been mostly gutted, and its future is highly uncertain. It is scheduled to disappear completely in 2010, to be replaced, oddly, with a new, more broadly based tax that hits smaller inheritances. Then, in a strange twist, the old estate tax is scheduled to reappear in 2011. This makes it likely that there will be fresh momentum to do away with the whole apparatus of estate taxes for good—a development that would amount to an enormous wealth transfer to the richest families in America at a time when the wealth of these families is already at an historic high.

All this has been accomplished through a masterful political campaign, funded and ultimately orchestrated by powerful wealthy interests. But this is not simply a story of behind-the-scenes machinations by wheelers and dealers buying off politicians with political contributions (although of course that's part of the story). Rather, the repeal of the estate tax was ultimately accomplished because those running the campaign figured out how to sell their case to the public by presenting it in a morally powerful way. They portrayed the tax as the enemy of hard-working citizens trying to live the American dream. A morally powerful *counter-argument* never really appeared; progressives had long since abandoned attacks on concentrations of wealth, thinking it strategically better to focus on making the case for helping the poor. So no effort was made to articulate a strong, principled argument along the lines of the one advanced by President Theodore Roosevelt in 1906 when he advocated a tax whose "primary objective should be to put a constantly increasing burden on the inheritance of swollen fortunes, which it is certainly of no benefit to this country to perpetuate."

The absence of this sort of moral critique in recent years has given conservatives virtual free rein to shape public opinion on the issue. In a comprehensive account of the estate tax battle, academics Michael J. Graetz and Ian Shapiro note that the campaign for repeal, which is a key part of a larger Republican anti-tax crusade, was able to gather steam with little opposition: "The anti-tax movement has built up a powerful philosophical attack on the very concept of progressive taxation ... an opposing philosophical case was never made."[7] As a result, a fundamental philosophical debate over progressive taxation—a debate that had apparently been settled nearly a hundred years ago and been considered uncontroversial for many decades— was suddenly thrown wide open. A new debate was abruptly staged, but this time only one side showed up to make its case, and won by default.

As that winning side now gears up for its bigger goal—to end all progressive taxation—the need for a powerful, compelling moral critique of the dangers of the extreme inequality that engulfs North America today couldn't be more urgent.

CANADIANS CAN WATCH the upcoming U.S. political battle over the estate tax like observers watching a strange, unfamiliar sport. Unlike the United States—and most other countries in the developed world— Canada has no estate tax, having quietly discarded the one we had back in 1972.

At the time, Ottawa was in the final stages of a major overhaul of the Canadian tax system that had been launched a decade earlier with the Royal Commission on Taxation, headed by Kenneth Carter. Although dominated by Bay Street types (Carter himself was an accountant at a blue-chip firm), the commission had enraged business by producing a far-reaching report that called for the elimination of the special tax deductions that allowed business and investment income to be taxed at advantageously low rates. That was wrong and unfair, said the Carter commission in its 1966 report, which made the radical recommendation that all sources of income should be treated the same for tax purposes. This approach became popularly known as "a buck is a buck is a buck."

For the next five years, business and wealthy interests kept up relentless pressure on the Liberal government in Ottawa not to reform the tax system along the lines recommended by the commission. The campaign against the Carter reforms became a pivotal experience for Canadian business in becoming an organized political force. Feeling the heat, the government produced its own white paper on tax reform and held extensive reviews of the issue by parliamentary and Senate committees. In the end, Ottawa backed off from almost all of Carter's proposed reforms. And tucked into the government's final tax reform package in 1971 was something that seemed to come out of nowhere, something that flew in the face of the fairness advocated by the Carter commission—the complete repeal of the estate tax.

Actually, the repeal idea hadn't come completely out of nowhere. Rather it had been recommended by the Senate banking committee—a group that was almost absurdly unrepresentative of the Canadian public in its close ties to the business world. The thirty-three senators on the committee, mostly well-to-do members of the Canadian establishment, held between them a total of 211 corporate directorships, sitting on the boards of many of the same corporations that appeared before them to protest the proposed tax changes. As their friends and colleagues (and even some relatives) testified before the committee, the sympathetic senators encouraged them to be more forceful still in their language of condemnation. One who needed little prompting was wealthy Toronto businessman Harry Jackman, who denounced the tax reform proposals as the first step toward socialism, and worse. "It was that way with Hitler. It has been that way many times in our history," said Jackman, who also complained to the committee that "because of the general affluence, domestic servants are almost impossible to get."[8]

It was Jackman who first floated the idea of abolishing the estate tax. He suggested to the Senate committee that this could be a trade-off for the introduction of capital gains taxes, which had been recommended by Carter. Up until this point, there had been no tax on capital gains in Canada—a situation very favourable to the wealthy, who could receive profits selling stocks and other capital holdings without passing a dime on to the government. In its attempt to remove this special privilege, the Carter commission had recommended that increases in the value of capital holdings be taxed when the holdings were sold or at the time of an individual's death, whether or not the holdings were actually sold. This meant that the taxation of capital gains would occur at death—at the same time as the estate tax. But this "double taxation at death" simply reflected the fact that the capital gains had not been taxed earlier. (The white paper avoided this double taxation problem by recommending capital gains on publicly traded shares be taxed every five years, whether the gains were realized or not—but only taxing them at half-rates.) In the end, the wealthy managed to win a particularly sweet deal: capital gains would only be taxed at half rates (not the full rates recommended by Carter), and only when realized or at death. And, in an unexpected move, the estate tax was also completely eliminated!

The removal of the estate tax was particularly striking. Since capital gains were only to be taxed starting in 1972, the tax would not apply to increases in the value of assets prior to this date. These pre-1972 gains would normally have been caught in the net of the inheritance tax. But now that it was gone, all wealth accumulated before 1972 escaped taxation entirely. University of Toronto economist John Bossons calculated that this resulted in a windfall for

Canada's richest families of about $12 billion—or $62 billion in today's dollars.

Among the beneficiaries was the family of Harry Jackman, who had first proposed the elimination of the tax to the Senate committee. His son Hal inherited an extensive investment empire worth more than $300 million. Today Hal Jackman is the fifty-seventh richest Canadian with a fortune of $967 million.

Yet, as in the United States, progressives in Canada have been reluctant to make an issue out of the rise of the new Canadian super-rich, or to urge a revival of the estate tax in Canada. The New Democratic Party briefly flirted with the idea of including a pledge to restore the estate tax in its party platform during the 2008 federal election campaign. But when the media heaped scorn on the idea, the NDP quickly beat a full retreat, ensuring that in Canada too the increasing concentration of wealth at the top would remain a subject all but banished from public debate.

OF COURSE, taxes are not the sole solution for the extreme inequality that plagues our society. As social justice advocates have been insisting for decades, tremendous gains in equality could be accomplished through more generous social assistance programs, as well as through improvements in our public education system, in more accessible child care, in more affordable university and college programs, in greater investment in public housing, and so on. We agree that there is a pressing need for all these reforms. But we also believe that the key to any solution involves making our tax system considerably more progressive. While reforms in education, child care, housing, and other areas would all contribute to the overall quest for a more equal society, their impact is likely to be gradual and slow-moving at best. The tax system, with its huge and comprehensive reach, has the capacity to reduce inequality much more quickly and decisively (while interfering minimally with the operation of the market economy, as

Henry Simons noted). Furthermore, progressive taxation provides a key source of income to pay for reforms in all these other areas.

In stressing the need for a more progressive tax system, we are not suggesting that the rich alone should bear the burden of paying for public services. On the contrary, we believe that we should all be willing to contribute to the costs of such services, given their importance to the quality of our lives and the vibrancy and cohesiveness of our communities. A willingness to pay for them collectively through the tax system—even to regard this as an important aspect of citizenship—reflects a sense of society as a shared project that benefits us all and imposes responsibility on us all.

In the Scandinavian countries, where there is strong appreciation of public services, there is little popular resistance to paying taxes. In fact, the social welfare systems in Scandinavia and northern Europe are primarily financed through sales and payroll taxes, not through progressive income taxes that take a big bite out of the rich. In other words, the working populations of these countries value their public programs, and are willing to pay for them. But then these are much more egalitarian countries, with income spread far more evenly throughout the population. The Anglo-American countries are in need of more progressive taxation partly because income is so concentrated at the top, making the rich a more important source of government revenue.

But the need for progressive taxation goes beyond simply revenue needs. Equally (if not more) important is its role as a vehicle for reducing inequality. The problem of inequality is not just a problem of too little money at the bottom, but also of too much money at the top. In recent years, we've been led to believe that the fortunes of those at the summit are benign, that any disgruntlement we feel about their wealth is simple jealousy. But, as noted, there is compelling evidence that these vast fortunes pose a threat to the health and well-being of the rest of society. Indeed, they significantly impair the functioning of democracy—a fragile enough institution at the best of times, but one that is seriously undermined by the presence of an extraordinarily rich elite controlling the political agenda, sometimes in highly destructive ways.

Perhaps this threat to democracy could be tolerated if there was some deep moral justification for it. But as we've seen, the distribution of income is really quite arbitrary, based on a whole range of man-made laws that, when tilted slightly in one direction or another, can produce vastly different results. This has become particularly problematic in the last few decades, as almost all the benefits of economic growth have gone to those at the top, with the biggest benefits way, way up at the apex. This hasn't happened because the high fliers have become more productive, hard-working, or innovative than the rest of the workforce—or than their peers were in the past—but rather because members of today's elite have managed to push through changes that have given them a much larger share of the economy's spoils.

Here then are a few key reforms that we propose:

- **The income tax system should be made more progressive. We propose adding a new rate of 60 percent to be applied to income above $500,000, and a new top rate of 70 percent for income above $2.5 million.**

   Recent years have seen an overall flattening of tax rates, so that the top marginal rate applies at a relatively low income level. In Canada, for instance, the top marginal rate of 46 percent kicks in at $127,000.[9] While this is certainly a good upper-middle-class income, it's not in the same league as incomes of the select few Canadians, who earn more than $500,000 a year (and all the way up to $51 million, in the case of Michael Lazaridis, the tallest person in the Canadian income parade). A top marginal rate of 46 percent may seem reasonable in the case of a person earning $127,000 a year, and a higher rate might seem onerous. But an individual earning above $500,000 a year has considerably more disposable income and could afford to pay a higher rate on part of that income. By applying the same rate to all income above $127,000, those with much higher incomes are being lumped in with the upper middle class, even though this richer group could easily shoulder a heavier tax burden.

Our proposal for a new top marginal rate of 60 percent (on earnings above $500,000) and 70 percent (on earnings above $2.5 million) is an attempt to re-introduce some meaningful progressivity to the income tax system. Someone earning $500,000 a year enjoys a very affluent income that is 12.5 times the Canadian median income (roughly $40,000). An income of $2.5 million is 60 times the median income, indicating tremendous abundance.

There is of course historical precedent for higher rates. In fact, the ones we are proposing are lower than the 80 and 90 percent top marginal rates that were in place during the prosperous early postwar decades in both Canada and the United States. And now, as then, these higher rates would apply only to very large incomes. In 1966, for instance, when the top marginal rate in Canada was 80 percent, it applied only to incomes above $400,000 (which in today's dollars would be about $2.5 million). Still, even if they only affect a small number of people, high rates are important symbolically as well as practically. They would not only collect significant additional revenue, but also send a message that society regards extreme inequality as a danger to the public good, and as something that is, in the words of Henry Simons, inherently "unlovely."[10]

- **Close the loopholes and remove the tax preferences that now riddle the income tax system and almost exclusively benefit the rich.**

The income tax base upon which the progressive tax rates are levied should be as comprehensive as possible, so that high-income individuals can't avoid high rates by taking advantage of tax loopholes and shelters.

The tax preferences currently enjoyed by Canada's rich are too extensive to detail here. But we'll briefly highlight two. First is the fact that only 50 percent of capital gains are included in an individual's income for tax purposes, providing enormous tax savings for the richest citizens. Nobel laureate Joseph Stiglitz pointed to the absurdity of favourable tax treatment for capital gains: "Why should those who make their income by gambling in Wall Street's casinos be taxed at a lower rate than those who earn their money in other ways?"[11] This is not only highly inequitable, it also provides an incentive for high-income people to come up with complex schemes to categorize as much of their income as possible as capital gains. Removing the special tax treatment for capital gains would eliminate a whole raft of tax avoidance opportunities, including employee stock options and the practice of hedge fund managers reporting their multimillion-dollar salaries for managing other people's money as capital gains.

Secondly, our tax laws also allow business people to deduct part of the costs of business-related meals, entertainment and travel, including flying in private jets and staying at luxury hotels. All this means that other Canadians end up subsidizing some very extravagant activities. Of course, it's impossible to know whether these activities are at all related to business. But even if some snippets of business are discussed during meals at five-star restaurants or in skyboxes at baseball games, this "business entertainment" provides immense personal benefit to the participants. Such indulgence should be enjoyed to the fullest. But it should not be subsidized by other taxpayers, who in many cases can only afford to eat at fast-food outlets or, very occasionally, to take their kids to a sports event and sit in the back row.

- **Support the international implementation of a financial transaction tax (sometimes referred to as the "Tobin tax.")** The idea of curbing financial speculation by imposing a tax on financial transactions has been attracting support from reformers ever since it was proposed in the early 1970s by Nobel Prize–winning economist James Tobin. Tobin's idea was ingenious: impose a tax so small (as little as a 0.05 percent) that it would have no impact on serious investors making long-term investments, but would amount to a million pinpricks in the flesh of those engaging in high-volume, quick-turnover, speculative activities—like the ones that have turned financial markets into wildly gyrating, high-risk casinos. The tax would thus have the added benefit of reducing inequality, since it wouldn't affect middle- or low-income investors, who tend to hold on to stocks and bonds for long periods. It would only hit people—mostly wealthy investors—who trade stocks on a daily or hourly basis.

  So it's hard not to love the Tobin tax: it could raise billions of dollars globally each year from financial speculators while leaving genuine investors unharmed—like a miracle cancer drug that leaves the healthy surrounding tissue undamaged. But if the idea of a financial transaction tax has always been a crowd-pleaser, these days it has the potential to go viral, given the extent of the public anger over reckless financial speculation in the wake of the Wall Street meltdown.

  Long resisted by Wall Street, the Tobin tax—or its new broader version, the financial transaction tax (FTT)—is now winning approval in the corridors of power. (The FTT should not be confused with other bank-related taxes being proposed in the wake of the 2008 Wall Street crash.) Since the fall of 2009, the

governments of Britain, France, and Germany have all indicated
support for an FTT-type tax. Even the United States, which had
been resisting, seemed to be moving in the spring of 2010 toward
at least considering it, after former Federal Reserve chair Paul
Volcker emerged as Barack Obama's leading advisor on financial
reform, pushing aside Tim Geithner, the Treasury secretary.
Geithner has been hostile to the tax; Volcker sees some merit in it.

But here in Canada, Stephen Harper's government opposes the
tax (and all other bank-related taxes) on the grounds that Canada's
banks weren't as reckless as Wall Street banks. So what? Canada still
suffered from the recession triggered by Wall Street's recklessness,
and is forced to deal with the resulting deficits. If we've learned
anything, it's that a crash on Wall Street can devastate economies
around the world, including ours. Past efforts by reformers—
including a strong contingent of Canadians—led to a U.N.–
sponsored international academic conference on the Tobin tax in
Halifax in 1995. If governments had gotten on board then, Wall
Street's financial speculation might have been discouraged, and we
might not be in the economic mess we're in today.

Yet, with some of the world's leading governments finally
onside, Ottawa is emerging as an obstacle—just as it has balked
at international efforts to tackle climate change. If ever there
was a moment for this sort of far-reaching financial reform, that
moment is now, while Main Street still has the whiff of the Wall
Street meltdown fresh in its nostrils.

- **Support international measures for a clampdown on tax
  avoiders and evaders.**
  When all the other arguments fail, the fallback position argued
  by people opposed to higher taxes on the rich is simply this: they
  will cut and run, moving their assets out of the country to a low-
  tax jurisdiction. Those pointing to this threat of "capital flight"

typically treat it as an unsolvable problem—the rich hold all the cards, we're told, and the only way to prevent them from leaving is to give them the lower taxes they want.

We propose a different approach: get tough on the use of tax havens, where trillions of dollars are stored beyond the reach of tax authorities. As we argued in Chapter 8, it would be easy to clamp down on these havens by setting up an international system for reporting financial transactions—a system that would be no more complicated than the international system of passports. Every time a financial institution made a payment to a client, an electronic copy of that payment would be automatically sent to the tax authorities of the country where the client resides, so they could make sure taxes were paid on the sum.

Such an initiative would have to be taken together with other countries. In the meantime, Canada should get much tougher on Canadians who use tax havens. This might prompt some wealthy individuals to relocate themselves and their assets to tax havens or lower-tax jurisdictions. But, as we saw in the case of the wealthy family (believed to be the Bronfmans), Canadian authorities have powers to tax assets being transferred out of the country. These rules should be tightened and enforced.

And there might also be some highly paid professionals who would depart, prompting business commentators to howl that a "brain drain" was depriving the country of its finest minds. No doubt we would lose some talented individuals—although probably not as many as expected, given that most people make decisions about their lives for reasons beyond simply taxation. Besides, if talented people did leave, it's almost certain that other talented individuals would step into the breach, thrilled at the chance to fill roles that otherwise had been closed to them. There's no shortage of gifted and educated people in this country, many of whom have never had the lucky breaks that have allowed others—particularly those born into privileged families—to get ahead of them. This might be their moment.

- **Strive to bring about a change in social attitudes toward taxation and its essential role in a democracy.**
  The neo-conservative movement has been successful in directing public anger toward taxes. It will only be possible to rebuild a properly progressive tax system once the neo-conservative misconceptions are exposed and an appreciation of the importance of taxation in a democracy is restored.

  This will involve not so much a new way of thinking as a revival of long-established notions of justice and democracy. While these notions have come under attack in recent years, they were originally championed by some of the leading thinkers of the modern age—including Adam Smith, John Stuart Mill, and Oliver Wendell Holmes Jr.—and were widely accepted even in North America in the early postwar years. In essence, taxes are about collectively creating things of value in a democracy. As Holmes, a former U.S. Supreme Court justice, succinctly put it, "Taxes are the price we pay for civilization." It could be added that they are also the price we pay for membership in the community and for citizenship in a democracy.

  So those who try to cheat their way out of paying them should be treated with disdain, as anti-social members of the community. In recent years, tax avoidance and even evasion have become socially acceptable. While there's nothing wrong with seeking to keep one's tax bill as low as possible within the requirements of the law, there's been a growing industry of tax professionals who push the envelope, coming up with ever more creative ways for clients to get around or subvert the law, including by parking assets offshore. What's striking is the lack of public outrage over this burgeoning industry and its schemes, which defraud the community of badly needed revenues.

It's interesting to note that the names of civil servants earning more than $100,000 are published each year in Ontario, and that the list inevitably leads to much hostile media commentary about overpaid public servants. Yet there is no equivalent attempt to publicly embarrass individuals who use exotic tax schemes to avoid paying income taxes, often reducing their tax bill to near zero. On the contrary, the secrecy of tax returns is treated as sacrosanct, for no clear reason. In Finland, by contrast, tax returns are public, allowing the citizenry to know who has, and who hasn't, contributed to the community's upkeep.

While neo-conservatives have done their best to erase the notion of society as a community, and taxes as a mark of citizenship, it is essential that we revive these powerful ideas.

Here, for instance, are two personal commentaries—one from a successful American businessman and one from billionaire author J.K. Rowling—that reframe the issue of taxation in a compelling way.

Martin Rosenberg, a New York–based software entrepreneur, explains why he is a supporter of the campaign to preserve the U.S. estate tax:

> My wealth is not only a product of my own hard work. It also resulted from a strong economy and lots of public investment, both in others and in me.
>
> I received a good education, and used free libraries and museums paid for by others. I went to college under the GI bill. I went to graduate school to study computers and language on a complete government scholarship, paid for by others. While teaching at Syracuse University for 25 years, my research was supported by numerous government grants—again paid for by others.
>
> My university research provided the basis for Syracuse

Language Systems, a company I formed in 1991 with some graduate students and my son Larry. I sold the company in 1998 and then started a new company, Glottal Enterprises. These companies have benefited from the technology-driven expansion—a boom fueled by continual public and private investment....

I was able to provide well for my family. Upon my death, I hope taxes on my estate will help fund the kind of programs that benefited me and others from humble backgrounds: a good education, money for research and targeted investments in poor communities. I'd like all Americans to have the same opportunities I did.[12]

And here's J.K. Rowling, who came from modest roots, explaining why she hasn't left high-tax Britain:

I chose to remain a domiciled taxpayer for a couple of reasons. The main one was that I wanted my children to grow up where I grew up, to have proper roots in a culture as old and magnificent as Britain's; to be citizens, with everything that implies, of a real country, not free-floating ex-pats, living in the limbo of some tax haven and associating only with the children of similarly greedy tax exiles.

A second reason, however, was that I am indebted to the British welfare state; the very one that [Prime Minister David] Cameron would like to replace with charity handouts. When my life hit rock bottom, that safety net, threadbare though it had become under John Major's government, was there to break the fall. I cannot help feeling, therefore, that it would have been contemptible to scarper for the West Indies at the first sniff of a seven-figure royalty cheque. This, if you like, is my notion of patriotism.[13]

- **Enact an inheritance tax, and use the proceeds to introduce a new education trust for every Canadian child.**
We've left this one to the last because in some ways it's the most ambitious—and it offers the chance to make a change that would have a fast and profound effect in reducing inequality in this country.

  The first part of the plan involves enacting an inheritance tax—which would affect only the wealthiest 1 or 2 percent of Canadian families. Canada has had no tax on inheritances for almost four decades. We propose a variation of the old estate tax—one that would tax those receiving the inheritance, rather than those leaving it. This would ensure that the tax achieves one of its purposes, to tax unearned wealth. To this end, we propose a tax that would be levied on the cumulative lifetime total of all inheritances (and gifts) received by an individual above a certain amount.[14] This would mean that an individual could receive a lifetime total of, say, $1.5 million worth of inheritances (and gifts) tax-free. For amounts above $1.5 million, a low rate of tax would apply, rising to a top rate of 70 percent on inherited grand fortunes worth more than $50 million. Among other things, a levy structured this way would encourage donors to leave their wealth to a larger number of individuals, since the amount of tax could be minimized by distributing the benefits more widely.

  The case for taxing inheritances is similar to the case for a more progressive income tax, except even stronger. As we've argued, the way the market distributes income is quite arbitrary. But at least income received in the marketplace is in some way connected to the individual's effort, labour, and skill. This is not true with inherited wealth, which allows individuals to become incredibly rich by doing nothing more than being born into the right family.

The circumstances of one's birth are always a key determinant of a person's financial well-being. Multibillionaire Warren Buffett has dubbed this the "Ovarian Lottery." Here's how he describes it:

> Imagine there are two identical twins in the womb, both equally bright and energetic. And the genie says to them, "One of you is going to be born in the United States, and one of you is going to be born in Bangladesh. And if you wind up in Bangladesh, you will pay no taxes. What percentage of your income would you bid to be the one that is born in the United States?" … The people who say, "I did it all myself," and think of themselves as Horatio Alger— believe me, they'd bid more to be in the United States than in Bangladesh. That's the Ovarian Lottery.[15]

Buffett also notes that if he had been born in some different epoch of human history, he (and, for that matter, Bill Gates) might well have ended up as some other animal's lunch, because both he and Gates have poor vision and can't climb trees well. Buffett also observes that his particular talent—knowing how best to allocate capital—would have been useless in many other eras and geographical locations. His point is that people lucky enough to be born with appropriate talents for their time and place are winners in the Ovarian Lottery.

But those who inherit wealth are particularly big winners in the Ovarian Lottery. The circumstances of their birth mean that they don't have to do anything at all to thrive materially. The money just falls into their hands. And then, in case this great blind luck isn't enough, the government of Canada tops it up by exempting inheritances from taxation, thereby allowing the leisured class to be spared the levies that apply to other forms of income earned by Canadians who are obliged to work for a living. As one of the few nations in the world without an estate or inheritance tax, Canada has created an Ovarian Lottery on Steroids.

Canadians would almost certainly support an inheritance tax, if they understood that it would not interfere in any way with the ability of roughly 98 percent of the population to leave a nest egg for their children. It would only affect the truly rich, and only reach high levels for the exceptionally rich. But let's not forget that there are some exceptionally rich Canadians. There are, for instance, ninety-seven Canadians with fortunes worth more than $500 million, including fifty-five worth more than $1 billion. This is an extraordinary amount of money. Taxing these grand fortunes would help prevent a small wealthy elite from exerting too much influence over our democracy. A small number of spectacularly wealthy families have dominated Canada's economic landscape for many decades, and our failure to tax their intergenerational transfers in recent years has only fuelled the growth of old and new dynasties. An inheritance tax is essential if we want to prevent them from turning into a kind of permanent aristocracy.

But now we come to the really exciting second part of our plan: an education trust fund for every Canadian child. The revenue collected from the inheritance tax would be sufficient to create individual trust funds for the next generation of Canadians. On their sixteenth birthday, every child would receive $16,000, deposited into an individual trust, which could be used exclusively for education or training.[16] This would mean that very large fortunes accumulated in previous generations would be taxed so that children in future generations would have a greater chance to develop their talents and skills to the fullest. It would amount to a direct transfer of wealth, taking from the very richest families and giving improved education possibilities to all Canadian children as they prepare to enter adulthood.

There would clearly be many benefits. Improving the education and skills of young people would greatly enhance their future work prospects, contributing to their own development and, ultimately, to the nation's productivity. It would also enhance the democratic nature of our country, by taking concrete steps toward realizing "equal opportunity"—a concept that is almost universally admired and celebrated, but that in practice has receded further and further from our grasp in recent decades as inequality has reached grotesque proportions in North America. Moving closer to the goal of "equal opportunity" would send a powerful signal to young Canadians, many of whom have become withdrawn and cynical, that we are serious as a society about our democracy and about their place in it.

This would be Robin Hood in grand style, achieving in one swoop a transfer of wealth from the very richest families to the next generation of Canadians, helping them in the most fundamental way. And it would in no way interfere with the push for other urgently needed reforms—such as creating programs for early childhood education and enhancing the existing public health care and education systems—which are funded separately out of general tax revenues. This proposal involves new revenues from a new tax, and would be handled separately. Such a clear relationship between the new inheritance tax and the new education trust funds would allow the public to see a direct connection, establishing a strong moral case for the inheritance tax as a vehicle for enhancing the prospects of young Canadians while creating a more democratic and egalitarian society.

It strikes us that this proposal fits very well with the values of Canadians, who respect hard work and effort and support the notion that individuals should earn their own way. Large inheritances are clearly unearned income—a gift that only a very few individuals, as a result of their lucky draw in the Ovarian Lottery, will ever be fortunate enough to receive. So imposing a limit to how much of this unearned income remains tax-free seems well in keeping with the moral principles and sense of fairness held by most Canadians.

In addition to being unearned, money left in large inheritances represents an enormous legacy from humanity's past. As we've argued in this book, the vast sums that the rich have been accumulating, particularly in recent decades, are based on the technological, scientific, and cultural advances achieved over many centuries, due to the work of countless scientists, innovators, and thinkers (and those who helped them, taught them, and nurtured them). The contribution of any one innovator or entrepreneur to the overall development of today's products is actually minuscule in the grand scheme of things—as his departure to a desert island would quickly clarify. Furthermore, it is only because of copyright and licensing laws—part of our man-made system of rules— that these individuals have been able to lay claim to such a large proportion of the benefits of this legacy.

It seems utterly appropriate then to use another man-made system of rules—the tax system—to ensure that the benefits are distributed much more widely, so that this vast inheritance ends up not in the hands of a privileged few but in the hands of many, all eager for a shot at a better life.

THE AMERICAN DREAM, despite its iconic stature in their land and ours, has always been more myth than reality. As it sadly fades further into mythology south of the border, Canada could emerge with an exciting new version—one that puts real heft behind the notion that society is a community and that everyone in the community should have a chance to live their dreams.

NOTES

1 Return of the Plutocrats

1 Adapted from Austan Goolsbee, "For the Super-Rich, Too Much Is Never Enough," *New York Times*, March 1, 2007. See also Marjorie Mader, "How school districts, towns share pain of Ellison refund," *The Almanac Online: Menlo Park, Atherton, Portola Valley, Woodside*, April 9, 2008.

2 Average income is the total income of all the individuals in a group divided by the number of individuals. Median income, on the other hand, is simply the income of the person exactly in the middle of all the income earners, with half earning more than that middle person and half earning less.

3 The data for today's income parade is from 2007.

4 One of the best-known attempts to reconstruct the distribution of income in pre-industrial societies relates to England and Wales in 1688. Prepared by seventeenth-century English civil servant Gregory King, it was based on confidential government information. Recently, economic historians led by Peter Lindert have revised King's data and used additional data to provide a fuller picture of income distribution in the seventeenth, eighteenth, and early nineteenth centuries. See Branko Milanovic, Peter Lindert, and Jeffrey Williamson, "Revising England's Social Tables 1688–1812," *Explorations in Economic History* 19:4 (1982: October), p. 385. See also Branko Milanovic, Peter Lindert, Jeffrey Williamson, "Measuring Ancient Inequality," Policy Research Paper #4412, World Bank (2007) online.

5 Interestingly, people confined to lunatic asylums had somewhat better incomes, averaging thirty pounds a year by 1801 (Lindert).

6 Actually, the comparison is between the top 398 income earners in 1961 and the top 400 income earners in 2006, since this is what is possible, given the available data. The U.S. Internal Revenue Service (IRS) has been releasing the data on the top 400 income earners since 1992. Financial writer David Cay Johnston combined this IRS data with other data from the U.S. Statistics of Income, going back to 1961. See David Cay Johnston, *Tax Notes*, December 21, 2009, pp. 1375–77.

7 Outer space is officially deemed to begin at seventy-three miles above sea level.

2 Why Pornography Is the Only True Free Market

1 John Arlidge, "I'm doing 'God's work.' Meet Mr. Goldman Sachs," *Sunday Times* (U.K.), November 8, 2009. See also Helia Ebrahimi, "Goldman Sachs teams could quit the City over taxes and regulations," *Telegraph* (U.K.), January 4, 2010.

2 The marginal tax rate is the rate applied to any extra income received by an individual. By raising the top marginal rate, the government is raising the rate of tax to be collected above a certain income threshold.

3 Iain Martin, "Britain is going to need far more people like Sir Michael Caine," *Daily Telegraph* (U.K.), April 27, 2009.

4 Liam Murphy and Thomas Nagel, *The Myth of Ownership: Taxes and Justice* (Oxford: Oxford University Press, 2002).

5 For an excellent discussion of the theories of Robert Hale, see Barbara Fried, *The Progressive Assault on Laissez-Faire: Robert Hale and the First Law and Economics Movement* (Cambridge, MA: Harvard University Press, 1998).

6 See Dean Baker, "The Reform of Intellectual Property," *Post-Autistic Economics Review*, no. 32, July 5, 2005.

7 All three are quoted in Louis Uchitelle and Amanda Cox, "The Richest of the Rich, Proud of a New Gilded Age," *New York Times*, July 15, 2007.

8 Richard Wilkinson and Kate Pickett, *The Spirit Level: Why More Equal Societies Almost Always Do Better* (London: Penguin Books, 2009), pp. 157–72. See also our Chapter 9.

9 Mark Jickling, "Causes of the Financial Crisis," Congressional Research Service, 7-5700, www.crs.gov R40173, January 29, 2009.

3 Millionaires and the Crash of 1929

1 Ferdinand Lundberg, *America's 60 Families* (New York: Vanguard Press, 1937), p. 102–3.
2 Ron Chernow, *The House of Morgan* (New York: Atlantic Monthly Press, 1990), p. 130.
3 Anna Rochester, *Rulers of America* (New York: International Publishers, 1936).
4 Matthew Josephson, *The Robber Barons* (New York: Harcourt, Brace and World, 1934), p. 449.
5 Lundberg, p. 95.
6 Chernow, p. 129.
7 Ibid, p. 130.
8 Lundberg, p. 147.
9 Ibid, p. 177.
10 Robert S. McElvaine, *The Great Depression: America, 1929–1941* (New York: Times Books, 1984), p. 23.
11 Louis Eisenstein, *The Ideologies of Taxation* (New York: The Ronald Press Company, 1961), p. 65.
12 Lundberg, p. 166.
13 Ibid, pp. 167–68.
14 John Kenneth Galbraith, *The Great Crash 1929* (Boston: Houghton Mifflin, 1961), p. 7.
15 Lundberg, pp. 231–35. See also Chernow, pp. 308–9.
16 Ibid, p. 221.
17 Cited in Chernow, p. 365.

4 Billionaires and the Crash of 2008

1 Paul Krugman, *The Conscience of a Liberal* (New York: W. W. Norton, 2007), pp. 7–9, 46.
2 Harold Ickes, *The Progressive*, January 8, 1938.
3 Thomas Piketty and Emmanuel Saez, "How Progressive Is the U.S. Federal Tax System? A Historical and International Perspective," *Journal of Economic Perspectives*, Vol. 21, No. 1, Winter 2007.

4 Quoted in Josephson, p. 441.

5 Chernow, p. 508.

6 David Moss, "An Ounce of Prevention: Financial Regulation, Moral Hazard, and the End of 'Too Big to Fail,'" *Harvard Magazine*, September–October 2009.

7 Federal Deposit Insurance Corporation, "Bank Failures and Assistance Transactions," *Historical Statistics on Banking*.

8 Simon Johnson and James Kwak, *13 Bankers* (New York: Pantheon Books, 2010), p. 35.

9 Kelly Fiveash, "Bank of England prescribes 'boredom,'" *The Register* (U.K.), October 22, 2008.

10 Doug Peters, author interview, November 4, 2009. Peters later got a Ph.D. from the University of Pennsylvania's Wharton School of Finance, and served as Canada's minister of financial institutions in the 1990s.

11 Nick Baker, "Ajay Kapur Quits Citigroup, Plans Hong Kong–Based Hedge Fund," Bloomberg.com, February 28, 2007.

12 James Livingston, "Their Great Depression and Ours, Part 2," *History News Network*, George Mason University, October 13, 2008.

13 Gregory Zuckerman, *The Greatest Trade Ever* (New York: Broadway Business, 2009), p. 14.

14 Chernow, p. 716.

15 Simon Johnson, "The Quiet Coup," *Atlantic Monthly*, May 2009.

16 Matt Taibbi, "The Big Takeover," *Rolling Stone*, March 19, 2009

17 Connie Bruck, "Angelo's Ashes," *The New Yorker*, June 25, 2009.

18 Johnson and Kwak, p. 7.

19 McElvaine, pp. 49–50.

20 Branko Milanovic, "Two Views of the Cause of the Global Crisis, Part 1," *Yale Global Online*, Yale Center for the Study of Globalization, Yale University, May 4, 2009.

21 James Livingston, "Their Depression and Ours, Parts 1 and 2," *History News Network*, October 7 and 13, 2008.

5 Why Bill Gates Doesn't Deserve His Fortune

1 Harold Evans, *They Made America* (New York: Little Brown, 2004), pp. 402–19.

2 James Essinger, *Jacquard's Web* (Oxford: Oxford University Press, 2004), p. 37.

3 Essinger, p. 249.

4 Thierry Bardini, *Bootstrapping: Douglas Engelbart, Coevolution, and the Origins of Personal Computing* (Stanford, CA: Stanford University Press, 2000), pp. 81–102.

5 Gar Alperovitz and Lew Daly, *Unjust Deserts* (New York: The New Press, 2008), p. 58.

6 Ibid, pp. 59–61.

7 Ibid, p. 60.

8 Cited in Alperovitz and Daly, p. 63.

9 Robert M. Solow, Nobel lecture, December 8, 1987.

10 Herbert A. Simon, "UBI and the Flat Tax," *Boston Review*, October/November 2000.

11 Cited in Alperovitz and Daly, p. 36.

12 Ibid, p. 5.

13 John Stuart Mill, "Land Tenure Reform," *Collected Works* (Toronto: University of Toronto Press, 1967), vol. 5, p. 691.

14 John Stuart Mill, *Principles of Political Economy*, vol. 2, book 2, chap. 1, section 3, p. 208.

15 L.T. Hobhouse, *Liberalism and other Writings*, ed. James Meadowcroft (Cambridge, U.K.: Cambridge University Press, 1994), pp. 91–92

16 Frank E. Manual and Fritzie P. Manual, *Utopian Thought in the Western World* (Cambridge, MA: Belknap Press, 1979), p. 466.

17 Bardini, pp. 6–14.

18 Alperovitz and Daly, p. 144.

6 Why Other Billionaires Are Even Less Deserving

1 Quoted in Zuckerman, p. 192.

2 Ibid., p. 95.

3 Martin Wolf and Simon Johnson, online interview, Yahoo Originals, April 21, 2010.

4 This analogy is an adaptation of one made by Phil Angelides, head of the Financial Crisis Inquiry Commission appointed by the U.S. government, and cited in Dean Baker, "Goldman's Scam #5476, Yes, It Can Get Even Worse," *Guardian* (U.K.), April 19, 2010.

5 Wolf and Johnson.

6 As noted earlier, Henry Paulson is not related to John Paulson, but is a former CEO of Goldman Sachs.

7 In fact, Goldman bought more of this insurance from AIG than any other bank. See Richard Teitelbaum, "Secret AIG Document Shows Goldman Sachs Minted Most Toxic CDOs," Bloomberg.com, February 23, 2010.

8 Les Leopold, "The Preposterous Reality," Alternet.org, April 10, 2010.

9 Joseph Stiglitz, "Skewed Rewards for Bankers," *Korea Herald*, March 30, 2010.

10 Evans, pp. 413–14.

11 World Wealth Report, Merrill Lynch, 2007.

12 Cited in Anatole Anton, Milton Fisk, and Nancy Holmstrom, *Not for Sale: In Defence of Public Goods* (Colorado: Westview Press, 2000), p. 3.

13 Ibid., p. 14.

14 Robert Nozick, *Anarchy, State, and Utopia* (New York: Basic Books, 1974), pp. 177–80.

7 Hank Aaron and the Myths about Human Motivation

1 After 1971, there was a separate higher top marginal rate for "unearned income"—that is, income not derived from employment but rather from dividends, rents, or interest payments. For most of the 1970s, the top marginal rate on this unearned income was 70 percent, while the top marginal rate on earned income (from employment) was 50 percent.

2 Joel Slemrod and Jon Bakija, *Taxing Ourselves: A Citizen's Guide to the Debate over Taxes* (Cambridge, MA: MIT Press, 2004), p. 116.

3 For details, see Neil Brooks, "Flattening the Claims of the Flat Taxers," 21 *Dalhousie Law Journal* 287 (1998), pp. 333–36.

4 Slemrod and Bakija, p. 118.

5 See A.B. Atkinson, "The Welfare State and Economic Performance," (1995) 48 *National Tax Journal* 171.

6 Lawrence Mishel, Jared Bernstein, and Heidi Shierholz, *The State of Working America 2008/2009* (Ithaca: Cornell University Press, 2009), pp. 26–27.

7 Dan Andrews, Christopher Jencks, and Andrew Leigh, "Do Rising Top Incomes Lift All Boats?" IZA DP No. 4920, Institute for the Study of Labour, April 2010.

8 Michael S. Derby, "Trickle-Down Economics Fails to Deliver as Promised," *Wall Street Journal,* digital edition, June 30, 2009.

9 Robert E. Lane, *The Market Experience* (Cambridge: Cambridge University Press, 1991).

10 Robert H. Frank, *Luxury Fever: Money and Happiness in an Era of Excess* (New York: The Free Press, 1999), p. 65.

11 Ibid, p. 73.

12 Lane, p. 345.

13 Ibid, p. 6.

14 Quoted in Uchitelle and Cox.

15 Quoted in Frank, p. 122.

16 Frank, p. 120.

17 Robert H. Frank and Philip J. Cook, *The Winner-Take-All Society* (New York: The Free Press, 1995), pp. 8–11, 101–15.

18 Richard A. Posner, "Are American CEOs overpaid, and if so, what if anything should be done about it?" *Duke Law Journal,* Vol. 58: 1023 (2009).

19 Posner, p. 102. See also Sanjai Bhagat and Bernard Black, *The Non-Correlation Between Board Independence and Long-Term Firm Performance,* 27 J. CORP. L. 231, 263 (2002).

8 Taking the Fun Out of Tax Havens

1 See studies referred to in Ronen Palan, Richard Murphy, and Christian Chavagneux, *Tax Havens: How Globalization Really Works* (Ithaca: Cornell University Press, 2010), pp. 61–62.

2 Neil King Jr. and Elizabeth Williamson, "Business Fends Off Tax Hit," *Wall Street Journal,* October 14, 2009.

3 The focus in this section is on Ottawa's recent lax approach to tax haven banking under the Conservative government of Stephen Harper, but it should be noted that the Liberals also have a very poor track record on this front. Most notably, former Liberal prime minister (and finance minister) Paul Martin did nothing to plug a loophole in the Canadian tax system that allowed his own family company, Canada Steamship Lines, to save millions of dollars by using a tax haven in Barbados. See

Diane Francis, "Martin's haven in Barbados legal but still questionable," *National Post,* January 15, 2004.

4 Linda McQuaig, "Tax Havens: Out of Sight, Out of Mind," *Toronto Star*, September 8, 2009.

5 Greg McArthur, "UBS Deal in Tax Case Unearths Canadian Connections," *Globe and Mail,* February 19, 2009.

6 For details see Linda McQuaig, *Behind Closed Doors: How the Rich Won Control of Canada's Tax System* (Toronto: Penguin Canada, 1987), pp. 331–46.

7 Ibid, pp. 294–99.

8 For details, see Doug Smith, *How to Tax a Billionaire* (Winnipeg: Arbeiter Ring Publishing, 2002), pp. 9–29.

9 Neil Brooks and Linda McQuaig, "Life's a Loophole Then Ya Die," *This Magazine*, December 1992.

9 Why Billionaires Are Bad for Your Health

1 John Kormos and Benjamin Lauderdale, "The Mysterious Stagnation and Relative Decline of American Heights After c. 1960" (2007), 88(2) *Social Science Quarterly* 283.

2 Thorvaldur Gylfason, "Why Europe Works Less and Grows Taller," *Challenge*, January–February 2007.

3 Richard Wilkinson and Kate Pickett, *The Spirit Level: Why More Equal Societies Almost Always Do Better* (London: Penguin Books, 2009), p. 18.

4 Michael Marmot, *Status Syndrome: How your social standing directly affects your health and life expectancy* (London: Bloomsbury, 2004), p. 39. The first Whitehall study examined only male civil servants; Whitehall II included female civil servants.

5 Redelmeir, D.A., and S.M. Singh, "Survival in Academy Award Winning Actors," *Annals of Medicine*, 2001, 134(10): pp. 955–62.

6 Ibid, p. 1.

7 Dennis Raphael, ed., *Social Determinants of Health: Canadian Perspectives*, 2nd ed. (Toronto: Canadian Scholars' Press, 2009).

8 Marmot, pp. 114–18.

9 S.S. Dickerson and M.E. Kemeny, "Acute stressors and cortisol responses: a theoretical integration and synthesis of laboratory research," *Psychological Bulletin* (2004) 130 (3), pp. 355–91.

10 Wilkinson and Pickett, pp. 51–53.

11 Ibid., p. 65.

12 James Gilligan, *Violence: Our deadly epidemic and its causes* (New York: Putnam, 1996), p. 110.

13 United Nations Crime and Justice Information Network, *Survey on Crime Trends and the Operation of Criminal Justice Systems* (New York: United Nations, 2000).

14 D. Dorling, "Prime Suspect: Murder in Britain," in P. Hillyard, C. Pantazis, S. Tombs, D. Gordon, and D. Dorling, eds., *Criminal Obsessions: Why Harm Matters More Than Crime* (London: Crime and Society Foundations, 2005).

15 Frank, pp. 1–5.

16 Wilkinson and Pickett, p. 223.

17 J. Blanden, J. Gregg, and S. Machin, *Intergenerational Mobility in Europe and North America* (London: Centre for Economic Performance, London School of Economics, 2005).

18 Lawrence Mishel, Jared Bernstein, and Heidi Shierholz, *The State of Working America 2008/2009* (Ithaca, NY: ILR Press, 2009), ch. 2.

19 See studies cited in Neil Brooks and Thaddeus Hwong, *The Social Benefits and Economic Costs of Taxation* (Ottawa: Canadian Centre for Policy Alternatives, 2006).

20 Reto Foellmi, Tobias Wuergler, and Josef Zweimüller, "The Macroeconomics of Model T," Institute for Empirical Research in Economics, University of Zurich, Working Paper Series, No. 459, December 2009.

10 Why Billionaires Are Bad for Democracy

1 Leo Kolber interview with Linda McQuaig, Montreal, March 4, 2010.

2 Nicholas Faith, *The Bronfmans: The Rise and Fall of the House of Seagram* (New York: St. Martin's Press, 2006), p. 142.

3 Leo Kolber and L. Ian MacDonald, *Leo, A Life* (Montreal and Kingston: McGill-Queen's University Press, 2003).

4 Ibid., pp. 153–54.

5 Interview with Kolber.

6 The committee recommended that only half of capital gains be included in income for tax purposes, so that they would be taxed at half the rate

of ordinary income. The committee also suggested that the rate might be reduced still further in the future.

7 Kolber, p. 147.

8 Interview with Kolber.

9 Brian Murphy, Paul Roberts, and Michael Wolfson, "Perspectives on Labour and Income: High-Income Canadians," *Statistics Canada*, Catalogue no. 75-001-XIE, September 2007, Chart H.

10 Peter Howitt, "Zero Inflation as a Long-Term Target for Monetary Policy," in *Zero Inflation: The Goal of Price Stability* (Toronto: C.D. Howe Institute, 1990), pp. 67–108.

11 Brian MacLean and Mark Setterfield, "Nexus or Not? Productivity and Inflation in Canada," *Canadian Business Economics,* Vol. 1, No. 2, Winter 1993.

12 The role played by the C.D. Howe Institute in the zero inflation campaign, and the impact of the zero inflation campaign on the deficit, is recounted in Linda McQuaig, *Shooting the Hippo: Death by Deficit and Other Canadian Myths* (Toronto: Penguin Books, 1995), pp. 72–164.

13 Johnson and Kwak, p. 11.

14 Robert A. Dahl and Charles E. Lindblom, *Politics, Economics and Welfare* (Chicago: University of Chicago Press, 1976).

15 Robert A. Dahl, Ian Shapiro, and Jose Antonio Cheibub, *The Democracy Sourcebook* (Boston: MIT Press, 2003), p. 385.

16 Task Force on Inequality and American Democracy, *American Democracy in an Age of Rising Inequality* (Washington, D.C.: American Political Science Association, 2004), p. 1.

17 Jacob S. Hacker and Paul Pierson, "Abandoning the Middle: The Bush Tax Cuts and the Limits of Democratic Control," in *Perspectives on Politics*, March 2005, Vol. 3, No. 1, pp. 33–53.

18 Cited in Hacker and Pierson, p. 40.

19 Quoted in Matt Bai, "Fight Club," *New York Times Magazine*, August 10, 2003, pp. 24–27.

20 *Too Much* newsletter, December 7, 2009.

21 Quoted in Louise Kinross, "Business schools look to private funding sources," *Financial Post*, April 24, 1996.

22 Uchitelle and Cox.

23 There is also a Peter Munk Cardiac Centre at Toronto General Hospital, following Munk's $6 million donation to the hospital in 1997. In 2006, Munk contributed an additional $37 million to the hospital to help support the cardiac centre.

24 That's because, under Canadian tax law, donors do not have to pay tax on the accrued capital gains, hence they get a charitable contribution deduction for amounts they have not paid tax on.

25 While there are no studies showing the incidence of charitable spending in Canada, U.S. studies reveal that only a comparatively small amount of philanthropy is directed to the poor, less than 1 percent by one estimate. See Estelle James, "Commentary," in Charles T. Clotfelter, ed., *Who Benefits from the Nonprofit Sector* (Chicago: University of Chicago Press, 1992). See also Christopher Jencks, "Who Gives to What?" in Walter W. Powell, ed., *The Nonprofit Sector: A Research Handbook* (New Haven, CT: Yale University Press, 1987).

26 Michael Valpy, "University of Toronto to reveal new School of Global Affairs," *Globe and Mail,* April 14, 2010.

11 The True Badge of Citizenship

1 Quoted in Frank Rich, "The Axis of the Obsessed and the Deranged," *New York Times,* February 27, 2010.

2 Hugh Stretton and Lionel Orchard, *Public Goods, Public Enterprise, Public Choice: Theoretical Foundations of the Contemporary Attack on Government* (New York: St. Martin's Press, 1994), p. 20.

3 Quoted in Stretton and Orchard, p. 51.

4 Karl Polanyi, *The Great Transformation* (Boston: Beacon Press, 1957), p. 163.

5 Quoted in Natalie Angier, "Taxing: A Ritual to Save the Species," *New York Times,* April 13, 2009.

6 For a discussion of the political views of Gerrard Winstanley and the Diggers, see Christopher Hill, *Liberty Against the Law: Some Seventeenth Century Controversies* (London: Penguin Books, 1996), p. 48–49.

7 R.H. Tawney, *Religion and the Rise of Capitalism* (Toronto: Penguin Books, 1990), p. 73.

8 Robert Nozick, *Anarchy, State, and Utopia* (New York: Basic Books, 1974), p. 169.

9 Henry Simons, *Personal Income Taxation* (Chicago: University of Chicago Press, 1938), p. 29.

10 Henry Simons, *Economic Policy for a Free Society* (Chicago: University of Chicago Press, 1948), p. 6.

11 Adam Smith, *The Wealth of Nations* (London: Penguin Books, 1999), p. 725.

12 Ibid, p. 842.

13 Ibid, p. 857. Interestingly, while Smith appears to support a progressive income tax, Karl Marx thought the idea was rather lame and that it fell considerably short of the kinds of changes needed. "Tax reform is the hobby-horse of every radical bourgeois, the specific element in all bourgeois economic reforms," Marx wrote. "From the earliest medieval Philistines to the modern English free-thinkers, the main struggle has revolved around taxation. The further it slips from his grasp in practice, the more keenly does the bourgeois pursue the chimerical ideal of equal distribution of taxation.... The reduction of taxes, their more equitable distribution, etc ... is banal bourgeois reform."

14 G.A. Cohen, *Self-Ownership, Freedom, and Equality* (Cambridge, U.K.: Cambridge University Press, 1995), p. 58.

15 John Gray, *Beyond the New Right* (London: Routledge, 1993), pp. 111–12.

16 Editorial, "Their Fair Share," *The Wall Street Journal*, July 21, 2008.

17 Rachel M. Johnson and Jeffrey Rohaly, *The Distribution of Federal Taxes, 2009–12* (Washington, D.C.: Urban-Brookings Tax Policy Center, August 2009).

18 Since the Tax Policy Center does not calculate the distribution of state and local taxes, the following numbers are from Citizens for Tax Justice.

19 Martin A. Sullivan, "Is the Income Tax Really Progressive?" *Tax Notes*, December 14, 2009.

20 Marc Lee, *Eroding Tax Fairness: Tax Incidence in Canada 1990 to 2005* (Ottawa: Canadian Centre for Policy Alternatives, 2007).

12 Revamping the Ovarian Lottery

1 Dalton Conley, "Don't Blame the Billionaires," *American Prospect*, December 15, 2009.

2 Benjamin Page and Lawrence Jacobs, *Class War: What Americans Really Think About Inequality* (Chicago: University of Chicago Press, 2009).

3 William Yardley, "Oregon Voters Approve Tax Increase," *New York Times*, January 27, 2010.

4 Quoted in Michael J. Graetz and Ian Shapiro, *Death by a Thousand Cuts: The Fight over Taxing Inherited Wealth* (Princeton: Princeton University Press, 2005), p. 241.

5 Graetz and Shapiro, p. 6.

6 Robert H. Frank, "The Estate Tax: Efficient, Fair and Misunderstood," *New York Times*, May 12, 2005.

7 Graetz and Shapiro, p. 10.

8 Leslie T. MacDonald, *Taxing Comprehensive Income: Power and Participation in Canadian Politics 1962–72* (Ph.D. thesis, Carleton University, Ottawa: 1985).

9 In Canada, the top marginal rate is a combination of both the federal and provincial income tax systems, so it varies somewhat from province to province. The top federal rate is 29 percent, while the provincial rates vary from a low of 10 percent in Alberta to a high of 17 percent in Ontario, creating a top rate of 39 percent in Alberta and 46 percent in Ontario. We are suggesting that the federal government add two additional rates to the federal income tax—a 43 percent and a 53 percent rate, to kick in $300,000 and $2.5 million respectively.

10 Henry Simons, *Personal Income Taxation* (Chicago: University of Chicago Press, 1938), pp. 18–19.

11 Joseph Stiglitz, "Scarcity in the Age of Plenty," *Guardian* (U.K.), June 15, 2008.

12 Quoted in Chuck Collins, Mike Lapham, and Scott Klinger, *I Didn't Do It Alone: Society's Contribution to Individual Wealth and Success* (Boston: United for a Fair Economy, 2004), pp. 1–2.

13 J.K. Rowling, "The Single Mother's Manifesto," *Times* (U.K.), April 14, 2010.

14 When Canada taxed inheritances prior to 1972, it did so through an estate tax, which was levied on the donor's estate—but the provinces had inheritances taxes, levied on the person who received the inheritance. These were eliminated along with the federal estate tax.

15 Warren Buffett has described his concept of the Ovarian Lottery on a number of occasions, including in a lecture at the University of Florida School of Business, October 15, 1998.

16 If anything, an inheritance tax similar to what exists in other OECD countries would enable a larger amount to be deposited in each trust fund, so the bequests could become larger over time.

ACKNOWLEDGMENTS

We'd like to thank a number of people for generously giving their time and expertise to help with this project, particularly Michael Wolfson, Daniel Wright, Barbara Nichol, Doug Peters, and David Peters, as well as Thaddeus Hwong, who provided helpful research assistance on a few key points.

The talented crew at Penguin Books did a terrific job. Right from the beginning, Diane Turbide showed enthusiasm for the subject and a keen sense of how to make it work. It was also a real pleasure working with Barbara Bower, Yvonne Hunter, Sandra Tooze, and Justin Stoller. Freelance copy editor Scott Steedman did great work on the manuscript. Our agent, Chris Bucci, was always helpful.

Linda also thanks Peter Langille, who made the last few months of heavy lifting really quite wonderful.

Toronto, June 2010

INDEX